The Wanderers F.C.

Five times F

AUTHOR

Rob Cavallini

Price £9.99

British Library Cataloguing in Publication Data
A catalogue record for this book is available from the British Library
ISBN 0-9550496-0-1

Published by Dog N Duck Publications

Printed by Apollo

Cover design by Hope Merris, concept by Steve Best

Cover picture shows the Forest F.C. in 1863

Contents

Introduction

The Wanderers Football Club has always fascinated and at the same time puzzled me. For although the club achieved five F.A. Cup wins and will be forever talked about whenever certain records are discussed, surprisingly little is known or written about it. Most things that I have read seem to have been reworded time and time again, as the same constant mistakes are made.

Most material mentions the F.A. Cup wins, the fact that they allegedly played at Battersea Park and the Oval. By way of passing they will mention Kinnaird and Alcock. What I have attempted to do is get inside the club and find out what really happened on a day to day basis. I have read countless texts, many written by Alcock in his publications and the 'Sportsman' newspaper and tried to establish a true picture.

It is amazing what can be discovered through analysing the statistics of the club, as it highlights trends, player movements and I believe the results section is the first time that an almost complete set has been published. The statistics alone highlight that the club, although always strong, was not invincible and struggled at times due to the same problems every club since has faced and even some strange ones that seem unbelievable in this day and age.

The Wanderers will always be quoted in everything from lists of clubs with the most wins, to Kinnaird who played in nine of the first twelve cup finals for Wanderers and Old Etonians. This fact was mentioned about five times by John Motson, in relation to Roy Keane's sixth appearance in a final, during the 2004 F.A. Cup Final radio broadcast which I was listening to while researching this book in the library.

The other objective I had in undertaking this project was to try and find out who the Wanderers were. As I mentioned previously, Alcock and Kinnaird always attract attention and Vidal and Wollaston also feature in more extensive works. There were however over 700 players who represented the club, by selection or just being in the right place at the right time on occasions. From my time at Corinthian-Casuals F.C., I was at times inundated with requests about old players' from interested parties or relatives and I hope this book will help people to clarify any questions they and the player's relatives have.

When researching this period the researcher is at the mercy of the newspapers: fortunately Alcock was sub-editor on The Sportsman, but still mistakes were made, initials were swapped around accidentally and there was the age old problem of deciphering people's hand writing which again leads to mistakes. I have wherever possible checked any other sources available to make sure as many errors as possible have been eliminated. It would be impossible to say there are no errors, and if you find any I apologise now. I hope you enjoy reading the story of the Wanderers Football Club and that it fills in certain areas that have not been previously covered.

Enjoy the book

Rob Cavallini   rob_cavallini@hotmail.com

4

British Social, Political and Economic History 1859-1883

Britain was a very different place in the era of the Wanderers Football Club, and this brief synopsis of the period aims to give the reader an idea of the circumstances in which sport developed in the early days. It was the age of the Industrial Revolution and the apogee of the British Empire.

During this period the country was a much less densely populated place. In 1851 there were only 17 million people in England. By 1871 this had risen to 21.5 million, of which 3.89 million lived in London or 20 per cent. By the end of the period in 1881 it had risen yet again to 24.5 million, approximately half of today's population [1].

The club was formed in 1859 whilst Britain and France were at war with China. This conflict finally ended in October 1860 when the allied armies entered Peking in triumph and later that month the imperial Chinese Government surrendered and agreed to implement the earlier treaty of June 1858, whilst paying a considerable indemnity to the allies towards the cost of the war. Further trouble overseas occurred in 1862 when troops were sent to Japan to secure compensation for the murder of a British citizen. This action led to the opening of Japanese ports to British trade. By the end of this period Britain had entered into and lost the first Boer War (1880-81) after the Boers revolted in protest over the annexation of the Transvaal region in 1877. The first Geneva Convention was only signed in 1864.

Closer to home, it was not until 1863 that future Prime Minister and current Chancellor of the Exchequer Gladstone, whose son also played for the Wanderers, opened the first section of the London Underground and it was 1882 when electric lights were first introduced to London streets.

Economically the period can be split into two periods. The Mid Victorian Boom from 1850 to 1873, and the Great Depression from 1873 to 1896. The first period saw dramatic growth with expansion in production, investment and exports. This in turn led to rising prices, profits and wages.

	%of total no. of families	% of national income received	Average Income per family
Upper Class (£1000+ per year)	0.5	26	£6079
Middle Class (£100-£1000 per year)	25	35	£154
Working Class	74.5	39	£58
National Ave.			£111

Distribution of national income between families in England and Wales 1867 [2]

There was still a huge concentration of wealth in the restricted but influential ranks from which the Wanderers members were primarily drawn. Leisure was becoming more available, but the time and facilities were more readily available to the richer classes. The period up to 1873 was seen as a golden age and real wages grew noticeably and wealth spread in a way never seen before.

From 1873, the period of the Great Depression took over. This is perhaps an over dramatic name for the period which perhaps could be regarded as recession. This term was coined without detailed and accurate records and it was only much later that it was disputed. It was based on the fact that prices fell from the 1870's until the mid 1890's. Formack-Peck argues that despite wholesale prices falling by 39 per cent from 1873 to 1896 the real reason was in fact the extension of arable farming in the New World and the transport revolution which lead to this situation 3.

If it really had been a depression falling agricultural prices would have been offset in their effect on the general level of prices by rising elsewhere 4. Another factor which backs this up is that money remained constant and wages actually improved during this period, although the working classes did face an increase in unemployment and as such the period could only be regarded as a recession.

It did however lead to the return of social tension, and trade unions began to emerge from the shadows. It gave a window for Socialist ideas which certainly made an impact in line with the questioning of Victorian certitudes and the similarities with that of the Liberal ideal.

Politically it was a time of reform in a period dominated by Gladstone and Disraeli. Palmerston was Prime Minister from 1859 to 1865, before he was followed in quick succession by Lord Russell (1865-66) and Derby (1866-68). Under Palmerston the process was started with key acts such as the Criminal Law enactments of 1861, the Companies Act of 1862 and Union Chargeability Act of 1865 which helped overhaul the Poor Law. Further progress was made with factory reform, local government reform, law reform and public health reform during his stewardship.

Lord Russell succeeded Palmerston on his death in what was to be destined to be a very short stay in office. The Reform Crisis of 1866 and 1867, led to his downfall as attempts were made to widen the scope of the people eligible to vote. Russell aimed to allow an extra 400,000 people to vote by lowering the property qualification for borough voters from £10 to £7, and lower the occupancy qualification from £50 to £14. These reforms alone would create an extra 60,000 voters. The balance would be made up by voters who earned the right by depositing £50 in a savings bank.

Uproar in the House of Commons eventually led to the Russell Cabinet resigning in 1866. Ironically a new bill which was pretty close to Russell's proposal was passed the following year, after Disraeli cleverly exploited the Liberal disunity, and thus Britain's journey towards democracy continued with 1.5 million men now having the vote, universal male suffrage did not occur until 1884.

Disraeli briefly became Prime Minister upon Derby's resignation in 1868, but Gladstone won the election later that year. Disraeli though was back in office following the 1874 election, before Gladstone returned following the 1880 election. Despite the comings and goings of these two famous politicians, the reforms continued to be one of the main focuses of British politics.

Gladstone in turn arranged the disestablishment of the Church of Ireland in an attempt to bring peace to that island. That meant that Irish Catholics did not need to pay their tithes to the Anglican Church of England. He also instituted Cardwell's Army reform that made peacetime flogging illegal in 1869, and the Irish Land Act and Forster's Education Act in 1870. Gladstone also instituted the University Test Act, instituted the Ballot Act for secret voting ballots and in 1873 he passed laws restructuring the High Courts 5.

Disreali's administration was responsible for the Artisans Dwellings Act (1875), the Public Health Act (1875), the Pure Food and Drugs Act (1875), the Climbing Boys Act (1875) and the Education Act (1876). His government also introduced a new Factory Act meant to protect workers, the Conspiracy and Protection of Property Act (1875) which allowed peaceful picketing and the Employers and Workmen Act (1878) which enabled workers to sue employers in the civil courts if they broke legal contracts 6.

There was a growing social mobility and the numbers of rich people continued to grow throughout these years. The existence of the numerous small enterprises or businesses meant that it was possible through skill, determination, hard work and a little bit of help from lady luck, for a working man to enter the ranks of the employers.

It is important to note the way the nature of business was changing and developing with the increase in 'white-collar' workers such as clerks, draughtsmen and salesmen whose ranks were compiled from other groups of workers, by either individual's career changes or by the recruitment of the sons of other workers into this employment sector. As this career path became more appealing and complex, it introduced much greater diversity into the social structure.

Trade Unions also became prominent although there was no one body which controlled them collectively. The Trade Union Congress is dated from 1868, but they did not enjoy complete control and there remained a suspicion of anything that would limit the independence of the local organizations. Despite the lack of unity, the Trade Unions did achieve a certain amount of success such as a shorter working week. By 1880 membership of such bodies did not reach 10 per cent of the adult male workforce.

Housing was also improving: legislation passed in 1875 meant that it was illegal to build houses without toilets. By 1876 four-fifths of the houses in Manchester had their own water taps and it is generally accepted that British workers enjoyed the best housing standard in Europe. Further developments such as wallpaper being made generally available from 1861, following the abolition of tax on paper, and floor covering in the guise of linoleum, which came into use from the 1870's onwards, meant conditions were certainly better.

Many people however still lived in old housing and did not get the benefits of the new innovations and reforms. This led to major issues in regard to public health and in particular, sanitation. Sewers were already in operation, but did little more than dump the waste into the nearest river. In short it did little more than move the problem and in no way solved it as the rivers became desperately unhygienic. Personal hygiene was improving which is highlighted by the fact that between 1841 and 1861 the consumption of soap per head doubled [7].

Public health was also helped by the emergence of voluntary general hospitals and by 1861 there were 130 of these across the country. There were also 23 hospitals with medical schools for training doctors. By the 1870's Tuberculosis deaths were in decline and so were deaths caused by Smallpox and Typhus. Vaccinations, which the government attempted to make compulsory in 1840, helped especially with the decline of Smallpox.

There were still however problems with illnesses such as Typhoid, Measles, Whooping Cough, Scarlet Fever and Diphtheria. One of the most prominent examples of this is the death of Prince Albert in 1861 from Typhoid. Alcoholism and venereal diseases remained serious causes of ill health throughout this period.

A combination of factors can be attributed to the improvement in public health by 1880. These were an improved diet, some improvement in housing standards, and, techniques in building. There was also some improvement in water supplies and medical facilities.

Law and order seemed to be largely intact and under control as well through self regulation:

7

'There is much evidence that it was a rough society, but little to show that people feared for their lives, or felt them selves unable to use the roads at night. There was roughness, much fighting, much casual violence and serious injury.... The forces of law enforcement were never very strong... and were certainly never strong enough to coerce the population into obedience. The system of law enforcement and administration of the criminal law could only have worked with the active co-operation or the passive acquiescence of the mass of the population- and the evidence suggests that the authorities received at least this passive acquiescence. The relatively peaceful, orderly and law-abiding Englishman seems to have been a reality by the 1880's already. [8]*'*

Leisure in these times was predominantly the privilege of the upper and middle classes, but in order to escape the previous images of sport they brought their own moral qualities. They embraced equal competition between equal numbers to well known published rules, and these rules had to be adhered to in a sportsmanlike manner [9]. The pursuit of leisure went hand in hand with prosperity as it made the granting of official free time a realistic option and it was here that Saturday afternoon became the prominent sporting day. With the leading public schools adopting the game of Association Football as their standard winter game the scene was set for the game to flourish.

The working classes held a healthy interest in sport, but it was not until much later that they got a foothold into the game of football. Absenteeism showed how keen they were on sport and it was not uncommon for a factory to be half full when a major sporting event was taking place. This of course was dependent on the job market at the time and whether there was a shortage of labour, which meant they could get away with it. Gradually though the government realized how important sport and leisure were to public health and the reforms helped enable the working classes to participate in organized sport and in particular football, although this occurred in the north of England, a long time before doing so in the gentleman amateur dominated south.

References

1   Crouzet   *The Victorian Economy* p20
2   Crouzet   *The Victorian Economy* p40
3   Formack-Peck *New Perspectives on the late Victorian Economy* p253
4   Formack-Peck *New Perspectives on the late Victorian Economy* p254
5   *http://en.wikipedia.org*
6   *http://en.wikipedia.org*
7   McCord *British History 1815-1906*   p342
8   Philips *Crime and Authority in Victorian England* p284-6
9   Brailsford *British Sport, A Social History* p83

Football in the Early Days

While reading this book, the reader should remember that football was very different from the game we know today. The rules were evolving constantly and to complicate matters many variations were in use locally. Football also did not carry the same importance as it does in this money-fuelled age of business, 'Sky' and agents' fees.

'Football at this period and indeed for some years yet to follow, in the main was a happy-go-lucky affair. It was a game for pure enjoyment, played in that spirit, but with no especial point to it beyond being an enjoyable method of exercise. Matches were arranged in a haphazard fashion, and teams turned up to honour their engagements, or they did not. It was largely a matter of mood, inclination or convenience. There was nothing to it. It was just an afternoon's good fun.'₁

From reading the reports of the games at this time, this is an accurate portrayal of the situation. There are numerous occasions when clubs turned up short of players, sometimes blamed on the transport or otherwise on the weather. There is an undoubted enjoyment factor which glows out of everything written by these early sportsmen.

The rules were very different in 1863 when they were first written by E.C. Morley, although you can identify similarities with today's game-

1) *The maximum length of the ground shall be 200 yards and the maximum breadth shall be 100 yards, the length and breadth shall be marked off with flags and the goal shall be defined by two upright posts, 8 yards apart, without any tape or bar across them.*

2) *The game shall be commenced by a place kick from the centre of the ground by the side winning the toss, the other side shall not approach with in 10 yards of the ball until it is kicked off. After a goal is won the losing side shall be entitled to kick off.*

3) *The two sides shall change goals after each goal is won.*

4) *A goal shall be won when the ball passes over the space between the goal posts (at whatever height) not being thrown, knocked on or carried.*

5) *When the ball is in touch the first player who shall touch it shall kick or throw it from the point on the boundary line where it left the ground in a direction at right angles with the boundary line.*

6) *A player shall be out of play immediately he is in front of the ball and must return behind the ball as soon as possible. If the ball is kicked past a player by his own side, he shall not touch or kick it or advance until one of the other side has first kicked it or one of his own side on a level with or in front of him, has been able to kick it.*

7) *In case the ball goes behind the goal line: if a player on the side to whom the goal belongs first touches the ball, one of his side shall be entitled to a free kick from the goal line at the point opposite the place where the ball shall be touched. If a player of the opposite side first touches the ball, one of his side shall be entitled to a free kick from a point 15 yards outside the goal line, opposite the place where the ball is touched.*

8) *If a player makes a fair catch he shall be entitled to a free kick provided he claims it by making a mark with his heel at once; and in order to take such kick he may go as far back as he pleases, and no player on the opposite side shall advance beyond his mark until he has kicked.*

9) *A player shall be entitled to run with the ball towards his adversaries goal of he makes a fair catch, or catches the ball on the first bound; but in case of a fair catch, if he makes his mark, he shall not then run.*

10) *If any player shall run with the ball towards his adversaries' goal, any player on the opposite side shall be at liberty to charge, hold, trip or hack him, or to wrest the ball from him, but no player shall be held and hacked at the same time.*

11) *Neither, tripping or hacking shall be allowed, and no player shall use his hands or elbows to hold or push his adversary, except in the case provided for by Law 10.*

12) *Any player shall be allowed to charge another, provided they are both in active play. A player shall be allowed to charge if even he is out of play*

13) *A player shall be allowed to throw the ball or pass it to another if he makes a fair catch, or catches the ball on the first bound.*

14) *No player shall be allowed to wear projecting nails, iron plates or gutta percha on the soles or heels of his boots.* [2]

Rules nine and ten were deleted following objections and as such they were brought in to line with those of Cambridge University. The deletion of these rules more commonly associated with Rugby, meant that a number of clubs such as Blackheath would take a different path.

As the 1860's wore on the rules were adapted and improved becoming much closer to those we now know. In 1867 the offside rule was changed to be in line with Charterhouse and Westminster School's. This meant that there had to be three defenders between the attacker and the goal line. Other improvements at this time included that tape was now to be placed across the goal at a height of eight feet to form a cross bar and the fair catch was expunged from the rules.

There were further changes –

1871	Goal Keeper was permitted to use hands
1873	The corner kick was adopted; previously it had been in the Sheffield rules.
1874	Umpires were mentioned in the rules for the first time
1875	The cross bar was permitted instead of the tape, but it was not compulsory.
1877	The Sheffield Association adopt the F.A. laws completely.
1880	The throw in (one handed) was allowed in any direction.
1881	The Referee is first mentioned in the rules.
1882	The throw in with both hands became permitted.

The tactics of clubs also evolved during this period but the 4:4:2 formation was a long way off. In 1863 it was common to have nine forwards, two behinds and no goal keeper. Within two years this had been modified so that there was one goalkeeper, one goal cover, one back and eight forwards. By 1870 the popular formation became one goal keeper, one back, two half backs and this time seven forwards. In 1875 the backs were increased to two and the forwards reduced to six. Eight years later the semi familiar 2:3:5, formation became the vogue and this was to survive in various guises until the 1960's.

These formations look suicidal in today's climate, although they may have suited the more attacking styles of Barry Fry or Kevin Keegan. The dribbling style was however the order of the day and players tended to dribble until they were tackled. Passing did not seem to be an option and was certainly not favoured amongst the early players. It was not until Queen's Park and Scotland had destroyed England's finest that the passing style was adopted in the period between 1881-1885: this no doubt sparked the 1883 change of formation to which it was better suited to.

The other thing that needs to be taken into account is where the games were played. There were no football grounds in the early days with stands and fences. Even changing rooms and washing facilities would have been a luxury. For the first five years the Wanderers under the Forest F.C. banner had a brief home at Snaresbrook, before going wandering. Many of the games were played at the public schools that they were playing, or on Clapham Common or Battersea Park.

Battersea Park has been described as follows. *'The area of the Park, was located on land, reclaimed from the marshes, in the 16th century, It was opposite, a Royal palace, and the Royal Hospital, at Chelsea.*

The land, was then known, as Battersea Fields, It was a venue for fairs, pigeon shooting, and donkey racing. The land, came under the jurisdiction, of H.M. Office of Works, in 1846. The area, was then, furthered drained. It was levelled, with soil excavated, from the Victoria Docks. The site covered 320 acres. However was sold, for housing.

Hence, Battersea Park was completed, over an area of 200 acres. There was a boating lake, with cascades, and Italian Gardens to the south. The area, by the river Thames, to the north, was reserved for Cricket Grounds. There were three, such sports areas. One for clubs, one for schools, and one for matches. It was in this location, that the Wanderers played their football.' 3 (sic)

This is inaccurate in that it claims Battersea Park was Wanderers home ground, but it does paint a picture of the venues where football was being played.

It was not until the Wanderers moved to the Middlesex County Cricket Ground for the 1868/69 season that they played on what could be regarded as anything close to a modern sporting venue. Lord's had a Pavilion lit by gas which although rebuilt after a fire in 1827 had been enlarged in 1865. During the period 1866-67 the first Grandstand designed by Arthur Allom was built, to be followed by the second tavern being built in 1867-1868. This was a sudden change for a club which had been used to playing on park pitches.

It would not be exaggerating to say that the early Wanderers players had to contend with conditions roughly on a par with the average Sunday League footballer today. Poor pitches, long walks to reach the pitch and being completely exposed to the elements. It is certain that when the club moved to playing home games at the Middlesex County Cricket Ground and then the Oval it must have come as a welcome relief for all those involved.

After all this, spare a thought for the club captain or secretary who was selecting the side for each game. There was no home ground that they owned and most players were scattered around London and the South East so even if they had one, it is unlikely they would have been leaving notices of fixtures and team selections on the club notice board. There was no training or regular meetings of players and information sharing. Whoever was selecting the side would have had to visit the players, send them letters by post or telegram and then wait for a response to see if they were available. It was the age before the telephone and certainly the mobile phone. If players got lost or had last minute emergencies, there was little hope of notifying the captain that they were not going to be playing that day. The whole exercise must have been both time consuming and a logistical nightmare.

Despite having to overcome all of this the game began to thrive and the Football Association increased in membership from the initial eleven clubs in 1863 to 29 by 1869. This increased dramatically as soon as the F.A. Cup started in the 1871/72 season.

References

1   Green *A History of the Football Association* p48
2   Green *A History of the Football Association* p34-5
3   Blythe Smart *The Wow Factor* p144

Forest Football Club – The Beginning

'Forest is usually regarded as the first football club of modern times and was certainly the first to make and impact in the south.' 1 This bold statement by Pawson certainly makes the Forest Football Club, who later would evolve into the Wanderers Football Club an intriguing proposition. Who were they? Why were they formed? What did they actually do? These are all questions which I will attempt to answer, both here and in the course of this book.

Football in the late 1850's, and early 1860's was little to write home about. For one thing there were no common set of rules to speak of, the earliest set being those of Cambridge University, which were laid down in 1848, but these had not extended themselves much further than the University city, and the public schools, all of which had their own variations. There were also very few clubs in existence, while the press coverage was limited. 'Bell's Life and Sporting Chronicle,' which was one of the leading newspapers of its type at this time, mainly reported on older more established sports such as Racing, Cricket, Pigeon Shooting and Boxing. When it did extend itself to football it quite naturally, at this time, looked to the public schools, primarily of Harrow, Charterhouse and Shrewsbury. The reports certainly make intriguing reading and some classic games took place including G.F. Harris Esq'. team verses E.H. Vaughan Esq' team or the more imaginative Light Hair versus Dark Hair which was played at Brighton College!

The Forest Football Club began life in 1859, the same year as their leading light Charles W. Alcock finished his schooling at Harrow. Alcock himself states *'the first club to work on a definite basis with the distinct object of circulating and popularising the game, I am inclined to think was a club known as the Forest Club. Founded in 1859 by a few Old Harrovians, it had an uninterrupted career of success.'* 2 Alcock explains further *'It was the winter of 1859/60 that really saw the first game of the great football revival. Great things, it is said, from trivial things spring. The trivial cause in this instance was the humble desire of a few Old Harrovians, who had just left school, to keep up the practice at all events of the game at which they had shown some considerable aptitude.'* 3

C.W. Alcock's role in the founding of the Forest Club is further enhanced in an interview with Bettesworth *'After leaving school, did you join the Wanderers?''Well, I started the Wanderers' Club, so that I can hardly be said to have joined it, I was captain of the team which won the Association Cup.'* 4 This quote is misleading in as much as C.W.Alcock certainly engineered the founding of the Wanderers club in 1864 out of the Forest Club, but the Wanderers were not around until five years after he left school, so it appears he viewed the Forest Club and Wanderers as one entity.

Who were the founder members of Forest Football Club? Alcock explains the early make up *'the first captain was J.F. Alcock, and among the original members of the team were J. Pardoe, who subsequently contributed largely to the development of Association football in Hitchin and Hertfordshire, C.W. Alcock, A. and W.J. Thompson.'* 5 Other early members of note were A.W. McKenzie who was Honorary Secretary certainly from the 1861/62 season onwards and represented the club with J.F. Alcock when the Football Association was founded in 1863. A.M. and C.M. Tebbut also gave many years service from an early stage. But, were they all Old Harrovians? Of the original team which took the field in 1861 only four appear to have been Harrow pupils, namely the Alcock brothers, the others being J. Pardoe and J. Morgan. What is usually not mentioned is that there was a strong connection with Forest School, with the following players all appearing under the banner of Forest Football Club namely Cutbill (although which brother is not known since there were five in total), G.H. Edmunds, D.J. Morgan and J. Robertson. There are also two possible players who could have come from Forest School, namely J. Elliott and F.C. Adams. Other prominent players such as W.J.B. Standidge went to King's College School, while A.M. and C.M. Tebbut, it has been suggested, were educated locally and did not in fact go to public school. The brothers did share a shipbuilding connection which could have brought them into contact with the Alcock's. The myth perhaps originated from C.W. Alcock himself, or from the fact that Old Harrovians without doubt dominated the membership throughout the life of the Wanderers Football Club.

A.G. Guillemard one of the early administrators in Rugby Union was a member, but not as previously claimed a founding member, as in 1859 he would have been only 14 years of age and still at school. Interestingly there is no record of him ever playing a game for Forest or the Wanderers, although he is listed on the fixture card for the 1865/66 season.

The first ground was at Snaresbrook which has been called *'a popular rendezvous for football clubs of the better class'*6 Several sources state that games were played in the shadow of the 'Seaman's Orphanage at Snaresbrook' This has opened up a debate as *'there is some confusion as there were at the time two orphanages in the vicinity, the Infant Orphan Asylum at Snaresbrook built by the Rev Andrew Read in 1841 (now Snaresbrook Crown Court) and the Merchant Seaman's Orphan Asylum opened in 1862 on Chigwell Road, Wanstead. It later became Wanstead Hospital.'*7 Gerald Wright the Forest School Archivist argues that is more likely that it was in fact the Infant Orphan Asylum due to it being built in 1841 and is actually in the Snaresbrook area, in contrast to the Merchant Seaman's Orphan Asylum which is based in Wanstead. It seems likely that the word 'Seamen's' inadvertently slipped into the equation probably through Alcock's mention of it in an article *'playing its home fixtures on a part of Epping Forest in the immediate vicinity of the Merchant Seaman's Orphan Asylum at Snaresbrook.'*8 Wright goes on to state that the orphanage at Snaresbrook was always, and still is, surrounded by open countryside. This also leads on to why the club was likely to be named Forest.

John Blythe Smart puts forward the only real theory on why the embryonic Forest Football Club chose Snaresbrook as their home ground. Smart states that John Pardoe lived two miles away at Leyton Manor House, and could well have known the land owner Lord Mornington who had property in Wanstead and as such he could have arranged it.

For two seasons Forest Football Club was a collection of friends playing football together in what which was probably little more than a kick about in the park. It is remarkable that the club managed to overcome this and start what was to become a voyage of discovery in the realms of the development of a game, which was soon to captivate a nation and then the world.

In 1861 Forest issued their first set of printed rules based largely on the Cambridge Rules of 1848. They did have however some wonderful additions.

1) *That Captains be chosen at the commencement of play, who shall have the direction of places, etc., etc., throughout the game.*
2) *That the length and breadth of ground be marked off with flags, and that the distance between goal-posts do not exceed eight yards.*
3) *That in the event of the bursting of the ball, a new one is to be placed in the centre of the ground, and that the side commencing the game have the kick off.*
4) *That any wilful infringement of the rules of the game, a fine of Two Shillings and Sixpence be inflicted.'*9

14

The final rule was no doubt good for the finances of the club, and surely led to some interesting debates among team members! They were however close to the rules played at Harrow School.

1861/62
By the time the 1861/62 season started in Alcock's words *'the Forest Club, having fulfilled its mission of pioneering work, after two winters had already begun to feel the necessity of a more extensive field of operations. It was gradually overstepping the circumscribed limits of a local habitation.'*[10] There was in fact a little bit more time to wait until the first external games took place in the Spring of 1862.

The Forest Club had little real chance of expanding their fixtures prior to this point in time. Two clubs were playing external games in the late 1850's and early 1860's namely Crusaders and Dingley Dell, but these clubs were never played by Forest. Furthermore all the clubs who were to make up what became the Forest Club and later the Wanderers fixture list had not been formed yet. The first club to be founded was the Crystal Palace Club which started life in 1861. Appropriately it was against this club that Forest made their competitive debut. Somewhat surprisingly the schools which did so much to foster the environment in which the game flourished in those early days did not start playing external games until 1863 at the earliest. Following on from Crystal Palace's formation came traditional rivals Barnes and Civil Service in 1862 and No Names, Kilburn in 1863. The Football Annual lists many other clubs formation dates from around this period, but these seem to relate to when they started playing internally or when the organisation such as the school was founded.

The Honorary Secretary of Forest Football Club, A.W. Mackenzie as a result had an extremely limited list of teams to invite to play matches against. Fortunately for the development of the game, Crystal Palace accepted the invitation and two games were arranged.

The first game took place on 15th March 1862 when J.F. Alcock captained the club and it is worth reproducing the report of this historic match.

Forest Club   ***1***   ***Crystal Palace Club***   ***0***

This match came off on Saturday, the 15th inst, on the ground of the former, at Leytonstone, Essex. Play began at about half-past two, and ended at five pm. The result was a victory for the Forest Club, who obtained one goal, their opponents none. The play on both sides was acknowledged to be very good, and that the game was hardly fought is shown by the fact that the only goal won was obtained after an hour and a half's play.

J.F. Alcock, C.W. Alcock, H. Bigland, C. Bigland, C. Jackson, G.W. Mackenzie, J. Morgan, J. Pardoe, J. Robertson, C. Tebbut, A. Tebbut, M. Savill, J.E. White, F.W. Woodward, A.W.Mackenzie
[11]

This fifteen a side game resulted in the first of many victories by the Forest Club, unfortunately the scorer of the first ever goal is lost in the mists of time. It was however a huge success and the return match followed three weeks later.

Forest Club   ***4***   ***Crystal Palace Club***   ***0***

The return match between these two clubs came off on Saturday week, on the ground of the latter, at the Palace. The weather which had been fine for the previous two or three days, was again wet, and that the ground was not in first rate condition. Despite draw backs, however, play commenced at three o'clock and continued till five. The result was another victory for the Forest Club, for at the conclusion of the game they had obtained four goals, their adversaries none. Three of these were kicked by Mr Pardoe and the other by C. Bigland. The play on both sides was good, but it was evident that the Forest Club were decidedly superior to their opponents, who admitted that they (the Forest Club) had it all their own way.

J.F. Alcock, C.W. Alcock, H. Bigland, C.Bigland, A.J. Burness, F.W. Connery, C.D. Jackson, D.J. Morgan, J. Pardoe, J. Robertson, W.J.B. Standidge, C. Tebbut, A. Tebbut, F.W. Woodward, A.W. Mackenzie 12

Forest successfully rearranged their team to record a convincing victory which included the first and only hat trick recorded by a Forest player in the five year life span of the club this was scored by J. Pardoe. This game also closed Forest's very short, yet important season where they finished with a one hundred per cent record.

1862/63
Forest Club under the stewardship of A.W. Mackenzie continued to look for expansion and issued an invitation to other clubs in Bell's Life in early 1862/63.

FOOTBALL – The Hon. Secretary of the Forest Football Club will be happy to make arrangements for matches to be played during the coming season, on the rules of the University of Cambridge. 13

Despite this invite, only Barnes Club was added to the fixture list for the coming season, with all games taking place again in the Spring. It appears likely that there were four games played, but only three were reported on. The clue appears in the Crystal Palace report, which states that the game was 'a return'. Whatever the result of this missing game, Forest did not lose as the Crystal Palace report closes by saying *'the Forest Club closes for the season, on 4ᵗʰ inst. It has been very successful during the present season, having suffered no defeat in any of its matches'* 14

The season as far as can be seen by articles of the time was a success, in particular for Charles W. Alcock who scored all four of the recorded goals. A goal was conceded for the first time, against the Crystal Palace Club. It was cancelled out however by C.W. Alcock and then the same player scored a winner in what was described as *'the final rush of this gentleman for the last goal was really magnificent, and won great applause'* 15

There are also clues which show that the game of football was beginning to become popular as a spectator sport and in a colourful description of the Barnes game in February 1863, which contains more about what was occurring in the proximity than the actual game it states

The ground is an excellent one, consisting of a large field with a noble avenue of trees running through it, which afforded a pleasant promenade for the spectators, of whom there was a goodly muster, including many of the fair sex, who added not a little to the attractions of the sport. 16

Unfortunately the quality of reporting was poor in this period and other than C.W. Alcock and suspicions about certain other players, it is not clear who was actually playing for the club at this time.

1863/64
1863 is a year which cannot be ignored in the history of football, as it was the year that the Football Association was founded. In keeping with the Forest Club's position as the leading club they played

a leading part in its formation. J.F. Alcock and A.W. Mackenzie were both present at the initial meeting on 26th October 1863 at the Freemasons Tavern, Great Queen Street, London. The meeting comprised representatives from the following clubs and institutions, Forest, No Names (Kilburn), War Office, Crusaders, Crystal Palace, Kensington School, Surbiton, Barnes, Blackheath, Blackheath School and Perceval House School (Blackheath). It was A.W. Mackenzie who seconded E.C. Morley of Barnes *'that it is advisable that a football association should be formed for the purpose of settling a code of rules for the regulation of the game of football.'*[17] Despite certain teething problems created by the public schools, Blackheath and Sheffield, the Football Association came into being and the rules were finally decided in December after a series of meetings based on the Cambridge Rules.

Forest Club was now in a very fortunate position with a number of club members in top positions with the newly formed Football Association. A. Pember was President although he does not seem to have played for Forest Club and J.F Alcock was on the committee.

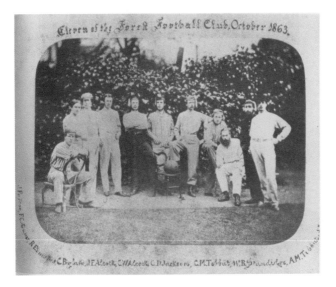

The only known picture of Forest F.C. or the Wanderers F.C. 1863

The season commenced on 7th November 1863 and it was raining goals for the Forest Club. It opened with a 3-0 thrashing of Richmond, who would soon take the Rugby route, Barnes were dispatched 5-0 as were Richmond in the return. Further convincing victories over No Names, Barnes, Thompson's XI and King's College followed before three drawn games against Harrow School, Thompson's XI and No Names rounded off the Forest Club season.

Forest Club, in keeping with their position in the Football Association and reacting to the fact that the first set of rules had been approved, immediately pronounced *'we have much pleasure in stating that the Forest Club have resolved 'That the rules of the Football Association be the rules of this club, and be used on all occasions with the exception of such matches as are already arranged.'*[18] This however was impossible to adhere in view of the lack of opposition and the Wanderers continued right until the end playing odd games under non Association rules.

The second half of the season was covered extremely well in 'Bell's Life' and 'Field' and as a result we can see a number of prominent and famous names playing for the club. C. Absolom, the famous England and Kent Cricketer as well as C.M. Tebbut who played Cricket for Essex. Charles W. Alcock was again top scorer with five although he had competition from Absolom and his brother J.F.Alcock.

During the eleven competitive matches only two goals were conceded, an impressive record, and both occurred in the penultimate game against Thompson's XI during a 2-2 draw. It was reported *'We think it is saying a good deal for Thompson's Eleven when we record the fact that in no other match have the F.F.C. lost a goal, and it must be a satisfaction to the members of the Forest Club to know that the only adversaries who ever got goals against them were able players and good fellows.'*[19]

The playing strength of the Forest Club can be assessed at this point in the first official game under F.A. rules, which was played on 9th January 1864. The game was perhaps the first representative game of sorts and consisted of elevens selected by the President and Secretary of the Football Association from the best players. For the President's XI A. Pember, C.W. Alcock and A.M. Tebbut were selected. Alcock got both the goals in a 2-0 win. Players selected for the Secretary's XI from Forest were J.F. Alcock and C.M. Tebbut. [20]

Forest Club played their last fixture of the season on 27th February 1864 and then something happened. Between this date and 2nd April 1864, Forest became the Wanderers. Why did this happen? There are several reasons which are commonly stated. The first suggested by Booth was that owning their own ground was too expensive a luxury.[21] Alcock stated *'a variety of causes led to the decision of the old Forest Club after four years of unbroken triumph, to seek a wider scope of football utility. The chief was the fact that the local element had become fine by degrees and beautifully less.'*[22] This is perhaps a romanticised version of events by Alcock himself which denotes harmony and the need to progress.

It does appear that there were certain elements of the club which did not share Alcock's vision *'some of the members openly opposed 'an organisation of ex-public schoolboys wandering from place to place' (the 19th Century equivalent it seems, of hanging around on street corners), but Alcock was equal to their complaints, and made a virtue of his team's rootlessness by renaming it The Wanderers.'*[23]

Did the name change result in a family split? J.F. Alcock only ever made one appearance for the Wanderers in 1867, which is strange when you look at his record prior to the name changing and the part he played in shaping the club and the Football Association. J.F. Alcock was to get caught up in a lengthy divorce battle from 1868, and that could explain why he disappeared from the scene. We are unlikely ever to get an answer on this, but it is worth pondering, as other notable absentees after the name change were J. Pardoe, F.C. Adams and the first Honorary Secretary A.W. Mackenzie.

The other reason given is the expansion of its membership to include all public school and university players and not just Old Harrovians, but this can hardly be the case when there were only seven Old Harrovians who featured during 1863/64 of the 29 known players i.e. the Alcock brothers, E.W. Burnett, A.K. Finlay, D. Gillespie, T.W. Greaves and J. Pardoe.

Alcock named the club The Wanderers by using the metaphor in the same way Wilson and Guillemard had done in naming the Butterflies Cricket Club. Alcock says *'the transmutation of the Forest chrysalis into the resplendent butterfly.'*[24] It certainly seems to be a play on words in that

18

they were technically homeless, as they did not own a ground, but they lingered on for another season at Snaresbrook, before playing a whole season away from home in 1865/66 season. Regardless of any club politics, which may or may not have occurred the Wanderers took the field on 2nd April 1864 in the fantastically coloured strip of Orange, Violet and Black for their first ever match as the Wanderers Football Club.

Wanderers   1   No Names, Kilburn   0

Responding as they always do with alacrity and cheerfulness to an invitation received at the eleventh hour, the Wanderers prepared their 'costumes de (foot) bal' on Saturday, April 2, and according to their usually wandering individual style of travelling started off by different routes to arrive at their destination, The Victoria Tavern, Kilburn, as may be expected, at widely different hours. Some, evidently relying on the old proverb that 'hansom is that hansom does' chartered the fashionable two wheeler and were quickly landed at the 'house of call', while others eager to take advantage of the opportunities for speedy (?) transit afforded them by the North London Railway, safely accomplished the distance (six miles) in the incredibly short space of one hour ten minutes. The roving band was at last, however, satisfactorily collected together, and soon made it's appearance on the field of battle, where it was very graciously received by a sharp cutting wind, which was blowing straight down from the upper to lower ground. By a happy acquaintance with the chief points of the art of tossing, as exemplified through the medium of a shilling piece, the choice of goal was won by the rovers, who, unwillingly as they always are to turn their backs on friend or foe, selected the upper goal, with the wind and sun (two valuable auxiliaries as it proved) behind them. For an hour, inspite of the heaviness of the ground, the game rages furiously, only one goal (kicked for the Wanderers by A.M. Tebbut) being obtained by either side.

C.W. Alcock, C. Absolom, C. Bigland, F. Desborough, G.H. Edmunds, T. Greaves, J. Hillhouse, A.M. Tebbut, C.M. Tebbut, A. Thompson [25]

Despite only having ten men, the Wanderers continued where Forest Club had left off and overcame a tough first hurdle. The report gives an interesting insight into the way the Wanderers players would have travelled to matches if nothing else. It also shows how much they seemed to enjoy their football. Throughout the research of this early period no one ever played a bad game and every one enjoyed it. The crowd always applauded something which sounds completely alien to the game we know today. It perhaps helped that most the reports seemed to have been penned by a member of the Forest or Wanderers Club, probably by Charles W. Alcock himself and that perhaps he was expressing his side's feelings more than the opposition who had just been trounced 5-0! The fact remains that the text of these early reports is littered with compliments, *'the spectators, of whom their were a goodly array, justly acknowledged it to be the finest match they had seen for a long time.'* [26] and *'both sides played beautifully'* [27]

At the same time the reports highlight that football was already showing signs of becoming a spectator sport and the Wanderers appear to have been building up a following as the writer or writers fondly mention the supporters frequently *'this being the first match since Christmas, a large number of spectators assembled'* [28] and *'Mr C. Alcock, of the Forest Club, elicited great applause from the spectators, of whom there were a large number present.'* [29] The Wanderers Football Club was now firmly established as the leading club in England and Charles W. Alcock was in charge of this progressive club which was seeking to expand the game further still.

References

1	Pawson *100 years of the F.A. Cup* pp5-6
2	Alcock *The Book of Football* p255
3	Alcock *The Association Game* p60
4	Bettesworth *Chats on the Cricket Field* p27
5	Alcock *The Book of Football* p255
6	Booth *The Father of Modern the Life & Times of Charles W, Alcock* p44
7	Reynolds *Forest School and the F.A.Cup*
8	Alcock *The Book of Football* p255
9	Witty *Association Football vol. 1* p144
10	Alcock *The Association Game* p62
11	*Bell's Life* 23.3.1862 p7
12	*Bell's Life* 13.4.1862 p 1
13	*Bell's Life* 7.10.1862 quoted in Williams *The Code War* p10
14	*Bell's Life* 29.3.1863 p6
15	*Bell's Life* 29.3.1863 p6
16	*Field* 28.2.1863 p193
17	Williams *The Code War* p17
18	*Bell's Life* 19.12.1863 p7
19	*Bell's Life* 20.2.1864 p3
20	*Bell's Life* 16.1.1864 p3
21	Booth *The Father of Modern the Life & Times of Charles W, Alcock* p44-5
22	Alcock *The Book of Football* p255
23	Mason *A Game for the People* p24
24	Alcock *Association Football* p62
25	*Bell's Life* 9.4.1864 p7
26	*Bell's Life* 26.12.1863 p6
27	*Bell's Life* 20.2.1864 p3
28	*Bell's Life* 20.2.1864 p3
29	*Bell's Life* 22.3.1863 p6

The Forgotten Years – 1864-1870

As described in the last chapter the Wanderers Football Club emerged out of the Forest Football Club in 1864, yet there is a surprisingly large gap of seven years before anything is written about them in detail. 1864-1870 could almost be described as 'the forgotten years'. The majority of people writing on the subject, including C.W. Alcock have ignored this period of the club's existence, except to mention that the club played in Battersea Park, and perhaps a brief note about the first defeat against Harrow School or the fact the park keepers used to kick them out the park if the game ended late.

This is perhaps because after 1866 the Wanderers Football Club declined steadily from their previous high standards before a spark returned at the start of the 1870/71 season. In one season shortly to be discussed the club struggled so much for players that they were short of a full complement of players in all but a couple of games. Perhaps in view of this, it was convenient for C.W. Alcock and the writers who followed him to gloss over this period and portray the more romantic version of events post 1871, which is so often relayed in books on the subject. It should be noted that the results were not disastrous, but the club's air of invincibility certainly disappeared over the course of these years.

It is however an important period of the Wanderers Football Club's history and should not be ignored. It witnessed the invention of the football tour, the establishment of the game and a huge expansion of the fixture list. It also was the time when the club sowed the seeds of their future success and legends of the game such as A.F. Kinnaird, T.C. Hooman and R.W.S. Vidal all made their debuts.

1864/65
For the 1864/65 season the Forest Football Club and the Wanderers Football Club seemed to have worked together at least at the start according to reports in Bell's Life. The reporting of games at this time was usually done by the Club Secretary, namely C.W. Alcock. This fact is substantiated by Alcock's quote in 1866 *'is the first I have ever yet seen published in any sporting paper as being a 'Wanderers' match which has not emanated from my pen or been published without sanction.'* 1 There is however a little bit of a mystery of how the team actually fared during the season. It is clear that they remained unbeaten from reports from the following season, but only four reports made the newspapers and only during the month of November 1864.

From that we can glean that Wanderers played two games, as did Forest Football Club. The Field newspaper lists the following fixtures which suggests, more games were played:

7th Jan	Wanderers v Forest F.C.	at Leytonstone
21st Jan	Forest v Crystal Palace	at Leytonstone
4th Feb	Forest v No Names	at Leytonstone 2

No reports followed these games, but it is interesting to see that the two clubs were due to face each other in January 1865 and that the Forest Football Club continued to play at Snaresbrook, while the Wanderers Football Club certainly did play at least one game at Battersea Park, although this was against Civil Service who could be regarded as the home club.

There is evidence to suggest that certain key club members also represented other clubs, which maybe explains why the Wanderers Football Club did not play many games. This exchange and sharing of players was made possible by the smaller fixture lists, which clubs undertook at the time through the lack of opponents, An example of this is the fact that the cream of the Wanderers Football Club all represented No Names (Kilburn) in February 1865, namely C.W. Alcock, A.M. Tebbut, C.M. Tebbut, A. Baker and W. Baker 3.

What is known is that the Wanderers Football Club opened the season with a game against 'The Officers' winning 1-0 with a goal by A.M. Tebbutt. This game has been quoted as the first Wanderers Football Club match in other literature, but this is not the case as the previous chapter highlights. The team, which opened the season, was as follows, C.W. Alcock, W.F. Baker, W. Cutbill, F. Elliot, F. Green, H. Green, H. Head, C.M. Tebbut, A.M. Tebbutt, A. Thompson and two unlisted others.

This was followed by a 2-0 victory over Civil Service at Battersea Park, before Forest Football Club fixtures resumed with an uncannily similar team. In the 1-0 win over Crystal Palace on 19th November 1864 the following is the team which represented Forest: C.W. Alcock, C. Absolom, R. Cotton, J. Elliot, C. Hamilton, C.D. Jackson, A.M. Tebbut, C.M. Tebbut and A.M. Thompson. This was followed by a 1-0 win over Civil Service and that is where the story ends for this season.

1865/66
The fixture card for 1865/66 lists the 42 members of the Wanderers Football Club who included an impressive array of contemporary sportsmen. C.W. and J.F. Alcock are both listed along with A. Baker, a famous sprinter, E.E. Bowen the famous Harrow School Master, C.F. Buller a well known Cricketer, A.G. Guillemard, one of the founding fathers of Rugby Union, J.B. Martin, later to become President of the London Athletic Club, A. Pember the Secretary of the F.A. and the Tebbut brothers of whom C.M. played Cricket for Essex County Cricket Club. It also gave the fixtures which were arranged at the start of the season, which incidentally were all played one week behind those published on the fixture card 4.

The Wanderers list of members and fixtures 1865/66

During the course of the season another club emerged, albeit briefly, using the name Wanderers and playing the game by Rugby rules no less. A report of 'Brookfield Club v Wanderers' featured in the Sportsman on 13th January 1866 and provoked a stormy response from C.W. Alcock:

'SIR – I note in your impression of last Saturday, immediately above the account of our match (Wanderers) against Crystal Palace Club, a paragraph headed 'Brookfield Club (Highgate) v Wanderers' and purporting to contain particulars of a game played between Brookfield Club as above and Wanderers.

Now, I am not going to enter into a dissertation on that well known question of the 'Devine Williams', what's in a name? Nor do I intend to argue on his assertation that 'that which we call a rose by any other name would smell as sweet.' I merely wish to enlighten your readers, some of whom, seeing accounts of two matches so closely attendant upon each other, both purporting to be played by 'Wanderers' and both played on the same day, might be lead to believe they were both matches of the same club. The account (Brookfield Club v Wanderers) to which I have above alluded is the first I have ever yet seen published in any sporting paper as being a 'Wanderers' match which had not emanated from my pen or been published without sanction. The 'Wanderers' Club' to which I belong and which club I can truthfully say has now obtained a (football) world renowned reputation – it's (sic) title has never been doubted or usurped by any other club- I will observe, for the information of your readers, is not in the habit of playing at Victoria Park, nor does it ever play Rugby rules.

After hard and severe contests, we have caused our names , 'Wanderers,' to be almost, as regards football players 'as familiar in their mouths as household words.' They say 'good wine needs no bush,' and we can of course lay no claim to our title except the claim first possession; but still we do not like to see the name which, has been rendered famous by repeated victories usurped by, I may almost say, an unknown club. I merely appeal to the spirit of fairplay which no doubt exists in the minds of the pseudo 'Wanderers', to refrain from player under a title which does no in justice belong to them. I give you below my name and address so that any communications on the subject may be made to me. I must apologise for thus trespassing on your valuable space, but I have done so merely from a desire to present your readers imagining the match v Brookfield Club to be one sanctioned by the real Wanderers, and thus turning the fictitious rovers

> *Into shapes, and giving to airy nothingness*
> *A local habitation and a name*

-Yours, & c.,   *C.W. Alcock*
155, Fenchurch Street, E.C. Jan 13 5

It is not known if anyone from the 'fictitious rovers' ever replied to C.W. Alcock, but it did spark a response from their opponents Brookfield Club:

SIR,- I was somewhat surprised to see the letter in your Tuesday's impression from a 'Real Wanderer' and complaining of another club (our opponents on the 6th) taking the same name without his sanction or knowledge. I was not aware that there was a rival club until I read the letter referred to; and now I find it is so, it is not for me (a member of Brookfield) to decide as to the prior right to the name, but I feel sure that our opponents will instantly re-christen their club on finding their title weak, and I hope to hear everything is amicably settled before our return match – I am, Sir, & c.,

> *John P.Chapman*
> *(captain Brookfield F.C.)* 6

On the football pitch the season was a success as the unbeaten run continued until December 1865. Prior to this Wanderers, played all games at their opponents grounds and got off to a great start

23

thrashing Civil Service, scoring five 'bases' to their opponents none. Bases seem to have been preferred to the word goals in describing a score. It was certainly a word used at Harrow School and could well have originated there although why it never appeared in any Wanderers reports prior to this time is not clear if this was the case.

Wanderers continued with a 1-0 win at Charterhouse, before a strange match at Penge against Crystal Palace resulted in a 1-1 draw. It was strange in that the report stated that the game kicked off at 3.15pm which in November would mean the game would have ended in pitch darkness had it lasted much more than 45 minutes and the report clearly indicates that it did. *'The Wanderers were kept at bay for nearly three-quarters of an hour. At last, however fortune smiled on them, and in one of their fine rushes the first goal was kicked by J.B. Martin.'*[7] Crystal Palace went on to equalise and the game continued in search of a winner before time was called.

A historic first visit to Vincent Square to face Westminster School followed and finished in victory. Forest School were the next victims and the report sheds more intriguing light on the Wanderers history. Contrary to what was claimed just two months later the report states *'the Wanderers inexperience in the School rules, which were a happy mixture of Rugby, Charterhouse, and Harrow.'*[8] It was a common theme that the Wanderers often adopted the home clubs rules and did not strictly adhere to the rules laid out by the Football Association. A nine man Wanderers side then beat No Names (Kilburn) 1-0 in what was to be the last match in the great unbeaten run of the club since starting playing competitive fixtures in 1862.

The defeat against Harrow School can be attributed to a number of factors: the first that Wanderers only had nine players, the second is that generally the case during the 1860's was that they would adopt Harrow rules, although the following report does not confirm it. Finally the coin toss was oft-times vital as there was a distinct advantage to the side defending the upper 'base'. The Harrow School magazine 'The Tyro' reported the game as follows:

Harrow School   4   Wanderers   0
This match was played on the last Saturday of the Christmas quarter. The Wanderers, hitherto invincible, were defeated by four bases to none. The first was obtained by Tupper with a capital 'three yards'. The next two were both kicked by Montgomery, off the ground, and the last by Noyes.

The Wanderer who most distinguished himself was Phipps; and Smith, who played against the School, played so well as to obtain the twelfth shirt.

C.W. Alcock, H.G. Phipps, C.F. Reid, W.M. Allfrey, Green, Cater, R.D. Elphinstone, J.B. Martin, Smith (emergency)[9]

The positive factor that the Wanderers Football Club could take from this game was that all the Harrow School goal scorers would go on to represent the club in future years.

Wanderers recovered well and duly beat Reigate before the Christmas break 3-1. The new year saw the introduction of one of the Wanderers most celebrated players, none other than A.F. Kinnaird, who brought a side specially selected by himself to face the Rovers as the Wanderers had been nick named at this time. His side held the Wanderers to a 0-0 draw and it would not be until the following season that he would make his Wanderers debut.

Wanderers went on to beat Crystal Palace (3-0), gain revenge over Harrow School (2-0), beat Crusaders (5-2), Charterhouse (1-0) and Forest School (4-0) whilst gaining draws with Civil Service and Westminster School. The season was reviewed in Bell's Life and concluded with the following:

THE WANDERERS CLUB

During the past season, commencing Oct 28th this powerful club has been engaged in 16 matches of which they won 11, four were drawn, and in one they were defeated by Harrow School, on which occasion they did not play their entire strength. In the return match the Wanderers retrieved their lost laurels, winning by two bases. In the 16 matches the Wanderers obtained 32 bases, and nine were scored against them. 10

There is a minor discrepancy on the writers adding up in the goals against column, but this may be attributed to Harrow stating the score was 4-0. No report of the defeat featured in the newspapers, perhaps denoting sour grapes, but because of this the goals against tally should read ten and not nine.

1866/67

After so much early success 1866/67 season was a real disappointment: the playing record was respectable to a point, but what was the real low spot for the club and C.W. Alcock, as the famed administrator was that on only two occasions did the club get eleven of their own players on the pitch at kick off time. Every other game saw either the late arrival of players or more commonly the need to borrow two or three players from the opposition to actually get a side on the pitch.

The side which, had gone nearly five seasons unbeaten, lost their opening two games against Forest School and Charterhouse. Forest School Magazine comments on the game and seems to have thought the Wanderers who turned up, somewhat aloof and stated *'had the Wanderers brought down their full number, I doubt if they would have beaten us, though **they** seem to have little doubt about it.'* 11

The ten man Wanderers recorded their first win in November against Westminster School and followed this up with a 1-0 win over Civil Service. Despite this success the report of the game was less than complimentary *'the Wanderers being represented by a team hardly worthy of their great reputation.'* 12 The Wanderers were struggling after seven games and had won only three and lost four.

Battersea Park has long been regarded as the Wanderers base in this period, but, apart from playing the Civil Service there until Christmas 1866, they could not realistically regard it as a home ground. The only brief period that it could be regarded as a home ground was December 1866 as Wanderers entertained the Old Etonians and Harrow Chequers on the 20th and 22nd December respectively.

The first of those games resulted in a 0-1 defeat to the Old Etonians with A.F. Kinnaird scoring the only goal. The game was played in dense fog and the report again questions the Wanderers, in particular one member's sportsmanship *'We must not omit to mention that a Wanderer, whose principles with regard to infringement of the rules are rather loose, was gently reminded by the captain of the Etonian team that 'fives' was a distinct game, and entirely separate from the game of football, with which he so often allied it.'* 13 This is somewhat appropriate given that the game of fives was invented in the cloisters at Eton College.

From the shambles of this season, though emerged one of the great grounds for optimism in the form of A.F. Kinnaird, who made his debut for the Wanderers two days later in the 1-1 draw with

Harrow Chequers. Although Kinnaird only made two further appearances this season, Wanderers form improved and they lost only one more game before the end of the season. The final record was as follows played fifteen: won six, drew four and lost five.

1867/68

By 1867 football was widely acknowledged as the popular winter sport. R.D. Norseman commented in his article Our Winter Game Chapter II, *'There is no English sport which can hold a candle to the winter game.'*[14] The Wanderers in turn were enjoying themselves, although 1867/68 was to be one of the worst playing record for a full season in their history, and one of only four seasons where they recorded a deficit of wins to losses, two of which were after 1878. Alcock's review of the season in the Football Annual was a positive one however.

'The Rovers kept the ball dribbling throughout the season with all their wonted energy, as will be evident from the large number of contests in which they were engaged. The Wanderers figure in 29 matches, of which they won nine, lost eleven and nine were drawn, the most memorable of their successes being the victory achieved by them over the Carthusians on Under Green, on Saturday 26th Oct., 1867. The Rovers appear to have been troubled with a run of ill-luck, the defeats they suffered at Cambridge, Oxford, against the No Names and the C.C.C. being rather attributable to caprices of fortune than to any superior skill of their opponents. No club has striven more energetically to extend the game than this band of Wanderers, whose name is now familiar to the veriest tyro in football matters. That the Wanderers have in no way lost strength since their last campaign the names of the following distinguished players who have represented them during the past season will best attest.

C.W. Alcock, E.E. Bowen, W.J. Dixon, K. Muir Mackenzie, M. Muir Mackenzie, C.E.B. Nepean, Quintin Hogg, J.M. Yates, C. Absolom, A.F. Kinnaird, Lord E. Fitzmaurice, G.G. Kennedy, J.T. Goldney, W.O. Hewlett, P.M. Thornton, C.F. Reid, E. Norman, P. Norman, J.B. Martin, A. Baker, C.M. Tebbut, J.E. Tayloe, E.W. Wylde, H.H. Montgomery, W.B. Money, Hon F.G. Pelham' [15]

Alcock was right in some respects in his review although it is a somewhat rosier picture than the results suggest. There was a dramatic increase in fixtures and the club played 29 as opposed to 15 the previous season. The season was extended to reflect this and started much earlier at the end of September to accommodate the extra games.

There is no mention of Battersea Park ceasing to be used as a home ground. However, it could not really be regarded as a home ground by today's standards, as between 1865 and 1867 they only played there on eight occasions. Four of these games were against the Civil Service who also used it as a home ground. The other visitors being Old Etonians, Harrow Chequers, Old Harrovians and the last ever visitors an Eton XI. It is interesting that the Rovers did not win any of the games in which they were regarded as the home club in this run!

The famous story about their very brief stay is that the park keepers used to end the games by locking the park gates when it was the end of their working day. This indeed was the case and on three occasions this happened, twice against Civil Service on 20th November 1866 and 7th November 1867 and finally against an Eton XI on 13th December 1867. The report versus Civil Service in 1867 states *'the game was not commenced until 3.15 – too late for the present early closing movement enforced by the park-keepers.'* [16] Against the Eton XI the report states *'Darkness, however, and the park-keepers put an end to the game.'* [17] Probably in view of these continuing problems it is no surprise that the Wanderers abandoned it as a home ground and never used it again.

The season can be viewed slightly more positively when you look at the defeats. Six occurred on the first ever football tours, which occurred at Cambridge and Oxford in 1867. Two were against the powerful Harrow School, while the remaining three games against No Names, C.C.C. and the Royal Engineers, which were no disgrace in themselves.

Wanderers were the inventors of the modern football tour and they undertook two, one to Cambridge in October 1867 and one to Oxford in November 1867. The Cambridge tour was the more extensive of the two and involved five games being played in five days. The tours have to be put in perspective as they were played under a variety of different rules depending on whom they were playing, while at the same time all the teams involved swapped and borrowed players.

The first ever tour game in football history took place on 28th October 1867 at Cambridge against Eton Club. It is hard to call it a tour, as such since most of the players involved were Wanderers members studying at Cambridge. A defeat followed, by three touchdowns to nil, while a report states *'only one recruit from the ranks of the metropolitan Wanderers appeared at Cambridge to sustain the reputation of the club.'* [18] The one Wanderer on this occasion was C.W. Alcock. The rules were again strange and the report dismisses them as *'a mixture of many good rules, good in themselves, but when strung together, unhappily, incongruous.'* [19] The rules were again in question the following day against Harrow Club, also at Cambridge, who defeated the tourists by one goal to one touchdown scored by W.W. Radcliffe.

A win materialised on the Wednesday against St. John's, coinciding with an improvement in the weather conditions. Thursday witnessed King's College defeating the Wanderers by one goal and one touch down to one touch down. Finally on Friday which was meant to be the grand finale, Cambridge University comprehensively beat the Wanderers by three goals and three touch downs to nil in what was described as a *'hollow victory for the University'* [20]

The Oxford tour was little better although much shorter and the club played two games, both at Oxford, one against Harrow Chequers under Harrow rules and one against Oxford University this time under Football Association rules. Both games resulted in 0-1 defeats.

Domestically Wanderers stayed unbeaten until losing to Harrow School in late November, a game in which there were two disputed goals. Prior to this the Wanderers had beaten some impressive opponents C.C.C., Charterhouse, Civil Service, Westminster School and also against numerical odds a Wanderers XI beat an Upton Park XV 1-0 with a little help from the wind.

On the Wanderers return from Oxford, they immediately went down 0-1 to No Names, before a 0-0 draw with an Eton XI in what was the last game at Battersea Park. Then came a 2-2 draw with the Amateur Athletic Club, despite going into a 2-0 lead. Wanderers then entertained and beat Royal Engineers 2-0; this was followed by a 1-2 defeat by C.C.C..

Wanderers then beat Hitchin 2-0, before losing 1-4 at Harrow School in what was to be their heaviest defeat of the season. Alcock was surprisingly missing from the side that lost to Royal Engineers as the Wanderers began falling back into bad habits only fielding eight men and having to find two substitutes on the day of the game to get a competitive side on the pitch. A 3-0 win over Westminster School followed and proved to be the last win of the season as three draws ensued against Charterhouse, an Upton Park XIII and Forest School. In all but one of these drawn games the Wanderers failed to put eleven men on the pitch. The Charterhouse game was significant as it was the first game the Wanderers played at Middlesex County Cricket Ground. Wanderers were to call Middlesex Cricket Club their home for the 1868/69 season and played a further seven games at this venue the following year.

Lords in 1842

The influence of the Wanderers though cannot be disputed and this was highlighted at the Football Association Annual Meeting held at the Freemason's Tavern, Great Queen Street on 26th February 1868. The Wanderers proposed that Rule 4 of the Football Association be changed in regard to the size of the committee and in the process defeated Crystal Palace's similar suggestion. It was reported as follows *'The proposal by the Crystal Palace to increase the number of the committee to twenty was rejected, and that put forward by the Wanderers (who wanted ten) unanimously carried.'* [21] At the same meeting C.W. Alcock and W.J.C. Cutbill were both re-elected to the committee, while Lord E. Fitzmaurice, A.F. Kinnaird, K. Muir Mackenzie, W.J. Dixon, G.G. Kennedy and J. Kirkpatrick were added to the committee all of whom had previously represented the Wanderers on the football pitch.

1868/69
1868/69 saw an improvement in the Wanderers playing record as the club won twelve and lost ten out of thirty games played during the course of the season. C.W. Alcock missed more games than he had ever missed before, being a virtual ever present in the preceding years. He was to feature in only two of the first eight games and then missed the last nine. It is interesting to note that when he played the Wanderers were defeated on only two occasions.

The season also saw the revival of a famous name from the past, Forest Football Club, who began playing regular games at the start of the season. The club was no relation to its more famous namesakes and although the two clubs did meet on the pitch, there were no great links in history or in sharing players.

Wanderers opened with a fixture against C.C.C., where they drew 1-1 and Alcock interestingly gave his name in report as *'T.H.E. Rover.'* [22] This game was followed by a 2-0 win over the Amateur Athletic Club. This game involved an extraordinary incident as revealed here: *'Very little time was now left, and part of this was taken up by the members of the 3rd Middlesex Rifles having to shoot at*

28

the 300 yards range, interfering with the game. However, they good-naturedly shot off their rounds as soon as they could, and play was resumed.' 23

Next up was Westminster School who defeated the Wanderers 1-0. This poor form continued and deteriorated badly in the next five games as the club went on its longest ever run without scoring a goal. R.M.A. beat Wanderers 2-0, Eton Club won by three goals to one touch down and then Harrow Club were held 0-0, the latter two games being part of a tour to Cambridge. Upton Park defeated an eight man Wanderers side 1-0 and this was followed by a 0-2 reverse at Harrow School, who won the toss and forced the Rovers to play up hill.

Alcock's return following these games certainly appears to have given the club a lift, if not a better organized set up, as in the next game at Hitchin a seven man Wanderers side held nine men to a 1-1 draw. The report criticized the fact that it was all too common for players just not to turn up. *'Absenteeism has now apparently become such an all-prevalent fashion among football players that it is perhaps almost superfluous to mention the Wanderers were severely crippled by the absence of three of their team who were expected from Cambridge.'* 24 The Rovers form steadily improved as did their attendances over the next few games, beating Crystal Palace, Forest School, Oxford Amalgamated Club and Civil Service. Sandwiched in the middle was a creditable draw with Royal Engineers despite *'the non-arrival of the expected ball play was not commenced until twenty minutes to four o'clock, a dense fog rendering a sight of the ball of the leather at any distance no easy matter.(sic)'* 25

A rare defeat in a game involving Alcock followed, but can be explained by the fact that the Wanderers only had eight men. The Christmas games saw a 3-0 win over Crusaders and a 0-0 draw with Civil Service.

The new year saw Wanderers stretch their unbeaten run to six games into February. 1869 opened with a 4-4 draw with Old Bradfield despite again being under strength and going 2-0 up, this time with nine men. Kinnaird's Old Etonian side was then held to a 1-1 draw before comprehensive wins over Bedouins and the newly formed Forest Club in what was to prove Alcock's last appearance of the season.

Without Alcock the Wanderers lost the next four games, the first of which was a 0-5 drubbing at Hampstead Heathens. This game marked the first time the Wanderers had conceded five goals in a game ever. Further defeats ensued against Harrow School, R.M.A. and Charterhouse. The run was ended with a 1-0 win over West Kent at Middlesex County Cricket Ground and was followed with a 3-1 win against Westminster School and the record win so far for the club, 8-0 against Upton Park. The game which saw Wanderers back at their best saw some inspired performances; *'the Wanderers got goal after goal in quick succession, chiefly by the dashing runs of A.F. Kinnaird, C.E. Nepean, and W.J. Dixon.'* 26 A victory over Charterhouse and a draw with Forest Club meant the club finished unbeaten in its last five games of the season.

1869/70
Wanderers good end of season did not continue into 1869/70 season as they failed to win any of their first four games and failed to register a single goal. This season will be remembered for other reasons as an exciting new development in the game of Association Football took place, the first ever England v Scotland International fixture, even if it was not official. The Wanderers themselves had exciting news when they moved grounds after their brief stay at Middlesex County Cricket Ground to the equally grand Oval, the home of Surrey County Cricket Club. It was to remain their home for the rest of their existence.

Wanderers helped make history by becoming the first ever opponents of the newly formed Clapham Rovers on the opening day of the season on Clapham Common. Clapham Rovers would go on to become powerful rivals of the Wanderers in the forthcoming years. The game ended in a 1-0 victory for Clapham. Poor finishing was to blame in the next game as C.C.C. were held 0-0. This was followed by Wanderers' first appearance at their new ground the Oval: unfortunately it was not a happy day as the club crashed 0-2 to West Kent. Their second game at the Oval was little better as Old Etonians went home with a 2-0 win. It was not until Wanderers third appearance in the following game that they recorded a victory, 3-0 over Rochester Club, A. Nash had the honour of scoring the club's first goal on what proved to be a very lucky ground.

The Wanderers form improved from this moment and the club only lost one of the next nine games, to Forest School, and included an impressive win over Royal Engineers despite only starting with eight men, although A. Baker turned up soon after the start and hit two goals in the 2-1 victory. The run ended with double defeats, the first at Parker's Piece against Cambridge University when under home rules the club lost by two goals and a touchdown to one touch down and then to what was becoming the traditional defeat at Harrow School.

Wanderers were still not playing every game by Association Rules and the Sportsman reported *'both sides using their hands throughout with all the freedom which has marked recent matches,'*[27] in the 4-2 victory against Civil Service. Revenge was sweet in the Wanderers next game as Hampstead Heathens were beaten 2-0 avenging the previous year's record defeat. Two more defeats followed: 1-2 against Crusaders, who had borrowed two of the Wanderers players prior to the game and 1-2 against Desperadoes, a club made of the cream of talent from bogey side Harrow School.

The beginning of 1870 saw Wanderers get back on track with victories over Crystal Palace, Harrow Pilgrims and Civil Service. In between was a 1-1 draw with the powerful Gitanos, one of Kinnaird's other clubs. Following this was yet another 0-1 defeat against Harrow School. Wanderers in fact added another three games to another poor goal less run which included a draw at Oxford Amalgamated Club and defeats against Crystal Palace, when Wanderers fielded only seven players, and Westminster School, when a certain R.W.S. Vidal scored for the School.

As was the case with the previous season Wanderers again finished strongly, their only defeat in the last five games being against Clapham Rovers on the same day as the first England v Scotland International. Forest Club were hit for seven in a game lasting one hour and an easy 3-0 win over Upton Park sandwiched the defeat. The Wanderers fielded two sides on the final day of the season, one which drew 1-1 at Charterhouse and the other which beat Hampstead Heathens 2-1 at the Oval. Remarkably Kinnaird played in both games for Wanderers 'Soon after the second change of ends the Hampstead Heathens enlisted A. Baker, who arrived in company with A.F. Kinnaird from Charterhouse, the latter at the same time joining the Wanderers.'[28]

The first England v Scotland fixture took place on 5th March 1870. It was not an official International as it was selected by members of the Football Association and only featured players with Scottish links based in London. Some of those links furthermore would hardly qualify a player in future years. In fact two players who represented Scotland that day would go onto play for England versus Scotland in official Internationals namely A.K. Smith and Will Lindsay [29]. It was however important as it was a series of five unofficial internationals which culminated in the birth of official International football in 1872. The game which ended goalless also highlights the strength of the Wanderers side as the club had fielded the following players for England, C.W. Alcock, E.E. Bowen, A. Baker, W.P. Crake, E. Freeth, E. Lubbock, A. Nash, J.C. Smith, A.H. Thornton and

R.W.S. Vidal, while for Scotland, J. Kirkpatrick, A.F. Kinnaird and A. Morten played during the course of the season 30.

Prior to this at the Football Association Annual Meeting on 23rd February 1870, the Wanderers had suggested the following rule change and had had it approved. It was as follows, *'Add to Law III- In the event, however of no goal having fallen to either party at the lapse of half the allotted time, ends shall be changed.'* 31 The club however was less successful in proposing to ban all handling including goal keepers and a motion by Civil Service was deemed to be more ideal which allowed handling. The season was concluded by the annual dinner on the 29th March 1870.

References

1	*The Sportsman* 16.1.1866 p7
2	*Field* 10.12.1864 p403
3	*Bell's Life* 18.2.1865 p8
4	*Wanderers Football Club –Season 1865-66– List of Members and Fixtures*
5	*The Sportsman* 16.1.1866 p7
6	*The Sportsman* 20.1.1866 p2
7	*Bell's Life* 18.11.1865 p7
8	*Bell's Life* 2.12.1865 p7
9	*The Tyro* – February 1866 Edition p111
10	*Bell's Life* 31.3.1866 p7
11	*The Forest School Magazine* 1866 p344
12	*The Sportsman* 24.11.1866 p4
13	*The Sportsman* 22.12.1866 p4
14	Norseman R.D. *The Sportsman–Our Winter Game Chapter II* 7.1.1868 p4
15	Alcock C.W. *Football Annual* 1868 p39
16	*The Sportsman* 9.11.1867 p3
17	*The Sportsman* 14.12.1867 p3
18	*The Sportsman* 29.10.1867 p3
19	*The Sportsman* 29.10.1867 p3
20	*The Sportsman* 2.11.1867 p3
21	*The Sportsman* 29.2.1868 p8
22	*The Sportsman* 29.9.1868 p3
23	*The Sportsman* 21.10.1868 p3
24	*The Sportsman* 28.11.1868 p2
25	*The Sportsman* 5.12.1868 p6
26	*The Sportsman* 17.3.1869 p3
27	*The Sportsman* 2.12.1869 p3
28	*The Sportsman* 23.3.1870 p4
29	Ward *Scotland The Team* p9
30	*The Sportsman* 8.3.1870 p3
31	*The Sportsman* 24.2.1870 p3

Recovery and Triumph 1870-1875

1870/71

The 1870/71 season firmly re-established the Wanderers as a force to be reckoned with, thanks to a dramatic upturn in performances and results on the pitch. This was achieved despite the worst winter that the infant sport had experienced. Due to the fact the pitches were iced over many games were cancelled and if they did take place, several times teams were under strength. Wanderers overcame this and in fact only lost five of their thirty-seven matches played this season. It was about this time in 1870 that the Wanderers changed their kit slightly when it became purple, yellow and black.

The season began, as had the previous season, with a game against the powerful Clapham Rovers club who visited the Oval and went home with a 1-0 win. The report of this game highlights the increasing interest in the sport *'in the presence of a large number of spectators, the popularity of this winter game being evidently on the increase, from the interest shown by the on lookers on this occasion.'*[1] Two wind affected victories followed, against C.C.C. and Civil Service, which both ended in narrow 1-0 results.

It would have been three victories in a row had C.W. Alcock's goal against West Kent not been disallowed. *'after a short scrimmage a few yards in front of the Kentish posts, a 'curly drop' kick by C.W. Alcock carried it between the posts. To this success, after the lapse of a few minutes, the captain of West Kent lodged an objection on the ground that the ball had been handled, and in the face of this plea the Wanderers conceded what was certainly a just claim.'*[2] The game ended goal less, but the ongoing confusion over the rules or, more to the point what rules were being played on the day continued. It is unlikely that C.W. Alcock, who was more conversant with the rules than most players, would not have known so he could have had few complaints.

The Oval as it would have been in Wanderers day (courtesy of Surrey Library)

The next game against Harrow Pilgrims at the Oval provided yet another curiosity as C.W. Alcock actually played for the visitors instead of the Wanderers: it was to no avail as the Pilgrims lost 2-0 after goals from R.S. Walker and A. Borwick. Forest School were the next victims when they succumbed 4-1 at Walthamstow. It would have finished 3-1 but the two sides were enjoying the game and decided to play an extra fifteen minutes and a fourth goal for the Wanderers was added.

The weather then upset the Wanderers' form as they were frustrated by the slippery conditions in the 0-0 draw at Upton Park and then lost 1-3 at Charterhouse School. The pitch was so bad it warranted this comment *'the scene of the action was Under Green, which, to treat the matter in the mildest manner, was in a condition utterly unfit for play, the centre of the ground being occupied by a circular patch of soft mud, of no mean width, through which it was almost impossible to wade.'*3 Spirits were lifted however three days later on Guy Fawke's Day when Harrow School were beaten for the first time since 1864. On the same day another Wanderers side, captained by T.C. Hooman, defeated the Forest Club 2-0 to round off a successful afternoon.

The two aforementioned games were the start of an impressive unbeaten streak in which the Wanderers won eight and drew two of a ten game sequence. The sequence included impressive wins over Brixton Club 5-1 in thick fog, a 2-0 win over Oxford Association Club and a 5-0 win over Gitanos at the Oval. It was ended in mid December when the Wanderers made their first trip to Brighton to face Brighton College. A weak side succumbed 1-0 to the hosts on this occasion.

In the middle of this run of form the second of the Pseudo Internationals involving England and Scotland was played. The Wanderers were well represented with C.W. Alcock, A.J. Baker, W.P. Crake, T.C. Hooman, E. Lubbock, R.W.S. Vidal and R.S.F. Walker representing England, while J. Kirkpatrick, A.F. Kinnaird, C.E.B. Nepean, Q. Hogg and G.G. Kennedy played for the Scots. A goal by R.S.F. Walker handed England a 1-0 victory in front of six or seven hundred spectators.

Following on from the defeat by Brighton College the Wanderers hit an indifferent patch defeating a Harrow Rovers side 4-0, then drawing with Eton College and then getting thrashed 0-5 at Hampstead Heathens in what was their joint heaviest defeat to date. Ironically the other 0-5 defeat was also at the hands of the Hampstead Heathens. The Wanderers did have the excuse that most of their strongest players were playing in the North v South game, which was also played the same day. Of the twenty two players selected for this game, sixteen had appeared for the Wanderers.

After an enforced break of a month, a game against Crystal Palace was arranged at short notice on 18th January 1871 and Wanderers won 3-0 thanks to two goals by A.F. Kinnaird and one by C.W. Alcock. This was followed by a second 0-0 draw with West Kent before four C.W. Alcock goals ensured a comfortable 6-1 win over Civil Service in a game which was novel in that it was six a side. Another 0-0 draw, this time against Harrow School was followed by a 2-0 win over an A.F. Kinnaird led, Gitanos side. Wins over Brixton Club, Hampstead Heathens and Westminster School ensued before a draw at Charterhouse School ended the run.

The second Pseudo International of the season also took place on 25th February 1871 and again the Wanderers were well represented as honours finished even in a 1-1 draw. C.W. Alcock, A.J. Baker, M.P. Betts, W.P. Crake, T.C. Hooman, E. Lubbock, C.W. Stephenson, R.W.S. Vidal and R.S.F. Walker represented England and for Scotland A.F. Kinnaird, W.H. Gladstone, Q. Hogg, J. Kirkpatrick and C.E.B. Nepean all featured.

The season closed with two defeats against Clapham Rovers and Royal Engineers, which both ended 0-1, before two wins on the same day against Forest Club and Upton Park. The defeat against the Engineers witnessed a goal which would never have stood in this day and age: *'a general scrimmage, in which hands appeared to be as prominent as feet, the goal-keeper finally, ball in* *hands, being literally forced through the posts by the overpowering onslaught of the opposite forwards'*4 The final game saw Wanderers draw with an ambitiously titled and somewhat grand 'The World'. The World it should be stated basically consisted of some of the better players from the South of England although R.Smith of Queen's Park did feature for them. The reports of the day though indicated that it was not the strongest team which could have been put out against the Wanderers.

The season was rounded off with the club's first meeting for athletic sports which was held at Lille Bridge, West Brompton on 8th April 1871. For each event the entrance fee was set at 2s. 6d., except for the 440 yards flat race and the 120 yards flat race when the fee was 5s. each. The attendance was however limited, due to cold weather and the counter attractions of Brighton. The following list details the winners of the events.

120 Yards Open Handicap	:	A.P. Wells
150 Yards Members Handicap	:	T.C. Hooman
440 Yards Open Handicap	:	W.H. Palmer
Putting the Weight	:	T.C. Hooman
120 Hurdles Race, Members	:	A.F. Kinnaird
One Mile Race, Members	:	F.A. Currie
300 Yards Race	:	A.F. Kinnaird
Football Race, dribbling	:	M.P. Betts

1871/72
After such a good season 1871/72 would have to go someway to better it. The Wanderers published a fixture list in the Sportsman and claimed in the Football Annual that covered this season to have 100 members as they ambitiously went on their way. It was the season when competitive football was born and as a result of this Wanderers lifted the first F.A. Cup, an achievement which was to mean their name was now permanently etched in the history of the game. The season had already commenced when the competition was approved and Wanderers had already played out two 0-0 draws with Clapham Rovers and Harrow Chequers, who would later scratch from the F.A. Cup, to the benefit of the Wanderers, and contained two players who would feature for them in the first final. This was followed by a weak Wanderers side overcoming Civil Service 1-0 and a 4-0 trouncing of Gitanos in an eight a side game.

On the 24th October 1871 The Sportsman published an article entitled *'FOOTBALL ASSOCIATION CHALLENGE CUP.'* At a meeting the previous night held at The Sportsman's offices the Football Association had approved the creation of what was to be the most famous cup competition the world has ever seen. The draw for the first round was made and is recorded as follows.

Wanderers	v	Harrow Chequers
Barnes	v	Civil Service
Crystal Palace	v	Hitchin
Donnington Grammar School	v	Queen's Park, Glasgow
Royal Engineers	v	Reigate Priory
Upton Park	v	Clapham Rovers
Hampstead Heathens (a bye)		

Note: Maidenhead v Marlow was omitted from the original draw listed in the Sportsman either in error or they were late entrants.

What the article does not give credit to is whose idea it was. It was C.W. Alcock who *proposed 'that it is desirable that a Challenge Cup should be established in connection with the Association, for which all clubs belonging to the Association should be invited to compete.'*[5] The concept though was based on the inter house competition at Harrow School which was competed for on a knock out basis. The entrance fee was set at one guinea and a trophy was purchased at a cost of £20, while rules were set stating that a player could only play for one competing club per season and a provision *'in the case of provincial clubs, it shall be in the power of the committee to except (sic) them from the early tie-drawings, and to allow them to compete specially against clubs in the same district, except in the case of the final ties.'*[6]

On the same day that this article was published Wanderers sent a team to Forest School their description was that *'the Wanderers' eleven was certainly the best they have ever brought against us.'*[7] A comfortable 3-0 victory was the result with C.W. Alcock, P. Morton and C.L. Huggins all scoring. Then after five matches without conceding a goal a weak Wanderers side lost 1-2 to Upton Park at the Oval and followed this up with a second successive defeat, losing at Harrow School by *'one luckily-acquired goal to none'*[8]

The Wanderers form improved however and following two 1-1 draws at Charterhouse School and at the Oval against future fellow finalists Royal Engineers got back to winning ways at Camberwell against the 1st Surrey Rifles. This 1-0 victory was achieved against all the odds as the report details. *'Three of their number, were hopelessly lost in their journey to the ground. Thus reduced by three, and further compelled to find a lamed substitute for a fourth unfortunate Wanderer, owing to a domestic bereavement of a rather remote character.'*[9] Two more wins came in quick succession against Cambridge University at Parker's Piece in a thirteen a side game and at Vincent Square where Westminster School unexpectedly were beaten easily 4-0.

The Wanderers then enjoyed a week off as a club, but due to the Psuedo International England against Scotland many were selected for this game. England triumphed 2-1 with the following Wanderers players being selected for England, C.W. Alcock, M.P. Betts, E. Lubbock, C.W. Stephenson, A.C. Thompson, R.W.S. Vidal and W.P. Crake. For Scotland, R.E.W. Crawford, F.H. Crawford, J. Kirkpatrick and E. Elliot all played.

In the lead up to the club's first F.A. Cup tie the Wanderers were in blistering form. An eight man Wanderers team saw off eleven of Windsor Home Park's finest 1-0, before Crystal Palace were beaten 1-0, Forest School 5-0, Hampstead Heathens 2-0 and Harrow Chequers 4-0. The latter saw an extra fifteen minutes added which was played under Harrow rules and saw both sides score once.

On the 16th December Wanderers made their F.A. Cup debut on Clapham Common against Clapham Rovers. Under Association Rules they had not conceded a goal for eight straight matches and were probably slight favourites, six of their side having appeared in the previous Pseudo International, while another four had represented London against Sheffield just two weeks previously, namely C.W. Alcock, C.W. Stephenson, W.P. Crake and P. Rivett-Carnac. The Wanderers were however fortunate that Harrow Chequers scratched from the competition in the first round as their numbers, and probably the outcome of the competition would have been severely altered, for example M.P. Betts would not have featured for the Wanderers as he would have been cup tied.

Despite some confusion over the kick off time which led to the match ending in pitch darkness and having to find late replacements for the absent A.C. Thompson and R.H. Benson the Wanderers triumphed 1-0. The side for this historic match was as follows,

E. Lubbock, R.C. Welch, C.W. Stephenson, C.W. Alcock, M.P. Betts, E.E. Bowen, A.G. Bonsor, W.P. Crake, T.C. Hooman, P.T. Rivett-Carnac and Hon. T.H. Pelham.

The goal finally came when *'the Wanderers' forwards had been working with praiseworthy energy, and at last, after some brilliant dribbling by W.P. Crake, a chance of a kick at goal was offered the Hon. T.H. Pelham, and steadying himself cleverly for the shot, the latter by a neat kick secured the fall of the Clapham goal.'*[10] Incidentally on the same day a Wanderers side lost 0-1 to Chiswick although the only record of this is in the Football Annual.

The Wanderers were through to face Crystal Palace in the third round. Before that though the club, still had two tough games to play, at home to Cambridge University and Hampstead Heathens. The Cambridge game was described as the toughest of the season so far and resulted in a 2-1 win after goals from C.L. Huggins and C.W. Alcock. The Heathens were easily seen off 3-0 with C.W. Alcock scoring a brace.

For the third round Wanderers were again back at Clapham Common, this time to play Crystal Palace as already stated. Wanderers had only beaten Crystal Palace two months previously, but were without their strongest forward line up while Crystal Palace had recruited several new players in an effort to progress. A close game ensued, ending 0-0 although C.W. Stephenson had a goal disallowed for the Wanderers following handling.

As a result of this both clubs progressed to the semi finals. Pawson argues *'the Wanderers were aided on their way to the Final by their power in committee as well as on the field. In the quarter-final they drew 0-0 with Crystal Palace and progressed under Rule 8 of the competition which stated: 'In the case of a drawn match the Clubs shall be drawn in the next round or compete again at the discretion of the committee.' This was, however a sensible decision to send Wanderers into one semi-final against Queen's Park, Glasgow and Crystal Palace into the other against Royal Engineers who would otherwise have a bye to the Final.'*[11] The Wanderers were also helped by the fact that many clubs were unable to enter due to the late commencement of the competition as they were already committed to fixtures elsewhere.

The Wanderers slipped into a poor run of form leading up to the semi-final. The same day as the Crystal Palace game a weak side had lost at the Oval to Gitanos. Two weeks later Wanderers beat Crystal Palace 1-0 according to the Football Annual, although no report has been traced. This game was made more bizarre by the fact that there is evidence that Crystal Palace played Barnes on the same day as did London play Sheffield. Next at the Oval, the 1st Surrey Rifles visited and won by the odd goal in three. Fortunately things improved as two of the next three games were won against Civil Service and Westminster School. These sandwiched a 0-2 reverse at Harrow School.

The Wanderers players also had to contend with an England v Scotland game and a London v Sheffield game in the run up to the semi-final. The latter was played just two days prior to the Queen's Park tie.

4th March 1872 was the date of the semi-final. It is significant in the history of the game in that it was the first time a Scottish side had come to London for a game and it could be argued that it was a more legitimate International fixture than the England v Scotland fixture that been played a couple of weeks beforehand.

Queen's Park arrived in London only because a public subscription was raised on their behalf in Glasgow 12, and they also cancelled a tour to the Tweed Valley. As a result of this the area turned to Rugby a tradition which still survives to this day 13. Queen's Park had in fact in their five year history only played seven games and had received a bye to this stage of the competition, but their performance in the semi-final not only helped spark the formation of the Scottish Football Association but also their passing game, as opposed to the dribbling game favoured in the South, was to influence the game as a whole.

The Wanderers were deemed to be favourites and won the toss which gave them the benefit of a slight wind for the first half. Although the Queen's Park side were smaller than their English opponents their energy certainly surprised and at times gave them an advantage. The Wanderers fought back into the game and play was even when the ends were changed at half time. In the second half C.W. Alcock came closest to scoring for the Wanderers, his shot going so close to the tape that it necessitated an appeal to the umpires. When time was called there was no score and the Wanderers offered Queen's Park the opportunity of thirty minutes extra time. This however was declined and as they could not fund another game in London, they had to withdraw from the competition, leaving the Wanderers a free path into the final.

The day was not quite over as *'after the close of the match the Glasgow eleven dined with their opponents. The toast of the Queen's Park Club was received with full honours, the enterprise and determination evinced in journeying so long a distance for the good of football being the subject of lengthy commendation from the chairman. The Football Association was also warmly received, and hopes expressed of a return match in Scotland during next season.'* 14

There was now a small matter of the first ever F.A. Cup Final to prepare for. Wanderers' next game paired them with Clapham Rovers and a W.G. Grace goal secured a 1-1 draw in game where two Queen's Park players R.H. Gardner and D.N. Wotherspoon featured.

The game also resulted in an amusing story involving C.W. Alcock and W.G. Grace, which was later recalled by the latter in the words of Alcock. *"Once,'* he says, *'W.G. played football on Clapham Common, when the Wanderers were playing a match against the Rovers. I was centre-forward, and had got the ball in front of the Rovers' goal, and was just going to kick it between the posts when, in his great rough sort of way, W.G. bowled me over and kicked the goal himself. It was'* Mr Alcock always adds – *'the most blackguard thing that happened to me during a long sporting career.'* 15

Cup Final day arrived on 16th March 1872 where the Wanderers were to face the Royal Engineers, who had crushed Crystal Palace 3-0 in the other semi final. The Engineers were quoted as 7 to 4 favourites as a result of their game against Crystal Palace and their playing record for the 1871/72 season which read played 19, won 15, drawn four and as such were unbeaten.

The final itself was to be played at the Oval which was the Wanderers home ground, and where the Royal Engineers had failed to win in November 1871. The make up of the Wanderers for this final *'was mainly made up of old Eton and Harrow boys, C.W. Alcock, M.P. Betts, E.E. Bowen, W.P. Crake, R. de C. Welch being Harrovians, and A.G. Bonsor, E.Lubbock, and A.C. Thompson, Etonians. The other members of the side were R.W. Sealy Vidal, an old Westminster boy, T.C. Hooman of Charterhouse, and C.H.R. Wollaston, of Oxford University. The Wanderers at this early period commanded the services of all the leading old Public School players.'* 16

2,000 people paid the one shilling admission charge, and Bell's Life suggested it might have been more had it not been for the charge and they were to see the Wanderers triumph in the first F.A. Cup Final.

The Wanderers captain won the toss and gained the advantage of the wind and having the sun at their backs. Wanderers then besieged the Engineers goal for the opening period and ultimately *'they maintained the attack, till at length, after some judicious 'middling' by R.W.S. Vidal, the goal of the Engineers fell to a well directed kick by A.H. Chequer.'*[17] A.H. Chequer was in fact the pseudonym of M.P. Betts and stood for 'A Harrow Chequer'.

The first F.A. Cup

Ends were now changed but it was the Wanderers who continued to attack and C.W. Alcock had a goal disallowed for a prior handling offence. Wanderers held out for a deserved win and the victory was attributed to the superior play of their backs. The Engineers were disadvantaged in that Lieutenant Cresswell broke his collar bone ten minutes into the game but he still managed to stay on the field for the whole match. T.C. Hooman later claimed that there was not one foul committed by either side in the 1872 final.

The team against the Royal Engineers was as follows:

C.W. Alcock, E.E. Bowen, A.G. Bonsor, M.P. Betts, T.C. Hooman, W.P. Crake, E. Lubbock, A.C. Thompson, R. de C. Welch, C.H.R. Wollaston and R.W.S. Vidal

Four days later the Wanderers were held 1-1 at Charterhouse School to round off a successful season. The Cup was presented at the Annual Dinner held at the Pall Mall Restaurant in Charing Cross on 11th April 1872, a ticket for which would have set you back 7s. 6d.![18]

The Sportsman published the results of this successful season the day prior to the dinner offering the following excuse for the defeats *'of the six matches lost, the two against Harrow were played according to Harrow rules, the remaining four being in each case played by the second eleven of the club, in three instances with short teams.'*[19]

38

1872/73

The fixture list for 1872/73 was dramatically scaled down by the F.A. Cup holders from 32 the previous season to just 23. This is mainly due to the fact there were so many representative games, Internationals and matches such as Old Etonians against Old Harrovians which gained preference.

Wanderers started the season in dominant mood and annihilated Clapham Rovers 4-0 in the first game. Wanderers never looked back once C.W. Alcock volleyed them in to the lead and this was followed by a devastating hat trick by C.H. Wollaston. Surrey Club, were the next opponents and their side was comprised entirely of members of Surrey County Cricket Club and were beaten 1-0 after W.P. Crake's goal fifteen minutes from time.

A 0-0 draw with Forest School at Snaresbrook marked a rare appearance by one of the original members of Forest F.C. when C. Absolom played in goal. Wanderers then faced Upton Park ultimately winning 4-1 after an intriguing episode *'not long after this, however, a plea was made by the captain of Upton Park, who had then got one goal to none, that half-past four o'clock was the hour appointed for the cessation, and for some minutes the play was suspended. Ultimately the visitors conceded the point, and the game was resumed with such success to the Wanderers that at five o'clock they had secured four goals without increase of score on the part of their opponents.'*[20]

Wanderers good form continued with wins over Forest School and Westminster School which in turn were followed by draws against Gitanos and Eton College. They were to suffer a huge blow when C.W. Alcock was severely injured whilst appearing for Old Harrovians versus Old Etonians; so badly indeed, that he played no further matches this season. There are contradictory reports of the injury: the Football Annual states it was his back, while the Sportsman says it was his knee.

The first defeat of the season came in the ninth game, at Parker's Piece against Cambridge University, and was quickly followed by two more as the Royal Engineers gained revenge 0-2 at the Oval, on the same day as the first official England v Scotland match, and then Harrow School convincingly beat Wanderers 1-4. The latter game was played in terrible conditions as the report states *'the swamp was perhaps more muddy than on the occasion of the Chequers' visit; and if the players were able to keep on their legs with more success in the previous match, it was simply due to the fact that at every step their feet sank some six inches in the mud, thus making slipping impossible.'*[21] The England game previously mentioned deprived the Wanderers of the services of R. de C. Welch and C.W. Alcock, who was the English umpire for the match.

Wanderers won their next game at Charterhouse School despite turning up with just seven players and having to borrow four. It was the start of another fine unbeaten run lasting seven games and saw victories over Cambridge University, Crystal Palace, Old Reptonians and Uxbridge. A bad performance during that run led to a 2-2 draw with Harrow School Vacation Club and a suicidal defensive performance meant a 4-1 lead over Harrow Chequers late in the game was surrendered and the game ended 4-4. The club was also due to play Charterhouse again during this run but failed to turn up for the match.

There was some very rare criticism of the referee in the victory over Crystal Palace. *'A once prominent Association player went through the farce of pretending to umpire, but as his opinion was rarely asked, and when asked was systematically overlooked and disregarded, it may be as well to refrain from mentioning his name. On the other hand in the case of the appeal, his back was either turned, or he was not looking at the exact moment, or he displayed either painful indecision or else absolute mental vacuity, it might have been better if he never appeared, or retired immediately after his appearance, instead of invariably getting in the way at the wrong moment and obstructing the game throughout.'22*

In early January 1873 a London side all of whom were past or present Wanderers recorded a fine 1-0 victory over Sheffield at the Oval. There was however a long break for the Wanderers who only played Uxbridge between the end of December and the start of March.

When games did resume in preparation for the cup, which the Wanderers as holders were exempted until the final, they started disastrously for the club. Royal Engineers defeated a very weak Wanderers side 0-4 at Chatham, before Westminster School won 2-4 at Vincent Square in a game where the visitors had to obtain three substitutes after turning up for the match several players short. Two draws followed against Gitanos and Upton Park when, in the week before the cup final, the Wanderers could only raise nine men for the game.

On 29th March 1873 the Wanderers faced Oxford University in the second final of the F.A. Cup at Lille Bridge. Lille Bridge, which is now covered by the railway lines at West Brompton, was chosen by the Wanderers, who as holders also had choice of venue, in an effort to subdue R.W.S. Vidal 'the prince of dribblers' and the most feared player in the Oxford side and one that the Wanderers knew well, as he had appeared for them in the previous season's final.

The Final was scheduled for an 11am kick off due to the fact that shortage of dates meant it had to be scheduled on Boat Race day. As a result the game was brought forward so that the players did not miss the race. The game did not in fact kick off until 11.30 due to the late arrival of several players. There was also a problem in finding two neutral umpires.

Wanderers were without A.C. Thompson and his first choice replacement, F.H. Wilson was also unavailable. The side was further weakened by the absence of W.P. Crake and T.C. Hooman. This explains why the Wanderers drafted in several players with L.S. Howell making his debut in the final and W.S. Kenyon-Slaney and C.M. Thompson playing only their second games.

The Wanderers did however, have A.F. Kinnaird who is described as giving *'a virile and flamboyant leadership'23* and *'almost half an hour had passed when A.F. Kinnaird took advantage of a favourable opportunity, and by a splendid run outpacing the opposite backs, he placed a very well obtained goal to the credit of the Wanderers.'* 24 Kinnaird scored the first goal of the game, not as commonly stated the second. W.S. Kenyon-Slaney then had a goal disallowed for the Wanderers. Oxford battled to get back into the game and moved their goal keeper up field in an effort to draw level. This however played into the hands of C.H. Wollaston who added a second goal for the Wanderers which was described *'as entirely owing to the absence of the man between the posts.'25* Wanderers won the Final 2-0 and lifted the trophy for the second consecutive year.

The team for the Wanderers second successive triumph was as follows:

A.F. Kinnaird, R.C. Welch, L.S. Howell, E.E. Bowen, C.H.R. Wollaston, R.K. Kingsford, A.G. Bonsor, W.S. Kenyon-Slaney, C.M. Thomspon, J.R. Sturgis, Rev. H.H. Stewart

1873/74

After the successes of the previous two seasons, season 1873/74 was somewhat average. The fixture list again reduced to just twenty games while the star of the side A.F. Kinnaird left to join the Old Etonians. It has been suggested that R.K. Kingsford took over the position of Secretary of the Wanderers for the 1873/74 season, but this can not be substantiated as there were no reports of this change in leadership in the papers, nor did his name replace that of Alcock's in the Football Annual's club directory.

The season started disappointingly with a defeat at the Oval against Clapham Rovers, which was followed by two games both against Forest School which ended 2-2 at Snaresbrook and in a 4-3 win at the Oval. October closed with a 0-1 defeat against the Royal Engineers who had not been defeated since the 1872 cup final.

November started with the first London versus Sheffield fixture of the season at Bramall Lane. A crowd of 5,000 saw the Londoners demolished 2-8 with a number of Wanderers players in the side. For the Wanderers however the month started brightly as despite only nine men turning up and again having to borrow players, Westminster School were beaten 3-1. The struggling Wanderers though could only raise seven players for the match against Swifts even though the fixture was at the Oval. A 0-5 defeat naturally followed.

For the visit of Gitanos in mid November, Wanderers finally got what they regarded as their first choice team on the field although they only had ten men. It paid dividends with a 1-0 win. The team that day was:

C.W. Alcock, R. Barker, F.H. Birley, A. Borwick, C. Colbeck, F.B. Howell, H.S. Otter, R.C. Welch, W.R. Bailey and C.H.R. Wollaston.

The Wanderers problems mounted after only six players turned up in the drenching rain at Charterhouse and despite borrowing five players they duly lost 1-4. Confidence was restored to a degree by a 4-0 win over Civil Service before the start of their defence of the F.A. Cup.

The rules of the F.A. Cup had been revised during the close season and the holders no longer enjoyed a bye to the final. As a result the full draw was made before the start of the competition and Wanderers had had the good fortune to progress to the third round without playing a game as both Trojans and Southall withdrew.

In the third round, Wanderers were paired with Oxford University, a strong side, but one they had beaten in the previous year's final. The game kicked off at 2.53pm and Wanderers took the lead through C.W. Alcock; unfortunately Oxford equalised to force a replay.

The replay was not scheduled until the end of January so the Wanderers had nearly two months to prepare for it. Cambridge University were beaten 2-1, before after a two hour long game against Harrow School, the school finally won 3-2. New Year's Day brought a 2-1 victory over the Harrow Chequers, before six days later Swifts destroyed a depleted Wanderers side yet again, this time 5-1 in a game which was played at Slough.

In the weeks leading up to the replay a 1-0 deficit was turned around against Uxbridge to record a 2-1 win, before two games on the same day against Upton Park and Gitanos both ended in defeat.

The anticipated replay was played on 31st January 1874 and the game finally saw a Wanderers defeat in the competition they had dominated since its inception.

The concluding heat of the third ties for the Association Challenge Cup was played in the 'Parks' at Oxford on Saturday last. This contest was looked forward to with much interest, not only on account of the great prestige of the two contending clubs, but as in their prior heats both had vanquished their then opponents with great ease, the meeting between these 'giants' was expected practically to decide who would finally hold the cup. The Clapham Rovers in their preliminary heats had been too closely pressed, and in two instances had to have an 'undecided' here they could claim victory, so their prospects are not regarded with much favour by unprejudiced followers of the game. To return, however to the match on Saturday. The Wanderers appeared at Oxford in a very forlorn state, as, though their captain had managed to bring together, the right number, he could but regard his team with mingled feelings, for they were by no means the flower of his flock. The University, on the other hand, played quite as a formidable team as it was imagined they would, all their best men being on the spot. Weak, however, as the Wanderers unquestionably were, they managed right gallantly to uphold the name of the club, and it appeared until nearly time for closing the match as if it would be left undecided, so well did the visitors work. If this had been the case the Wanderers would have been very fortunate, as in the play off they doubtless would have been materially strengthened. Just before an hour and a half's play had been concluded R.W.S. Vidal managed to get the ball in the middle, and by a general rush it was sent through the Wanderers' goal. After this success for Oxford no further advantage was gained by either side up to the call of 'time.' [26]

The team for this game was five short of the eleven who competed in the original tie. Only R. de C. Welch, C.W. Alcock, R. Barker, C.J. Chenery, W.P. Crake and R.K. Kingsford survived from the first game and were joined by A.H. Stratford, S.R. Tatham, H.S. Otter, W.F. O'Shaughnessy and A.F. Kinnaird. Although Stratford and Kinnaird were no mean players, the loss of C.H. Wollaston, E. Lubbock and A.C. Thompson was certainly a major blow.

Although it being only January, the Wanderers merely played one more game which was a 4-0 win against Westminster School. The repeated call up of players for representative sides seems to have curtailed the season, but whether it was these circumstances or actually the Wanderers choice is not clear.

They did schedule two more games which are retold here. The first against Charterhouse was due to be played at the end of February. *'On Wednesday last the Wanderers were to have played Charterhouse at Godalming, but as only two of them turned up they joined in the school game which was Singers v non-Singers.'* [27] A similar occurrence happened for a fixture against Upton Park. *'This match was arranged to have taken place on Saturday last, but unfortunately the Wanderers failed to put in an appearance. In order, therefore not to disappoint a large number of people who had assembled to witness the play, a scratch team was chosen to represent the missing team. A ridiculously one-sided game ensued, and the Uptonians scored eleven goals against nothing, and strange to say each of the winning side secured one goal.'* [28] The report then cheekily lists the names of the scratch players under the banner of Wanderers.

1874/75

Wanderers improved dramatically during the 1874/75 season, although the ultimate goal of winning the F.A. Cup again eluded them. The fixture list was slashed to just thirteen games as all the matches against the public schools, with the exception of Harrow, were deleted from the fixture list. The seeds of the club's future successes were sown as seven of next year's cup final side all featured this season, while the future goal keeper was discovered in unfortunate circumstances.

A good forward display enabled the Wanderers to complete an impressive opening day 5-0 victory over Clapham Rovers. A weak side then drew with Uxbridge in appalling weather conditions, before the customary defeat to the Royal Engineers followed.

Wanderers F.A. Cup campaign started with a 16-0 annihilation of Farningham. R.K. Kingsford scored an impressive five goals and he was followed closely behind by C.H.R. Wollaston who hit four. The poor goal keeper who was on the receiving end of Wanderers record ever victory was a certain W.D.O. Greig who must go down in history as having the biggest turn around of fortunes in the history of the F.A. Cup as he received a winners medal the following season.

The goals were flowing as Civil Service were thrashed 7-0 four days later even though Saturday's five goal hero was unavailable due to him missing the train. C.W. Alcock scored a hat trick and W.D.O. Greig playing outfield scored two.

The Sheffield v London fixture followed with C.W. Alcock, F.T. Green and A.H. Stratford all selected for the 1-2 defeat at Sheffield. There then came a free weekend prior to the 2nd round of the F.A. Cup when Wanderers were to face Barnes at the Oval. It was the first time Wanderers had faced Barnes since 1863, which is somewhat surprising given the lack of suitable opposition during the early years. The eleven year wait for a repeat fixture saw little changed as Wanderers recorded a 5-0 win as they had done in the last meeting, with C.W. Alcock scoring his second successive hat trick for the club.

Wanderers continued in this fine form despite a three week wait for the visit of Harrow School to the Oval who were soundly beaten 5-0. Another three weeks wait ensued and this time Harrow Chequers were the victims, Wanderers scoring nine to the Chequers one as J. Kenrick hit a hat trick.

The strength of the club can be seen in the January representative games as C.W. Alcock, R.K. Kingsford, C.H. Wollaston and F.H. Birley were selected for London who defeated Sheffield 3-1. Two weeks later C.W. Alcock, C.J. Chenery, J. Kenrick, R.K. Kingsford and J. Kirkpatrick were all in turn selected for Surrey against Berkshire.

Wanderers drew 1-1 with Gitanos prior to their F.A. Cup 3rd round tie with the previous two seasons adversaries Oxford University. The Wanderers were favourites going into the game as a result of their previous blistering form, but quickly found themselves behind to two early goals. An own goal got them back into the game but despite being on top in the second half they could not find the elusive equalizer although they did have a goal disallowed. It should be noted that A.H. Stratford, one of the better players, had to withdraw at the last minute, while R.K. Kingsford was injured early in the game and later on so was F.H. Birley.

As was the case in the previous season the club virtually closed down for the season after this defeat. In early February the club was deemed worthy opposition for the England Trial Team and the Wanderers beat the trialists 2-1. The final game in mid March was against the Royal Engineers; unfortunately the only trace of this game is found in the Engineers results list for this season.

The club received further representative honours as four players were selected for England to face Scotland namely C.W. Alcock, H. Heron, C.H.R. Wollaston and F.H. Birley. Then eight Wanderers players were selected for London's 2-0 win against Sheffield.

References

1	*The Sportsman* 4.10.1870 p3
2	*The Sportsman* 19.10.1870 p 4
3	*The Sportsman* 3.11.1870 p4
4	*The Sportsman* 15.3.1871 p3
5	Fabian & Green *Association Football* v3 p4
6	*The Sportsman* 24.10.1871 p3
7	*The Forest School Magazine* p162
8	*The Sportsman* 8.11.1871 p3
9	*The Sportsman* 15.11.1871 p3
10	*The Sportsman* 20.12.1871 p3
11	Pawson *100 Years of the F.A. Cup* p7
12	Fabian & Green *Association Football* v3 p9
13	Williams *The Code War* p44
14	*The Sportsman* 5.3.1872 p3
15	Grace *Cricketing Reminiscences and Personal Recollections* p322
16	The Sportsman *British Sports & Sportsmen* p226
17	*The Sportsman* 19.3.1872 p4
18	*The Sportsman* 23.3.1872 p3
19	*The Sportsman* 10.4.1872 p3
20	*The Sportsman* 23.10.1872 p3
21	*The Sportsman* 17.12.1872 p3
22	*The Sportsman* 19.12.1872 p3
23	Pawson *100 Years of the F.A.Cup* p9
24	*The Sportsman* 1.4.1873 p3
25	*The Sportsman* 1.4.1873 p3
26	*The Sportsman* 4.2.1874 p4
27	*The Sportsman* 28.2.1874 p6
28	*The Sportsman* 11.3.1874 p3

Treble F.A. Cup Winners: 1875-78

From 1875 to 1878 the Wanderers dominated English competitive football and won three consecutive F.A. Cups, one of only two clubs ever to achieve this feat. This was achieved with a stable side aided by the return of A.F. Kinnaird for the last two successes.

1875/76

The period did not exactly start in a blaze of glory as the 1875/76 season opened with a 0-0 draw at Balham against Clapham Rovers and *'there was an evident want of training throughout, especially on the side of the Wanderers'* 1. This comment would come back to haunt them a week later when the club made its first visit to Scotland to face Queen's Park at Hampden Park. A crowd of 12,000 paid the one shilling entrance fee to see the Wanderers simply brushed aside 0-5 and their fitness was highlighted again, *'the date of the fixture was obviously all in favour of the Scottish team, as while they are hard at practice throughout the Summer, and were consequently on Saturday in rare fettle, the majority of their opponents had not seen a football since last season.'* 2

The programme from Queens Park v Wanderers 1875

There was a tremendous spirit within the Wanderers camp in these days and C.W. Alcock recalls an episode relating to the trip to Queen's Park. *'I can vividly recall the details of a visit I made to Gresham Street one Friday afternoon to get a goal keeper to play against Queen's Park at Glasgow the following day.*

'Can you play to-morrow, G------- ?' was my salutation.
'Yes,' was the reply; *'where?'*
When I responded *'At Glasgow,'* he said cheerily:
'All right! When do we go?' It was late in the afternoon.
'From Euston at eight.'
'I shall be there,' he returned with a smile.

And he was there. Very much there in fact, in a more than usually stubborn contest. No wonder that the club made history as it did with such splendid material.'3

C.W. Alcock went on to say *'To go to Glasgow – a railway journey of over 800 miles there and back – in the good old days for an hour and a half's football and at one's own expense was not in a way grateful and comforting. How we did it is not easy to say. But it was done, and plenty of fun it brought with it, if one had to travel through the night in draughty carriages with hard seats – in fact in severely economical style.'4*

The F.A. Cup 1st round draw saw Wanderers paired with the 1st Surrey Rifles at the Oval, in what could potentially have proved a tricky tie, but the two goals by J. Kenrick and F.B. Maddison and one by C.W. Alcock secured a 5-0 win. This was followed by a 3-2 win over Westminster School who made a return to the fixture list for this season. Harrow School then beat the Wanderers 0-1, before a 4-0 win over Gitanos and another 1-3 defeat ensued this time at The Parks versus Oxford University. This was to signal a turn around which saw the Wanderers lose only two more games before the end of the season.

There was still room for improvement as the report shows following a 0-0 draw with Aldershot Division in the next game. *'they played badly, especially the forwards, who were wanting in dash, and systematically from first to last adhered to the policy of keeping the ball to themselves at all hazards.'* It continued, *'but generally the eleven preferred to get in the way of each other rather than in that of their opponents.'5*

It did not take long for the Wanderers to click, as Cricklewood were thrashed 7-0 in the next game, which must have restored confidence prior to their F.A. Cup 2nd round tie with Crystal Palace at the Oval. A physical game saw Wanderers win 3-0 and W.D.O. Greig in goal did not touch the ball. Three draws followed against Harrow School, Royal Engineers and the Swifts in what was to be C.W. Alcock's last game for the Wanderers. Then A.H. Stratford, C.H. Wollaston and J. Kenrick were all selected to represent London against Sheffield, which with their help, the former won convincingly 4-0.

After leading the club since its inception, C.W. Alcock finally stood down in an announcement made in the Sportsman on 26th January 1876 and took up position as President of the club.

THE WANDERERS
MESSRS F.H. Birley (Winchester) and J. Kenrick (Lancing) have been elected captain and Hon. Secretary respectively of this club, the offices vacated by Mr C.W. Alcock. It is requested that all communications relating to the club be addressed to the hon. sec., J. Kenrick, Reigate, Surrey. 6

At the end of January the Wanderers found themselves again on F.A. Cup duty. This time it was against Sheffield F.C. at the Oval in the third round. *'A quarter of an hour after the kick off by the Wanderers matters assumed a very dull aspect both for players and spectators, as the fog again asserted its supremacy, and during the rest of the afternoon it was almost totally impossible to discern the ball at even short distance.'7* It made little difference to the Wanderers who won 2-0 thanks to two second half goals by F. Heron.

One week later the Wanderers faced a rematch with Queen's Park, this time on home ground at the Oval. Queen's Park were still unbeaten since their formation and had only conceded four goals up to this point. The build up for the game was described as follows. *'Special interest was therefore* *attached to the meeting of Saturday last, and no stone had been left unturned by the executive of either club to ensure success by the collection of their most able representatives. The Queen's Park had all its best men, while the Wanderers had judiciously chosen a fast and hardworking list of forwards, besides strengthening their back play by the aid of W.S. Rawson, the captain of the Oxford University team, and a Wanderer of some years standing. The executive of the Surrey Cricket Club, in honour of the occasion , apportioned for the match a piece of ground parallel with the pavilion, and a judicious arrangement it proved, as there was not only shelter from a cutting wind, but ample room for a large number of spectators, each side of the ropes being, besides, marked by an unbroken line of onlookers.'*₈ The game ended in a hard fought 2-0 win for the Wanderers who as such not only ended Queen's Park unbeaten run, but gained revenge for the 0-5 drubbing handed out to them the previous October.

Wanderers enjoyed a three week break in the lead up to the next big match, an F.A. Cup semi final against Swifts at the Oval. F.H. Birley and C.H. Wollaston scored first half goals to secure a 2-1 win and a third appearance in the F.A. Cup final. Three days later on 29th February, the Wanderers lost their first game since November during their visit to Westminster School at Vincent Square. Wanderers had a goal disallowed as the home side won 1-0.

Before the F.A. Cup final three more Wanderers players were capped by England in their game against Scotland, F.T. Green and the Heron brothers.

The F.A. Cup was scheduled for 11th March 1876 when the Wanderers were due to face Old Etonians. The Old Etonians side actually contained five players who had previously played for the Wanderers namely A.F. Kinnaird, Q. Hogg, W.S. Kenyon-Slaney, A.G. Bonsor and E. Lubbock. It is also interesting to note that the 1876 final saw one of only two instances when two brothers played together in an international and in a cup winning side when H. and F. Heron appeared for the Wanderers.

The final ended in a close fought 1-1 draw which had seen Wanderers take the lead following a goal by J.H. Edwards. The Etonians equalised in dramatic circumstances *'the result was a scrimmage, in which the Eton forwards scored a goal though the posts had been overturned in the rush. (sic)'*₉ The replay saw the Old Etonians struggle with real injury problems losing three players before the start and then having to carry the lame A.F. Kinnaird. In those circumstances the Wanderers proved far too strong for them and two quick goals during the first half by C.H.R. Wollaston and T.B. Hughes meant it was an uphill struggle. T.B. Hughes scored a third as the Wanderers ran out comfortable 3-0 winners.

The team in both games was as follows:

W.D.O. Greig, A.H. Stratford, W. Lindsey, F.B. Maddison, F.H. Birley, C.H. Wollaston, H. Heron, F. Heron, J.H. Edwards, J.Kenrick, T.B. Hughes

A.H. Stratford, F.H. Birley, J. Kenrick and W.D.O. Greig were all selected to represent London the following week against Sheffield which ended in a drastic 0-6 defeat in front of 7,000 spectators at Bramall Lane. The last Wanderers game on 1st April 1876 was against Royal Engineers and ended in 0-3 defeat; no details are known of this game other than on the Engineers' results list.

1876/77
The 1876/77 season heralded the return of the prodigal son in the form of A.F. Kinnaird who rejoined the club from Old Etonians who had withdrawn from the F.A. Cup. Kinnaird was by far the

greatest player of his day as his record of nine cup final appearances stands testament and it is no surprise that his ability, added to the already impressive Wanderers side, meant only one thing: more success. Unfortunately, the reporting of games this season was somewhat lacking, which may be attributable to the new secretary, J. Kenrick. It seems unlikely that C.W. Alcock in his influential position as sub-editor of Football for 'The Sportsman' would have omitted any reports sent in to him.

The season started with a defeat at the Oval against Barnes, but was swiftly followed by the club's first success over Royal Engineers since the 1872 cup final. A good second half performance accompanied by goals from C.H.R. Wollaston, H. Wace and a rushed goal secured a 3-0 victory. Further wins followed against Westminster School 2-0 and Civil Service 7-0.

Queen's Park were the next visitors to the Oval, but this time the Wanderers were no match for them. After conceding two early goals, the goals quickly racked up and by full time the score was 0-6 in favour of the Scottish side. This was now the Wanderers record defeat to date and as it turned out the joint record margin of all time.

Maybe because of this only A.F. Kinnaird was selected for the London representative side to face Sheffield the week after. Wanderers on the other hand, bounced back in style by beating Gitanos 5-1 when H Wace hit a hat trick. A visit to The Parks to face Oxford University ended in disappointment as the club entered an indifferent patch. Forest were beaten, a draw at Upton Park and defeat at Harrow School all followed before a 4-0 win at 1st Surrey Rifles.

In the return against Oxford University at the Oval, the students returned home happy with another 0-1 victory and then the Wanderers turned around their season by winning nine of the next eleven games starting with a 2-0 win over Cambridge University.

The Wanderers who had been lucky enough to have free passage into the second round of the F.A. Cup thanks to Saffron Walden withdrawing, were drawn away to Southall. The result has been the centre of much debate as some sources put it as 6-0, others 5-0 while yet others state it was 6-1. As per 'The Sportsman' the game ended 6-0; one goal was disputed however which may explain how 5-0 might have emerged from some sources.

In a game described *'as in no way interesting'*10, Wanderers then lost 0-1 at the Oval to Old Bradfieldians. An easy win followed 5-0 against Harrow School and then in a nine a side game, South Norwood were beaten 2-0. This good form continued as victories over the Swifts and Old Wykehamists followed although there appear to be no reports for these games.

Pilgrims were drawn to play Wanderers in the F.A. Cup 3rd round and certainly put up a good show in this early 'David and Goliath' tie. It was not until 20 minutes from the end that Wanderers were able to turn their authority into goals and F.B. Maddison, C.H.R. Wollaston and a scrimmaged goal sealed a 3-0 victory. This result and a bye for Wanderers in round four meant the club was through to the semi-finals.

There was however to be a two month wait for the semi final against Cambridge University. Old Harrovians thrashed the Wanderers in the next game, but no details are known. Two more victories followed, against Clapham Rovers and Harrow School, the latter was not reported on.

Wanderers next visited Upton Park and lost 0-1. The same result followed against Royal Engineers, although they did score a disputed goal which even the Wanderers themselves discounted when publishing their results for the season. From this point on the club was to have a perfect record until the end of the season.

South Norwood were soundly beaten 9-0, before two close 1-0 wins over Westminster School and Barnes came shortly afterwards. A 2-0 win over 1st Surrey Rifles and a 4-1 win over S.R. Bastard's Team, all of which were yet again not reported on, meant the Wanderers were in top form going into the semi final.

Cambridge University were a side that had not beaten the Wanderers since November 1872 and they certainly started the game with the intention of putting this statistic right. Cambridge dominated the early proceedings, before the Wanderers got into their stride and won courtesy of a 40th minute goal by H. Heron.

Four days later on 24th March 1877, Wanderers met Oxford University in the final of the F.A. Cup. The game at the Oval was watched by 3,000 spectators and the result was by no means cut and dried. Oxford University had already beaten Wanderers twice so far that season, and Wanderers had not even scored a goal in the process. The form book certainly looked as if it was going to plan when *'Waddington drove the ball sharply into the centre of the posts, and Kinnaird inadvertently stepped back between the posts with the ball in his hands. An immediate appeal was made to the umpires, and after some consultation the verdict was given in favour of Oxford.'*11

Trailing 1-0 the Wanderers fought back, but it was not until a few minutes from the final whistle that they got the equaliser. *'A fine run by Heron along the upper side, followed by a good kick, placed the ball neatly to Kenrick, and the latter got it securely through the Oxford posts.'*12 The score stood at 1-1 at the end of ninety minutes and the game entered extra time where the Wanderers proved too strong for their opponents and *'Lindsay planted the ball well in the centre, and when it was headed out by Oxford he had a second kick, again directing it into the centre of the Oxford posts, this time so cleverly that the goal keeper could not save his charge.'*13 The Wanderers had now won the F.A. Cup for the second successive year and for the fourth time in six attempts.

The team who played in the final was:

F.H. Birley, F.T. Green, T.B. Hughes, J. Kenrick, C.H.R. Wollaston, A.H. Stratford, W. Lindsay, C.A. Denton, H. Heron, H. Wace and A.F. Kinnaird.

1877/78
1877/78 was to be the Wanderers swan song as a major footballing power, with the club dominating throughout the season and only losing three games all year. The first two and the last game sandwiched a fourteen match undefeated run, which saw the club lift the F.A. Cup for the fifth and final time. It should be noted that five games are unaccounted for and all that is known is that they resulted in four wins and a draw.

The season opened as stated with two defeats. The first against Old Harrovians ended 1-2 in favour of the former Harrow pupils. This game was used as a trial for the new throw in rule. *'The new rule relative to the throw in from touch in did not seem to be well understood by the two sides, but as this was its first trial at the Oval it was hardly to be expected that it would at once work easily.'*14 Then in a game when only four of the previous season's cup final side played, Clapham Rovers were victorious 3-1 at the Oval.

49

Wanderers returned to winning ways with a 7-0 win over Runnymede, and followed this up with a comprehensive 4-0 victory over Royal Engineers. The result was not quite as clear cut as the scoreline suggests as, although the Wanderers were in control for much of the game, two goals were scored in the last five minutes.

It was back to F.A. Cup duty for the fifth game of the campaign and the Panthers were easily beaten 9-0 at Sandhurst and H. Heron hit four goals in this game. Westminster School were then dismissed 1-0 in a game which finished in darkness.

Five players were selected for London's 6-0 win over Sheffield just prior to the Westminster game, A.F. Kinnaird, J.G. Wylie, C.H.R. Wollaston, H. Heron and H. Wace being the players involved. Another four were also selected for London's next game against Birmingham which ended in complete humiliation for the midlands team, 11-0. The players selected were as follows, J.G. Wylie, H. Wace, H. Heron and C.H.R. Wollaston.

The second round of the F.A. Cup dictated that the Wanderers had to travel to High Wycombe. This game ended in a 9-0 win in very awkward conditions due to the frozen pitch. A 3-1 win over Harrow School and a 0-0 draw at Snaresbrook against Old Foresters either side of New Year set the Wanderers up nicely for their F.A. Cup third round tie with Barnes on 12th January 1878.

The Wanderers struggled with players being unavailable for this tie however, as J.G. Wylie and A.F. Kinnaird missed the game. The game ended 1-1 and in the replay two weeks later the Wanderers with their players now available stormed into a 4-1 half time lead. No further scoring occurred in the second half and the Wanderers progressed into round four.

There were two games scheduled in the weeks following the cup ties, against Clapham Rovers and Runnymede, but there is no evidence that these were played. In preparation for the fourth round Wanderers beat Westminster School 5-2.

Wanderers were again on top form when they met Sheffield F.C. in the fourth round of the F.A. Cup and some enthralling attacking play meant they made short work of their opponents who played well below their usual standard. The result meant that with an odd number of teams, the Wanderers received a bye in the semi-final and as such had arrived in their third successive F.A. Cup final unscathed.

Clapham Rovers were beaten 5-1 before three Wanderers players were selected for England who were playing Scotland. The game did not end happily for the English as the Scots ran out 7-2 winners. H. Heron, H. Wace and J.G. Wylie were the players involved. The Wanderers won 9-1 against the 1st Surrey Rifles in their final warm up game for the final.

Wanderers now faced Royal Engineers in the F.A. Cup final, a repeat of the inaugural final of 1872. The outcome was to be little different as Wanderers scored after only five minutes. This was in complete contrast to their reputation which had been acquired as slow starters. J. Kirkpatrick in the Wanderers goal then fractured his arm but continued regardless. The Engineers did equalise before the captain A.F. Kinnaird restored the lead in time for the interval. The Engineers continued to fight and had a goal disallowed for offside before J. Kenrick sealed the victory with 25 minutes remaining.

Wanderers' third straight success meant that the Football Association awarded them the cup outright as per the rule13 which stated *'unless the holders shall have won the cup three years in succession, when the cup shall become the absolute property of the club so winning it. '.* It was however *'handed back on condition it could never be won outright,'*15 in what can be regarded as highly sporting and honourable gesture.

The side for the historic third straight F.A. Cup victory was as follows:

J. Kirkpatrick, A.H. Stratford, W. Lindsay, A.F. Kinnaird, F.T. Green, C.H.R. Wollaston, H. Heron, J.G. Wylie, H. Wace, C.A. Denton and J. Kenrick.

There was still more excitement to come as Wanderers faced Vale of Leven in their last game of the season, in what could be described as an unofficial British championship game. Vale of Leven were dominating Scottish football at this time and had just lifted their second successive Scottish F.A. Cup. They would in fact emulate the Wanderers' feat the following season of three successive Scottish F.A. Cup triumphs.

So on boat race day the two clubs met at the Oval in front of 2,000 spectators. The Wanderers though did not put their full strength side out and only seven of the cup final side were on show. Wanderers found themselves trailing 0-2 at half time. Wollaston pulled a goal back, to no avail as a goal keeping error led to a third and decisive Vale of Leven goal. The report puts the whole defeat down to *'the goal-keeping, as before stated, lost them the match beyond all doubt, as the first and the last of the Scottish goals ought to have been easily saved, and the second might have been stopped by an active player.'*16

References

1	*The Sportsman* 5.10.1875 p3
2	*The Sportsman* 12.10.1875 p4
3	Alcock *The Book of Football* p255
4	Alcock *The Book of Football* p256
5	*The Sportsman* 25.11.1875 p3
6	*The Sportsman* 16.1.1876 p4
7	*The Sportsman* 1.2.1876 p3
8	*The Sportsman* 8.2.1876 p3
9	*The Sportsman* 14.3.1876 p4
10	*The Sportsman* 19.12.1876 p4
11	*The Sportsman* 26.3.1877 p4
12	*The Sportsman* 26.3.1877 p4
13	*The Sportsman* 26.3.1877 p4
14	*The Sportsman* 8.10.1877 p4
15	Fabian & Green *Association Football* v2 p10
16	*The Sportsman* 15.4.1878 p3

The Decline and End of the Wanderers Football Club 1878-1883

The Wanderers decline occurred over an astonishingly short period. To go from winning the F.A. Cup three times in succession to nothing in the space of five seasons almost defies belief. It was however a club run by the players, for the players and as football evolved and the old school tie began to dominate the club had little chance of surviving.

The vast expansion of 'Old Boys' sides in this period effectively ended the club. There were early signs when A.F. Kinnaird left in 1873 to join the Old Etonians, but 1878 can be regarded as the watershed.

Club	Year Formed	Year F.A. Cup Entered
Old Carthusians	1876	1879/80
Old Etonians	1871	1873/74
Old Foresters	1876	1877/78, then not again until 1881/82
Old Harrovians	1859	1876/77
Old Westminsters	1880	1882/83
Old Wykehamists	1875	1876/77, then not again until 1883/84

Table showing formation dates of the 'Old Boy' clubs and when they entered the F.A.Cup

As can be seen the six major contributors of the Wanderers players were all in existence in 1878 except Old Westminsters, who still had an impact at the only time when the Wanderers looked as if they could make a come back. As soon as these clubs entered the F.A. Cup they began to drain the Wanderers existing talent and at the same time, which was perhaps more of an issue, stopped the Wanderers recruiting good standard replacements.

Pawson described 1878 as *'the eve of dissolution. Composed as it was of a collection of members of other clubs, it found increasing difficulty in securing players.'* He goes on to quote Gibson and Pickford's 'History of Association Football'. *"'Old School Clubs' were being formed in growing numbers and it became almost mandatory in the etiquette of the day for a player leaving school or university to offer himself to his 'Old Boys Club''*[1]

1878/79
At the start of 1878/79 A.F. Kinnaird left the Wanderers to rejoin the Old Etonians: he did make occasional appearances for his old club, but his F.A. Cup loyalties remained firmly with his old school from this point. Wanderers started the season in the same way that they always had, but after the F.A. Cup debacle it appears that the club was shell shocked and the playing side collapsed well before Christmas 1878. There is no evidence from newspapers, school magazines or results lists published at the end of the season to suggest that the club played any more than nine games this season, of which they managed to win just one.

Wanderers opened the season with 2-3 defeat at the Oval against Old Harrovians, but only nine players arrived at the ground. *'The Wanderers only mustered nine to ten Harrovians, though the numbers were equalised by the addition to the former of a substitute, who kept goal without taking off his hat or coat, and proved rather an expensive luxury for his side.'*[2] The next two games saw a second half collapse against Clapham Rovers who eventually won 1-5 and a 1-1 draw against Old Foresters.

52

The two most interesting games of this short season occurred within the space of a week in early November. Amid much speculation about a forthcoming floodlit match the following announcement was made.

FOOTBALL BY ELECTRIC LIGHT

We are requested by the secretary of the Surrey County Cricket Club to state that no match as has been announced will be played at the Oval on Monday evening next. A match, under the joint auspices of the Surrey County Cricket Club and the Football Association, will be played at the Oval during the week after next, probably Tuesday, November 5th. The Wanderers and the Clapham Rovers will be the contending clubs .3

Floodlit football at the Oval

The game ended in a 2-2 draw and it is worth recalling the report to fully appreciate the occasion.

THE ELECTRIC LIGHT MATCH AT THE OVAL

For the last fortnight the public has been liberally treated to announcements of an Electric Light Football Match at the Oval. Almost every hoarding in the metropolis bore on it a placard or placards testifying to the extraordinary illuminating powers of the electric light, which was said to equal thousands on thousands of sperm candles. The success that attended the committee of the Sheffield Association on the occasion of the first venture of the kind at Bramall Lane Ground a few weeks ago had fired the ambition of some of the London authorities, and encouraged by the glowing reports that had appeared in the newspapers with regard to the brilliant light at Sheffield. A match was arranged for last night at the Oval, between the Wanderers and Clapham Rovers, under the joint auspices of the Surrey County Cricket Club and the Football Association. Every preparation had been made for a vast crowd – a military band had been engaged, a strong body of police was on the ground, the gates were announced to be open an hour and a half before the commencement of the game, and in fact every provision had been taken for the expected thousands who never came. The light was managed on the same principle as at Sheffield, by Siemen's machines, and it was arranged that four lights should be used, the first to be ignited at six o'clock, another at seven, and the two remaining to be reserved for the commencement of the match at half-past seven o'clock. One light was placed on the roof of the pavilion, one at the Press box, one on the box by the Vauxhall gate, and the fourth on a scaffolding specially erected, so that one was at each corner of the ground. Prior to the commencement of the game the Clapham Rovers were photographed by Messrs Elliott and Fry, but what the result of the picture will be remains to be seen. By a quarter-past seven o'clock there were about three thousand spectators on the ground, and before the close this number must have been increased to four thousand, a gathering far short of what had been anticipated. At twenty minutes to eight o'clock the ball was kicked off, and at first the play was of a very peculiar kind, as the lights were anything but reliable, the shadows over the ground causing the players to make curious mistakes. After the first quarter of an hour the electricians were a little more successful in their manipulation of the lights, but that on the pavilion seemed to be hardly low enough, and every now and again at the most critical moment a sudden transition would take place, causing the ball to disappear out of a bright light into almost total darkness. The game was carried on for the allotted period of an hour and a half, but it was not in any way the success that had been expected, and unless some considerable improvement is made in the arrangements for lighting, football under such influences will be more of a burlesque than real sport. The game ended in a tie, each side scoring two goals. 4

Five days later the Wanderers were to face A.F. Kinnaird's Old Etonians in the F.A. Cup first round. A lot has been said about the exodus of players from the Wanderers, but for this game there were only three missing from the side that lifted the cup the previous March. A.F. Kinnaird as previously stated had departed; J. Kirkpatrick had retired at the age of 37 and was actually an umpire for this game and lastly H. Heron.

Wanderers failed to perform and found themselves one down after five minutes. A brief recovery followed as the Wanderers forwards hit the posts twice, but following a J. Kenrick own goal, it was always going to be an uphill struggle. Another Old Etonian goal, meant it was 3-0 at the break. Three more Etonian goals followed on the resumption and although J. Kenrick and a scrimmaged goal reduced the arrears for the Wanderers, there was still time for another by the Etonians who eventually ran out 7-2 winners.

Wanderers did manage to finally win a game when Barnes were beaten 5-0; a defeat at Harrow School and two draws against Westminster School and Oxford University followed and the season was finished by the 30th November 1878.

Wanderers did however still have players selected for England. H. Wace appeared against both Wales and Scotland. C.W. Alcock was umpire for the former game and A.F. Kinnaird for the latter. Interestingly both had 'the Wanderers' placed after their names in brackets in the reports. This was also the case in an article about the A.G.M. of the Football Association. 5

The London representative side also drew from the Wanderers ranks during the season. H. Wace and J.G. Wylie both appeared in the 1-1 draw at Sheffield, A.H. Stratford and H. Wace appeared in the 8-0 win over Birmingham and finally A.H. Stratford was again selected for the return which ended 7-0.

1879/80

The Wanderers again attempted to regroup for the 1879/80 season and showed their intentions by publishing an extensive fixture list of which they at least managed to play fifteen games. The reporting of these games was sketchier than at any time in the club's history and most evidence has been found in results lists to confirm that games actually were played.

Wanderers first game ended with their record defeat as Clapham Rovers destroyed them 8-2 at the Oval. Things improved however as Old Foresters were held to a 2-2 draw the week after. It is not clear if the scheduled game against Cambridge University was played at the end of October, but November opened with a 4-0 win over Barnes. Royal Engineers then defeated the Wanderers 2-1 at Chatham.

The F.A. Cup started later that month and Wanderers had little trouble in disposing of Rochester at the Bat and Ball Ground 6-0. Westminster School and Old Harrovians were defeated and defeats against Oxford University and Upton Park marked the build up to the second round.

Old Carthusians who were playing their first season of F.A. Cup football were the visitors to the Oval and a H. Wace goal secured the Wanderers passage through into the third round. The result perhaps hinted at a revival, but it was not to be as in the next round Wanderers were drawn to face Old Etonians for the second year running. The Wanderers only had five of the 1878 team left to call upon, J.G. Wylie now 36 years old was only playing occasional friendly games, J. Kenrick had stopped playing the previous season and was now 38 years old as had 39 year old F.T. Green.

The side was also at a great loss due to the unavailability of W.S. Rawson; on the positive side it had been strengthened by the return of T.B. Hughes who had played in the 1876 and 1877 finals. Wanderers lived up to their slow starter's reputation by going a goal down on five minutes, but held out before conceding two second half goals. H. Wace scored the consolation and what was to be the Wanderers last ever F.A. Cup goal late in the game. This game sealed the fate of the Wanderers Football Club, as it was the spark for more players to depart the following season.

The side for this final F.A. Cup tie was as follows:

C.E. Hammond, A.H. Stratford, A.G. Kennedy, W. Lindsay, F.W. Stratford, C.H. Wollaston, T.N. Tyndale, T.B. Hughes, H. Wace, C.A. Denton, D.B. Roffey

Wanderers completed the season by beating Westminster School 1-0, before going three games with out a goal. Two 0-0 draws with Royal Engineers and Forest School sandwiched a 0-3 defeat at Upton Park. C.H. Wollaston was also selected for the England game against Scotland.

1880-1883

By 1880/81 Wanderers were in serious trouble, C.H Wollaston had succeeded J. Kenrick as Secretary, but he faced an uphill struggle. It was a post he would hold until the end. From the outset the Wanderers started as normal in early October with a 6-2 win over Old Harrovians, but the side was almost unrecognizable from previous years. The only players of any note to remain were Secretary, C.H. Wollaston, A.H. Stratford and T.B. Hughes. H. Wace had joined Clapham Rovers and was in their F.A. Cup side and even C.H. Wollaston was appearing for them.

It was Clapham Rovers, the F.A. Cup holders, who faced Wanderers in their second game, and easily beat the expiring club 4-0. Old Foresters were defeated 3-1 the following week, before a 0-2 loss at Upton Park preceded the final indignity.

55

The Wanderers had gone from winners in 1878 to having to scratch from the F.A. Cup competition in 1880. Having drawn Rangers F.C., London in the first round the club was unable to field a team as players were all committed to other sides. The club played five more games before the end of the season, one an impressive 3-2 win over Oxford University, another a 2-1 win over Harrow School while the other three games ended in defeats against Westminster School twice and Harrow School.

The Wanderers lingered on, however, and even entered the F.A. Cup in 1881/82 season. The draw paired the club with St. Bartholomew's Hospital, but again a lack of players meant they were forced to withdraw before playing a game. Harrow School were defeated 2-1 in the only game that has been traced.

In February 1882 the London Football Association was created in order to deal with local footballing issues. Wanderers are listed among the 52 founder members. The first President of the London F.A. was A.F. Kinnaird and C.W. Alcock became a vice-president.

The Wanderers lasted for two more years, playing one game a season against their traditional opponents Harrow School. This is confirmed '...and Harrow School year after year came to Kennington on the first day of the Christmas vacation to meet the Wanderers, playing their one match of the season according to Association rules.'6

In 1882/83 a side containing M.P. Betts, T.B. Hughes, C. Holden-White of Corinthians, A.F. Kinnaird and E.E. Bowen drew 1-1 at the Oval with the School. By this point it had almost become a veterans side, who were keeping up old school connections and catching up with friends the week before Christmas.

The final Wanderers game took place on 18th December 1883, the report is reproduced below:

WANDERERS v. HARROW SCHOOL.

In rather dreary weather a smart team of boys from Harrow-on-the-Hill played their annual match, under Association rules, at Kennington Oval yesterday (Tuesday) against a singularly mixed-up eleven supposed to represent the almost defunct Wanderers, which naturally enough, resulted in favour of the latter by six goals to one, after playing for an hour and twenty minutes. The Wanderers won the toss and Kinnaird having chosen the western side of the Oval, to take advantage of a rather strong wind that blew from that quarter, the young Harrovians made a start from the Clayton-street end at ten minutes to three. When the Wanderers received the ball it was at once returned, but before it could reach its destination Cox, putting forth his powers, took it in hand, and, running down the side, made good way towards the opposite end, but the Wanderers' backs drove him back again, and, following up, a claim of hands close in front of the Harrow goal gave Kinnaird a free kick, but the ball flew wide of its mark. At length after playing for about ten minutes, from a rush made by the Wanderers, Parry drove the ball under the bar. On resuming hostilities, Holden-White, Bain, Whitfield and Sandwith showed to great advantage for the Wanderers, while Cross, Cox, Rendell, Wright and Lafone worked hard, but ineffectually, to uphold the reputation of the old school. The Wanderers still pressed their adversaries with unrelenting vigour, and Holden-White soon added another goal to the one already gained. A few minutes later on Sandwith did likewise, and immediately afterwards Parry kicked two almost consecutively. Having changed ends at half-time, the contest continued to be carried on still in favour of the Wanderers and Parry, after some heavy charging, easily avoiding the keeper, sent the ball through the posts. All hope for the boys was now over, and with the exception that Cross a short time before the game came to an end made a successful shot for Harrow, nothing else occurred worthy of mentioning, and the Wanderers therefore retired winners as previously mentioned.

C. Holden-White, W.F.G. Sandwith, F.W. Bain, C. Colbeck, J.L. Nikisson, H. Whitfield, E.H. Parry, Hon. A.F. Kinnaird, C. Fletcher, E.E. Bowen, J.F.P. Rawlinson [7]

C.W. Alcock was appropriately umpire as he saw his club through from its birth to its death. In the team that day were two of the great Wanderers stalwarts E.E. Bowen and A.F. Kinnaird. The book 'British Sports and Sportsmen', which was produced by 'The Sportsman' newspaper states *'the Wanderers ceased to exist in 1884'*[8]. During the course of my research, I have found no indication that any game was played against Harrow School before Christmas 1884 and as such can only conclude that the club ended with C.W. Alcock's final whistle in the above game.

References

1   Pawson *100 Years of the F.A. Cup* p10
2   *The Sportsman* 7.10.1878   p4
3   *The Sportsman* 26.10.1878 p8
4   *The Sportsman* 5.11.1878 p4
5   *The Sportsman* 28.2.1879 p4
6   Alverstone & Alcock *Surrey Cricket – It's History and Associations* p437
7   *The Sportsman* 19.12.1883 p4
8   The Sportsman *British Sports & Sportsmen* p237

The Wanderers Achievements and Legacy

The previous five chapters have highlighted how the club evolved and the path it took during the 24 years of its existence. The game of Football was influenced and steered to a large extent by the Wanderers and their members, and by 1883 when the club finally closed, the rules had been accepted universally, the F.A. Cup was firmly established and legalized professionalism was only a couple of years away.

From those early games against Crystal Palace in 1862, the Wanderers' pioneering work built up a head of steam, and more opponents were added to the fixtures, no doubt inspired by the thought of beating the all conquering club. The missionary work in the public schools such as Harrow, Westminster, Eton and Charterhouse certainly must have influenced these schools to sticking to the dribbling game rather than the handling game.

The Football Association's foundation in 1863 gave the Wanderers a unique position in the game thanks to the drive and enthusiasm of certain members who took up key positions within the infant organisation. A. Pember was the first President, between 1863 and 1867. C.W. Alcock was Secretary between 1870 and 1895, while A.F. Kinnaird was President from 1890-1923. Furthermore, C.H. Wollaston, J.F. Alcock, A.W. Mackenzie, M.P. Betts and J. Kirkpatrick were all committee members so the Football Association still bore the Wanderers mark forty years after the last game was played in 1883 and for the first sixty years of the F.A.'s existence.

The Wanderers combined with the Football Association did much to create the right atmosphere whereby the new unified rules would be accepted. Although willing to compromise the Wanderers more often than not played by the rules, laid down by the Football Association, and this along with the creation of organized competitive football was a major factor in the rules of Association Football being accepted by the mass of clubs springing up around the country.

C.W. Alcock's idea for creating the F.A. Cup was a catalyst in the development of uniform playing rules, and from this point onwards, except in certain public schools who still preferred there own variations of the game, disputes became less and the game progressed and grew at a dramatic rate.

Wanderers were never afraid to try new ideas, and as such in 1879 they featured in the first floodlit game in London. This revolutionary concept was not a success, but with improved technology the idea was not as misguided as initially thought, just 70 years ahead of its time and is now something taken for granted.

The club invented the football tour although on a limited scale. While they did not quite match the Corinthians' scope when it came to touring, the idea became firmly rooted in the culture of the early game. From those humble beginnings in 1867 when Oxford and Cambridge were visited for several days, by the turn of the century the Corinthians had toured South Africa for three months spreading the footballing gospel. This was later expanded by the Corinthians between 1900 and the Second World War, when Brazil, America and practically every country in Europe was visited in an effort to spread the word.

It is easy to spot the links between the Wanderers and the Corinthians. The two clubs briefly exchanged players in C. Holden-White and N.C. Bailey during the last two seasons of the Wanderers. The two clubs essentially enjoyed the same make up in membership, with both clubs' membership being composed of ex-public school boys and certainly the gentlemanly classes. The

Corinthians without doubt could be seen as natural successors to the Wanderers as they too aimed to attract the best players from Universities and the public schools. There was one exception between the two clubs however in that the Corinthians refused to enter the F.A. Cup. They too shared their players with other clubs, as had the Wanderers and the lessons from history meant the new club would not last long if they had entered the F.A. Cup. The Corinthians did of course change their stance on competitive football in the 1920's, but times had changed. Prior to this period the amateur dominated and amateur players regularly were selected alongside their professional counterparts for International duty. The split in 1907 ended this when a dispute about professional clubs' membership of the county football associations led to the leading amateur clubs withdrawing from all activities with the Football Association and its remaining members, and the formation of the Amateur Football Alliance.

The most lasting tradition adopted by the Corinthians was the Wanderers sporting ethic. This became embodied in what is commonly known as the 'Corinthian Spirit' which has itself spawned so many stories and myths. Only once was there any criticism of a match official in any report I have studied and even then he was unnamed. There were also very few references to bad sportsmanship; any that were mentioned are open to debate and could potentially have been tongue in cheek. Any disputes seemed to have been settled amicably between captains in the early days and later by the umpires and referee. Furthermore, having been presented with the F.A. Cup trophy on a permanent basis following their third successive triumph, the club handed it back to the Football Association with the proviso that no team could ever win it outright again. This principle has been maintained ever since although the F.A. Cup trophy is in its fourth incarnation through various mishaps: no club has ever become owners of the trophy.

The Wanderers playing record in this period was second to none. Five F.A. Cup wins in seven years is testament to that. That is not to say the club was unbeatable, because it clearly had weaknesses and was susceptible to defeat. The problem the club faced was the sharing of players with other teams, thus causing divided loyalties. The Wanderers though could call on so many great players of the day that when it mattered they proved to be the best club. In nine seasons of F.A. Cup competition the Wanderers only lost to two sides, twice to Oxford University and twice to the Old Etonians when the club was in decline.

Wanderers' involvement in the F.A. Cup allowed the southern clubs first to come into contact with Queen's Park who were busy dominating Scottish football in the same way as their London counterparts. It was during the 1872 semi-final that the passing game played north of the border first came to the fore. In fact in subsequent games, including the first time an English club had played in Scotland, the benefits of this passing style were clearly highlighted by the score lines. Combine this with the North v South fixtures and the biannual London v Sheffield games and football became the national game through having a universally standard set of rules.

These five F.A. Cup wins means the Wanderers are joint eighth in the all time list of F.A. Cup winners with Everton and West Bromich Albion. It seems unlikely that they will slip outside the top ten for some time to come as only Chelsea look capable of catching and overtaking them from the chasing pack. In today's footballing climate the F.A. Cup is dominated by the big clubs, Manchester United, Arsenal, Liverpool and Chelsea. Only once since 1991 has a team other than these won the trophy and consequently it is unlikely in the near future that any of the closest teams, (Bolton Wanderers, Sheffield United, Wolverhampton Wanderers and Manchester City) will win the trophy enough times to remove the Wanderers name from this prestigious list.

One record associated with the club which is highly unlikely to be beaten is A.F. Kinnaird's record of nine cup final appearances in eleven years. Roy Keane has closed the gap and has now played in seven, winning four; he however is running out of time to beat this record. Nevertheless Keane could well equal the joint record of A.F. Kinnaird and C.H.R. Wollaston who both received five winners' medals. Kinnaird won two with the Old Etonians while Wollaston was never on the losing side in a final while with the Wanderers.

Team	No of F.A. Cup wins
Manchester United	11
Arsenal	10
Tottenham Hotspur	8
Aston Villa	7
Blackburn Rovers	6
Liverpool	6
Newcastle United	6
The Wanderers	**5**
West Bromich Albion	5
Everton	5
Bolton Wanderers	4
Manchester City	4
Sheffield United	4
Wolverhampton Wanderers	4
Chelsea	3
Sheffield Wednesday	3
West Ham United	3

Table of F.A. Cup wins

It is also interesting to see how the name Wanderers has lived on in the names of other clubs. The name and fashion for the name must clearly have influenced various teams such as Wolverhampton Wanderers and Bolton Wanderers to mention but two. The name however seemed to be adopted almost immediately as 'The Sportsman' contained details around 1879 of the following clubs, Manchester Wanderers, City Wanderers, Thursday Wanderers (Sheffield), Edinburgh Wanderers, Free Wanderers (Manchester) and in 1881 Grimsby Town's reserve side had added Wanderers as a suffix. The Wanderers were also known by the nickname 'The Rovers' in the 1860's which potentially led to naming of yet more clubs. Initially Clapham Rovers, but latterly Blackburn Rovers, Bristol Rovers and Doncaster Rovers all bear the name. This nickname died out in the 1870's probably due to the fact it may have caused confusion with Clapham Rovers.

The International game also is indebted to the Wanderers as they made a valuable contribution to making the pseudo-internationals a success. In this series of five games the Wanderers supplied many member players to both England and Scotland. The first game in 1870 saw no fewer than thirteen players who had represented the Wanderers play on either of the sides. This trend continued to throughout the series. After the Wanderers game with Queen's Park in 1872, the Scottish Football Association was founded and from this point the England v Scotland fixture became official.

The official games saw twenty three players from the Wanderers capped between 1872 and 1880. The figure would be higher if you take into account those who also represented the Wanderers in the same season they were capped. Regardless of this it is still an impressive total, given that only ten internationals were played between the first and last Wanderers player to be capped so only 110 caps were available in all.

Wanderers as can be seen were involved in everything that emerged and developed in football from 1859 until the late 1870's. Their influence is beyond question and the roots of the game we enjoy today stem from Wanderers' ideas. The global game, the International fixtures and World Cup, the mass spectator sport and most importantly the F.A. Cup all have had the Wanderers mark on them either directly or via concepts that they introduced. Take the Wanderers out of the equation and the F.A. would probably never have evolved in the way it did; without Alcock's drive and vision and the Wanderers undoubted ability, the game would be very different. A revolution at the F.A. occurred after Alcock's appointment and his vehicle was the Wanderers Football Club.

Player Profiles – The Top 50 Wanderers F.C. Players and Significant Others

This section deals with profiles of the top 50 Wanderers. This is done purely on appearances as it is impossible to calculate it on ability although the leading players tend to feature further up the list. There are also several additional profiles added for players who appeared in F.A. Cup Finals for the club, but did not make it on to the list. There are of course gaps in the statistics, but I believe this is a fair reflection of the players who made the Wanderers F.C. the leading club of its day.

C.W. Alcock

Date of Birth	2nd December 1842
Died	26th February 1907
Place of Birth	Sunderland
School	Harrow
Position	Forward
Other Clubs	Surrey, Upton Park, Harrow Pilgrims, Gitanos, Crystal Palace
Debut	15th March 1862 Forest 1 Crystal Palace 0 @ Leytonstone
Last Game	22nd December 1875 Wanderers 2 Swifts 2 @ Oval

Season	Apps	Goals	Season	Apps	Goals
1861/62	2	0	1862/63	3	4
1863/64	8	5	1864/65	3	1
1865/66	16	6	1866/67	14	2
1867/68	20	3	1868/69	15	5
1869/70	22	9	1870/71	33	17
1871/72	23	10	1872/73	7	3
1873/74	13	4	1874/75	11	11
1875/76	9	2	Total	199	82

'A hardworking forward player and usually a safe shot at goal.'
Football Annual 1875

Charles William Alcock was the leading Wanderers player in terms of both appearances and goals. He undoubtedly played more than the 198 games which have been traced, and possibly could have been responsible for a few more goals. Alcock however is not remembered for his football, but instead for his ability as an administrator, journalist and sports promoter. Without Alcock it is unlikely that the game of football would have progressed and spread so rapidly, as he is credited with turning around the fortunes of the Football Association.

Alcock was one of five sons of a Sunderland shipbuilder. The family relocated to Essex and between 1855 and 1859 he attended Harrow School where he first discovered the infant game of football. His health hampered his sporting activity while at school and it is often commented that he did not make the school team. It is unlikely however that the school were playing external opponents at this time.

On leaving school Alcock played a prominent part in the creation of Forest Football Club, while working in the family business. He married Eliza Caroline Ovenden in 1864 a marriage which was to produce eight children. By 1866 Alcock was on the Football Association Committee having replaced his brother John, and became Secretary in 1870. A year later at Alcock's suggestion the F.A. Cup was agreed upon and started. Alcock was Secretary of the F.A. until 1895 when he resigned and became Vice-President. He did however remain in a consultancy role for another year. He had become the first paid Secretary of the F.A. in 1887 when he started to collect a £200 a year salary.

In 1871 Alcock defied the Football Association Committee and took a team to play Sheffield. The controversy had begun due to the fact that the game was to take place under Sheffield rules. Had Alcock not done this the game's development is likely to have been delayed for several years; as it was he who oversaw the amalgamation of rules in 1876.

During this time Alcock continued to captain and act as secretary to the Wanderers who by March 1872 had captured the first ever F.A. Cup. This was to be the only final Alcock would play in as injuries and age began to creep up on him. He was also chosen to captain England on four occasions in full internationals, but again injuries prevented him from playing in all but for the March 1875 match against Scotland, a game in which Alcock scored in a 2-2 draw. Prior to the official internationals starting he had played in all five pseudo internationals between 1870 and 1872. Alcock gained other representative honours by appearing in the Middlesex versus Surrey & Kent game in 1867 and Middlesex versus Surrey in 1868, not to mention numerous times in the London versus Sheffield series.

Alcock was a prolific goal scorer of the dribbling school of play, hitting 82 for the Wanderers alone. His greatest scoring feats were four goals against Civil Service in 1871 and an F.A. Cup hat trick against Barnes in 1874. He retired from playing in 1875 following a 2-2 draw with Swifts, although he did make a comeback briefly in 1880 when he featured in a Rugby Veterans verses Soccer Veterans fixture. His career also saw him playing in a number of representative fixtures for London and Middlesex, which were organised by the F.A. prior to the formation of the County Associations.

Another string to Alcock's bow was that he was an accomplished referee and umpire. The referee was a point of appeal only if the two umpires, one in each half of the field, did not agree, prior to the introduction of the more active referee. He was umpire for the first official international and also refereed the 1875 and 1879 F.A. Cup Finals. He also was referee for the Wanderers' last ever game in 1883. Later Alcock was the first President of the Referees' Association and also was President of the Surrey F.A. and Vice-President of the London F.A..

As stated earlier he is more renowned for his achievements off the football pitch rather than on it. His journalism and sports promotion were two key qualities which helped the game grow. By the late 1860's Alcock was editor of the 'Football Annual' and in 1872 became editor of 'James Lillywhite's Cricketers' Annual'. Alcock was also a sub editor for 'The Sportsman' newspaper as well as publishing many books such as 'Football: Our Winter Game', 'Football: The Association

Game' and 'Famous Footballers and Athletes'. He also published a magazine called 'Cricket', worked for 'The Field' and launched the magazine 'Football'.

Cricket was another of Alcock's loves and in 1862 he played at Lords for M.C.C. against Middlesex. He is also known to have represented the Gentlemen of Essex and the Butterflies. He also has the distinction of captaining France against Germany at Cricket! In 1872 Alcock became secretary of Surrey County Cricket Club and he was able to make that club rich, thanks to his influence within football as the Oval was hired out regularly and became the primary venue for sport in the capital. W.G. Grace stated that Alcock once played Rugby for Blackheath as well, highlighting what an all round sport enthusiast he was.

Alcock died in 1907 following two years of illness of a heart and bronchial nature. A friend of Alcock's wrote this account of the man at the turn of the century:-

'When the flashing meteors have come and gone, when the League tables are full and complete, and when the present fades into the past the name of C.W. Alcock will stand out all the more prominently like a rugged rock in a sea of bubbles. Like a thread of gold his career runs through the weaving of the story of Association football, and his tall and dignified form strides the river of the game from its source. When needed, he can deliver a telling speech with the best, and it will contain as much truth and fact and information to the square inch as most. His face still mirrors the moving joy of the tough conflict which he loves to watch from the Grand Stand; his censure of evil practices that sometimes disgrace the game he loves is as caustic as ever; his advice is much sought after and his opinion as highly esteemed. He is as good a judge of a player's form and abilities now as when he himself took part in the rough and tumble early days, just as he is as keen to note a weak point in an argument or a loophole in a rule as the most astute football lawyer. Still a jovial comrade with a wealth of football anecdote; still as determined to probe to the bottom anything that reflects upon the game, but with a blend of good nature that declines to press too hard upon a luckless defender, he is the Grand Old Man of The Football Association, loved and respected by everybody.'[1]

A.F. Kinnaird

Date of Birth	16th February 1847
Died	30th January 1923
Place of Birth	London, Hyde Park Gardens
School	Eton College & Trinity College, Cambridge University
Position	Played in all positions
Other Clubs	Old Etonians, Trinity Coll., West Kent, Crusaders, Civil Service, Gitanos
Debut	22nd December 1866 Wanderers 1 Harrow Chequers 1 @ Battersea Pk
Last Game	18th December 1883 Wanderers 6 Harrow School 1 @ Oval

Season	Apps	Goals	Season	Apps	Goals
1866/67	3	0	1867/68	4	0
1868/69	3	7	1869/70	13	5
1870/71	13	4	1871/72	0	0
1872/73	10	4	1873/74	1	0
1874/75	1	0	1875/76	3	1
1876/77	13	1	1877/78	12	3
1878/79	2	1	1882/83	1	0
1883/84	1	0	Total	80	26

'Without exception the best player of the day; capable of taking any place in the field; is very fast and never loses sight of the ball. An excellent captain.'
Football Annual 1873

'Is still first amongst the football players of the day; very fast, with great pluck, and plays hard to the last.'
Football Annual 1875

Arthur Fitzgerald Kinnaird was the greatest player of his day. He played in nine of the first twelve F.A. Cup finals where he collected five winners' medals. After he retired he gave great service to the Football Association until his death.

A.F. Kinnaird

Kinnaird was born in 1847, the only son of a Scottish peer. He attended Eton College before progressing to Cambridge University where he achieved a B.A. in 1869 and a M.A. in 1873. In 1887 he became Lord Kinnaird and he went onto become prominent in the House of Lords being very influential on religious matters. A Merchant Banker by profession, Kinnaird went to work for Ranson & Co. where he was made a partner in 1877. This later became Barclay, Ransom & Co. and then Barclays Bank where he finished as a director. He was also a Justice of the Peace for Perth, Kent and London, President of the Y.M.C.A. and Lord High Commissioner of the Church of Scotland from 1907 to 1909.

In 1866/67 Kinnaird became captain of the Eton Club at Cambridge University and in the same year made his debut for the Wanderers in a 1-1 draw with Harrow Chequers. A year later he was elected on to the committee of the F.A.

As organised football developed Kinnaird began to collect honours. He appeared in the first three pseudo internationals for Scotland and also in a full international in 1873. He also played on numerous occasions for London's representative side, four times for Middlesex and also Kent.

It was the F.A. Cup where Kinnaird shone and he collected his first winners' medal in 1873 when Wanderers beat Oxford University. He was to appear in another eight finals winning a total of five winners' medals. He was a winner with Wanderers in 1877 and 1878, and with Old Etonians in 1879 and 1882. He was a runners up on four occasions with the Old Etonians in 1875, 1876 (against the Wanderers), 1881 and 1883.

Kinnaird had several spells with the Wanderers, and tended to yo-yo between them and Old Etonians of whom he was the founder. He did however enjoy his greatest success while playing for the Wanderers in a period which lasted 17 years. During his time with the club he played in every position, yet still managed to score 26 goals which is the third highest in the club's history. His greatest scoring exploits came when he scored a hat trick at Upton Park in an 8-0 mauling in 1869.

Kinnaird played until he was 43 years of age, finally retiring from playing in 1890. He was already on the F.A. Committee at this point and had been treasurer since 1877, but his retirement signalled his promotion to F.A. President. In this position he used his influence to promote the sport and encourage a class less game. Kinnaird was also to become first President of the London F.A. In 1911 Kinnaird was presented by the F.A. with the second F.A. Cup which was replica of the original which had been stolen. This was in recognition of his services to the game of football.

Kinnaird will always be remembered for being one of the great characters and extroverts of the early game. He was unmistakable with his long red beard, and blue and white cap which he pulled down over his eyes. Following the 1882 F.A. Cup final when Old Etonians defeated Blackburn Rovers, Kinnaird stood on his head in front of the Oval pavilion to celebrate. One story which is often quoted about Kinnaird is as follows. *'One day Major Marindin called on Mrs Kinnaird, and she expressed her fear that 'Arthur will one day come home with a broken leg.' 'Don't be alarmed,' replied the Major, 'for if he does, it will not be his own.'*[2]

Lord Kinnaird died on 30th January 1923, just eleven days after his wife by whom he had had seven children.

C.H.R. Wollaston

Date of Birth	31st July 1849
Died	22nd June 1926
Place of Birth	
School	Lancing and Trinity College, Oxford University
Position	Inside Forward
Other Clubs	Oxford University, Clapham Rovers, Middlesex, Lancing O.B.
Debut	9th March 1872 Clapham Rovers 1 Wanderers 1 @ Clapham
Last Game	23rd October 1880 Wanderers 0 Upton Park 2 @ Oval

Season	Apps	Goals	Season	Apps	Goals
1871/72	2	0	1872/73	9	7
1873/74	8	6	1874/75	8	8
1875/76	9	5	1876/77	10	4
1877/78	12	7	1878/79	5	1
1879/80	8	2	1880/81	4	0
			Total	75	40

'Guides the leather with the most consummate skill, and is unerring in his shots at goal.'
Football Annual 1873

'A very pretty and effective player; usually acting as a 'wing' especially good as a dribbler and always about goal when the ball is in the way.'
Football Annual 1875

Charles Henry Reynolds Wollaston was another outstanding player of his day who gave excellent service to the Wanderers Football Club. During his ten seasons with the club, he collected five F.A. Cup winners' medals and four England caps for whom he scored one goal. He also appeared in London versus Sheffield and served on the F.A. Committee from 1879 to 1886.

Wollaston was educated at Lancing before progressing to Trinity College, Oxford. In 1878 he went to work as assistant secretary to the Union Bank in London and was promoted in 1885 to secretary. By 1898 he had been elected a director. He continued working there, even after the bank amalgamated with the National Provincial Bank, until his death in 1926.

Wollaston was a regular with the Wanderers for ten years and in his last two seasons was Secretary of the club. By this time he was facing an uphill struggle to turn the club's fortunes around and he finally left the club after the 1880/81 season and played for Clapham Rovers. He was the second top scorer in the club's history and games which stand out are his four goal showing against Farningham in 1874 and hat tricks against Clapham Rovers in 1871 and Civil Service in 1873.

His obituary described his later life as:-

'He shrank from any form of public appearance, or anything which he regarded as savouring or self-advertisement. He never had his photograph taken except for the purpose of his passport, he never spoke in public, and never spoke about himself at all. He had no liking for general society and his pleasantest hours were spent with small groups of old and intimate friends, or wandering in the Alps with Swiss guides. He had strong affections for his family, for certain chosen friends, for the hills, music and the sea; he also had a hearty hatred for particular men, particular kinds of men, and particular manners of life and particular kinds of food – aversions which were as violent as they were whimsical and prejudiced. He was a firm of purpose and determined to the verge of obstinacy. He had no doubt about what was right and what was wrong, and followed unswervingly, both in small things and in great, that which he believed to be right.'[3]

Rev. A.H. Stratford

Date of Birth	5th September 1853
Died	2nd May 1914
Place of Birth	Kensington
School	Malvern
Position	Full Back
Other Clubs	Swifts, Middlesex
Debut	31st January 1874 Oxford University 1 Wanderers 0 @ The Parks F.A. Cup 3rd round replay
Last Game	17th November 1880 Westminster School 1 Wanderers 0 @ Vincent Square

Season	Apps	Goals	Season	Apps	Goals
1873/74	1	0	1874/75	9	1
1875/76	15	0	1876/77	11	0
1877/78	16	1	1878/79	5	0
1879/80	9	0	1880/81	4	0
			Total	70	2

67

'Can play forward and back; plays well as full back, being a good strong tackler.'
Football Annual 1875

Alfred Hugh Stratford joined the Wanderers at the start of the 1874/75 season having previously attended Malvern College from 1870 to 1873. Whilst at Malvern Stratford was a prefect and played in the Cricket XI from 1871 to 1873 and the Football XI from 1870 to 1873, where he was captain in his final year.

During his time with the Wanderers he was an undoubted stalwart of the club, rarely missing a game during his seven seasons, and collecting three successive F.A. Cup medals along the way. In 1874 Stratford made his only appearance for England against Scotland in a 1-2 defeat; he also made several appearances for London versus Sheffield.

Stratford was also a successful Cricketer and enjoyed a seven year first class career between 1877 and 1884 whilst playing for Middlesex. His cricket career saw him play in 33 matches. In 55 innings he scored 577 runs, being not out on eight occasions. On the bowling side of things he took 83 wickets in these games. Stratford went on to play for the United States of America after emigrating there. He died there in Newark, New Jersey in 1914.

C.M. Tebbut

Date of Birth	24th December 1839
Died	27th December 1898
Place of Birth	Wanstead
School	Unknown
Position	Forward (probably)
Other Clubs	No Names
Debut	15th March 1862 Forest 1 Crystal Palace 0 @ Leytonstone
Last Game	1st October 1870 Wanderers 0 Clapham Rovers 1 @ Oval

Season	Apps	Goals	Season	Apps	Goals
1861/62	2	0	1862/63	0	0
1863/64	7	2	1864/65	2	0
1865/66	8	0	1866/67	11	0
1867/68	14	0	1868/69	11	0
1869/70	3	0	1870/71	1	0
			Total	59	2

Charles Mansfield Tebbut was born on Christmas Eve 1839 in Wanstead close to Forest Football Club's first ground. Information is in scarce supply as to his life in general. It has been suggested he could have been educated locally or at home, but it is known that his family owned a ship building company and this is possibly how he came into contact with the Alcock brothers.

Tebbut was one of the original Forest Football Club members and played on through their evolution into the Wanderers. A regular in the side for many years, he was the brother of A.M Tebbut who scored the winner in the Wanderers' first ever game against No Names in 1864. Tebbut gained representative honours when he appeared for Middlesex versus Surrey in 1868.

Tebbut also enjoyed fame as a first class cricketer with Middlesex between 1866 and 1870 and featured in six matches, scoring 38 runs in nine innings, being not out once. He was described as *'a great patron of cricket, he was for many years on the committees of both Middlesex and Essex and advanced a considerable sum of money to the latter.... Which saved it from extinction.'*[4] He died in 1898 at South Hampstead in London.

J. Kirkpatrick

Date of Birth	22nd March 1841
Died	10th November 1899
Place of Birth	Dumfries
School	Unknown
Position	Goal Keeper
Other Clubs	Civil Service, Gitanos
Debut	28th September 1867 C.C.C. 0 Wanderers 1 @ Clapham Com.
Last Game	23rd March 1878 Wanderers 3 Royal Engineers 1 @ Oval F.A. Cup Final

Season	Apps	Goals	Season	Apps	Goals
1866/67	1	0	1867/68	4	0
1868/69	7	0	1869/70	8	1
1870/71	2	0	1871/72	6	0
1872/73	3	0	1873/74	10	0
1874/75	2	0	1875/76	3	0
1876/77	4	1	1877/78	8	0
			Total	58	2

'As a goal-keeper is always excellent, and Surrey owes much to him in that position.'
Football Annual 1875

'A very useful goal-keeper; fields well, and does not lose his head.'
Football Annual 1879

James Kirkpatrick was the second of eight sons born to Sir Charles Kirkpatrick, 6th Baronet of Closeburn, County Dumfries. In 1880 he succeeded his brother to become the 8th Baronet; prior to this he was the Private Secretary to Lord George Hamilton, 1st Lord of the Admiralty.

He was the Wanderers favoured goal-keeper for a number of years and helped the club to win the 1878 F.A. Cup final in what proved to be his last game for the club. He played during this game against the Royal Engineers with a fractured arm sustained during the game.

It can also be seen by looking at the statistics that he did not always play in goal and actually scored two goals during his time at the club against Forest Club in 1870 and Gitanos at the Oval in 1876.

Kirkpatrick was selected for the Scotland side during the pseudo international period and appeared in the first four of these unofficial games and also represented Surrey. Kirkpatrick served on the F.A. Committee from 1869 to 1872.

As a cricketer Kirkpatrick played one first class game in 1867 for the Gentlemen of the South, scoring ten runs and taking three wickets.

A & A.C. Thompson

Date of Birth	13th July 1848
Died	20th March 1894
Place of Birth	Vale of York
School	Eton College & Cambridge University
Position	Back
Other Clubs	Gitanos, Old Etonians
Debut	2nd April 1864 No Names 0 Wanderers 1 @ Kilburn
Last Game	6th December 1873 Wanderers 1 Oxford University 1 @ Oval F.A. Cup

Season	Apps	Goals	Season	Apps	Goals
1863/64	1	0	1864/65	2	0
1865/66	12	4	1866/67	2	0
1867/68	2	0	1868/69	3	0
1869/70	4	0	1870/71	4	0
1871/72	16	0	1872/73	9	0
1873/74	1	0	Total	56	4

'Facile princes, the king of backs. The ease with which he kicks the ball in the most difficult positions suggest the belief that at one time of his life he must have gone into training with a view to an acrobatic career'
Football Annual 1873

'Played principally for Cambridge, and was unable to take part in many of the principal matches of the year, but still holds his own as a half-back, one of the most brilliant kickers of the day.'
Football Annual 1875

There is a lot of confusion over A and A.C. Thompson. They were clearly two different players, but statistically it is impossible to separate the two due to the way the names were given in the press. A. Thompson was certainly an individual as it is quoted he was the brother of W.J. Thompson another early player; on two occasions, both A. Thompson and A.C. Thompson featured in the same side. A. Thompson played in the first Wanderers game in 1864 when he made his debut against No Names.

Albert Childers Thompson was born in 1848 and grew up in the Vale of York. Thompson attended Eton College (1862-65) at the same time as Kinnaird. Like Kinnaird he progressed to Trinity College, Cambridge. Whilst at Eton he played the Wall game in 1866 and made the shooting XI in 1865 to 1867. In 1872 he was called to the bar at the Inner Temple. In 1874 his father altered the family name to Meysey-Thompson.

In 1872 he won his first F.A. Cup final winner's medal. Thompson left the Wanderers for good after a brief appearance in the F.A. Cup side of 1873/74 which lost to Oxford University after a replay. The following season he was a cup winner with Old Etonians although he did not play in the deciding replay and in 1876 was on the losing side against the Wanderers. Other honours include appearing for London versus Sheffield in 1872 and for Surrey versus Kent in 1868.

A.C. Thompson died in 1894 the first of the 1872 side to pass away.

A.J. Baker

Date of Birth	Unknown
Died	Unknown
Place of Birth	Unknown
School	Unknown
Position	
Other Clubs	No Names
Debut	12th November 1864 Civil Service 0 Wanderers 2 @ Battersea Park
Last Game	25th March 1871 Wanderers 1 The World 1 @ Oval

Season	Apps	Goals	Season	Apps	Goals
1864/65	1	0	1865/66	0	0
1866/67	1	0	1867/68	9	1
1868/69	13	4	1869/70	17	9
1870/71	17	1	Total	58	15

A.J. Baker was another early Wanderer about whom little is known. He made a valuable contribution to the club over a period of six years. Baker however was a famous sprinter and appeared in two of the early pseudo internationals and also played in the South versus North game in December 1870. He also represented Middlesex versus Surrey & Kent in 1867, Middlesex versus Surrey in 1868 and Kent versus Surrey in 1868. Baker was on the F.A. Committee from 1871 to 1872.

J. Kendrick

Date of Birth	13th November 1852
Died	29th January 1949
Place of Birth	Chichester
School	Lancing
Position	Forward
Other Clubs	Forest Club, Clapham Rovers, Old Lancing
Debut	14th January 1874 Wanderers 2 Uxbridge 1 @ Oval
Last Game	20th November 1878 Westminster School 1 Wanderers 1 @ Vincent Sq.

Season	Apps	Goals	Season	Apps	Goals
1873/74	1	0	1874/75	7	7
1875/76	14	4	1876/77	12	2
1877/78	13	5	1878/79	4	2
			Total	51	20

'A very promising forward; played very well for London at Sheffield in the third match of last season; wants rousing at times.'
Football Annual 1875

'Fair down a side; rather slack at times, but generally near the goal when the ball is there.'
Football Annual 1879

Jarvis Kenrick was educated at Lancing College, where he was a prefect in 1869 and in the Cricket XI in 1868 and 1869; he left Lancing in July 1869 and by 1875 had qualified as a Solicitor. By this time he had already joined the Wanderers where he was steadily establishing himself as a key member of the side.

At the end of 1875 he succeeded Alcock as Secretary of the club, which was an honour in itself following such a prestigious name. Under his leadership the club went from strength to strength and collected a hat trick of F.A. Cup successes. He remained playing and as Secretary until the end of the 1878/79 season. He made his mark early at the Wanderers hitting a hat trick in the 9-1 demolition of Harrow Chequers in January 1875, but never equalled this scoring feat again. Kenrick however remains fourth in the all time scorers' list. Kenrick gained representative honours player four times for Surrey versus Essex and four times for London versus Sheffield. Kenrick served on the F.A. Committee from 1877 to 1879.

Kenrick also had a brief stint in first class Cricket in 1876. Very brief in fact, as he only played one match for Surrey scoring 11 runs and taking one wicket.

Kenrick died in 1949 in Blatchington, Sussex, the last member of the great Wanderers sides to pass away.

R. de C. Welch

Date of Birth	17th October 1851
Died	4th June 1939
Place of Birth	Unknown
School	Harrow
Position	Full Back, Goal Keeper
Other Clubs	Harrow Chequers, Remnants, Middlesex, Old Harrovians
Debut	27th November 1869 Harrow School 3 Wanderers 1 @ Harrow
Last Game	November 1878 Harrow School 4 Wanderers 2 @ Harrow

Season	Apps	Goals	Season	Apps	Goals
1869/70	1	0	1870/71	0	0
1871/72	21	0	1872/73	11	0
1873/74	6	0	1874/75	6	0
1875/76	1	0	1876/77	1	0
1877/78	0	0	1878/79	1	0
			Total	48	0

'Played little last year, but is still a good safe goal keeper.'
Football Annual 1875

'Played well back in the cup-ties, working hard and kicking accurately; can keep goal well'
Football Annual 1879

Reginald de Courtenay Welch attended Harrow School from 1864 to 1871, where he represented the school at football in 1870 and Cricket in 1871. Welch also was a school monitor and editor of the 'Harrovian' from 1869 to 1871. He had grown up in Twickenham before going to Harrow.

From 1871 onwards Welch became a regular feature of the Wanderers sides and featured in the first two F.A. Cup finals which the Wanderers won. After the second of those victories he appeared less probably due to him becoming Honorary Secretary for both the Harrow Chequers and Old Harrovians the latter being between 1872 and 1874. The last major game he played in was the 1874 England versus Scotland fixture where he earned his second cap while also representing both Middlesex and London. Welch was on the F.A. Committee form 1873 to 1876 and 1879 to 1881.

He continued to feature for the Wanderers until the 1878/79 season making only occasional appearances after the 1874/75 season. His last game, as was his first was against his old school, Harrow.

After 1880 he retired from football to concentrate on his career and he was listed as a School Army Teacher at the Army College, Heath End, Farnham from 1883 to 1895.

E. E. Bowen

Date of Birth	30th March 1836
Died	8th April 1901
Place of Birth	Glenmore, Ireland
School	Blackheath School, Kings College, London & Trinity College, Cambridge
Position	
Other Clubs	Kings College, London, Trinity College, Harrow Pilgrims
Debut	28th October 1865 Civil Service 0 Wanderers 5 @ Battersea Park
Last Game	18th December 1883 Wanderers 6 Harrow School 1 @ Oval

Season	Apps	Goals	Season	Apps	Goals
1865/66	2	0	1866/67	3	0
1867/68	4	0	1868/69	5	2
1869/70	5	0	1870/71	4	1
1871/72	6	0	1872/73	5	1
1873/74	2	0	1874/75	0	0
1875/76	3	0	1876/77	2	0
1877/78	1	0	1878/79	0	0
1879/80	0	0	1880/81	2	0
1881/82	0	0	1882/83	1	0
1883/84	1	0	Total	46	4

Edward Ernest Bowen was born in Glenmore in Ireland in 1836, making him the oldest of the early Wanderers. He worked as a school master at Marlborough College from 1858, before moving to Harrow School in 1859.

Bowen served the Wanderers for eighteen years, a period which covers virtually the whole existence of the club. At the age of 36 years, he played in his first F.A. Cup final and followed that with a second triumph a year later. He was to play in the last ever Wanderers game in 1883 at the grand age of 47 years. Bowen also played in the first pseudo international in 1870.

In 1864 he played his one and only first class Cricket match for Hampshire, but did not score any runs. He was also an accomplished Skater and Mountaineer.

Bowen continued in his sporting activities literally up until his death in 1901. He died in Moux, Cote D'or in France whilst on a cycling tour.

C. F. Reid

Date of Birth	Unknown
Died	Unknown
Place of Birth	Unknown
School	Harrow School
Position	
Other Clubs	Hitchin
Debut	28th October 1865 Civil Service 0 Wanderers 5 @ Battersea Park
Last Game	14th February 1872 Wanderers 6 Civil Service 1 @ Oval

Season	Apps	Goals	Season	Apps	Goals
1865/66	6	1	1866/67	4	0
1867/68	5	1	1868/69	8	0
1869/70	4	0	1870/71	11	1
1871/72	6	0	Total	44	3

Virtually nothing is known about C.F. Reid except that he went to Harrow School and played for Hitchin. This latter fact may suggest that he was perhaps living in or in the proximity of the Hertfordshire town.

Despite the lack of factual evidence about the player's life, he played a substantial number of games for the club. He was never recognised in any representative games or pseudo internationals as far as can be established.

G. H. H. Heron

Date of Birth	30th January 1852
Died	5th June 1914
Place of Birth	Uxbridge
School	Mill Hill School
Position	Wing Forward
Other Clubs	Uxbridge, Swifts, Middlesex, Windsor Home Park
Debut	4th March 1874 Westminster School 0 Wanderers 4 @ Vincent Square
Last Game	23rd March 1878 Wanderers 3 Royal Engineers 1 @ Oval F.A. Cup Final

Season	Apps	Goals	Season	Apps	Goals
1873/74	1	0	1874/75	10	8
1875/76	13	0	1876/77	12	3
1877/78	7	4	Total	43	15

'As a wing player is useful and at times brilliant; is fast and dribbles skilfully, used to be a little selfish in his style of play, but of late very much improved in this respect.'
Football Annual 1875

George Hubert Hugh Heron was more commonly known as Hubert Heron and he played for the Wanderers during the club's most successful period. Hubert gained a place in the history books as he and his brother Frank were the first set of brothers to play in the same England team, against Scotland in 1876. He gained five England caps in total, although finishing on the winning side only once. He also represented Middlesex and appeared for London versus Sheffield.

Hubert played in three F.A. Cup finals during his four year spell at the club, bowing out after the 1878 victory over Royal Engineers. His goal scoring record was a reasonable one, with him scoring on average one goal for every three games played. The biggest scoring achievement came when he scored four goals in a 9-1 F.A. Cup win over Panthers in his last season.

Between 1873 and 1876 Hubert Heron was a member of the F.A. Committee where in 1873/74 he was listed as representing Uxbridge and then 1875/76 as representing Swifts. It is believed that he played for both clubs whilst in membership of the Wanderers.

F.T. Green

Date of Birth	**21st June 1851**
Died	**6th July 1928**
Place of Birth	**Unknown**
School	**Winchester & Oxford University**
Position	**Half Back**
Other Clubs	**Oxford University, Middlesex**
Debut	**31st October 1874 Wanderers 16 Farningham 0 @ Oval**
Last Game	**9th November 1878 Wanderers 2 Old Etonians 7 @ Oval F.A. Cup**

Season	Apps	Goals	Season	Apps	Goals
1874/75	7	0	1875/76	11	1
1876/77	12	0	1877/78	10	1
1878/79	2	0	Total	42	2

'A reliable half-back, being a sure kick and never irresolute.'
Football Annual 1875

Frederick Thomas Green was born in 1851 the son of Reverend Frederick Septimus Green of Wrexham and attended Winchester College between 1864 and 1869 when he then progressed to New College, Oxford, where he stayed until 1874. Green certainly took an active role in school life whilst at Winchester and participated in theatricals in 1867 when he played Banquo in MacBeth; he was a member of the debating society, a prefect of the Chapel and also was a member of the committee for athletic sports.

Green's ability as a sportsman also came to light whilst at Winchester and he represented the school at racquets (1868-69), Cricket (1868-69) and Rowing (1868). Despite all this extra curricular activity he still managed to finish third top of his class. He gained a B.A. whilst at Oxford which he

75

completed in 1874. From here he went on to qualify as a Barrister at the Inner Temple in 1877 and later became Inspector of Schools in 1880.

During five seasons with the Wanderers Green collected two F.A. Cup winners' medals to add to the one he won whilst at Oxford University in 1874. He certainly had a debut to remember as the Wanderers destroyed Farningham 16-0. Green stayed on after the 1878 exodus and featured in the first floodlit game of football in London when Wanderers played Clapham Rovers at the Oval. Five days later came his last game for the club as Wanderers were humbled by the Old Etonians. In 1876 he gained his solitary England cap in 0-3 defeat against Scotland. Green represented Middlesex and London twice against Sheffield.

G. G. Kennedy

Date of Birth	9th May 1844
Died	2nd January 1909
Place of Birth	Unknown
School	Harrow School & Trinity College, Cambridge University
Position	Forward
Other Clubs	Harrow Chequers
Debut	20th December 1866 Wanderers 0 Old Etonians 1 @ Battersea Park
Last Game	17th January 1874 Upton Park 2 Wanderers 1 @ Upton Park

Season	Apps	Goals	Season	Apps	Goals
1866/67	4	0	1867/68	8	1
1868/69	9	4	1869/70	0	0
1870/71	6	0	1871/72	8	3
1872/73	4	0	1873/74	2	0
			Total	41	8

'No mean forward, and very great in front of the enemy's goal.'
Football Annual 1873

Gilbert George Kennedy attended Harrow School before progressing to Trinity College, Cambridge. Whilst at Cambridge he is known to have rowed in the 'Head of the River Race' in 1867. After leaving Cambridge he went onto become a Metropolitan Police Magistrate and was a Justice of the Peace in London, Essex, Hertfordshire, Middlesex, Kent and Surrey.

Kennedy was never the most prolific of scorers, but he did receive recognition in 1870 when he was picked to represent Scotland in the second pseudo international. Kennedy also gained recognition when he appeared for Middlesex versus Surrey & Kent in 1867 and also for London versus Sheffield. Furthermore, Kennedy was a F.A. Committee member between 1869 and 1870.

Although not playing in the 1872 final, Kennedy did at least make a contribution to the cup run as he appeared in the 0-0 draw with Crystal Palace. A game which saw both teams progress into the semi finals.

C. A. Denton

Date of Birth	October 1852
Died	1932
Place of Birth	Unknown
School	Bradfield College & Oxford University
Position	Wing Forward
Other Clubs	Oxford University, Casuals
Debut	13th January 1872 Wanderers 3 Hampstead Heathens 0 @ Oval
Last Game	12th February 1880 Westminster School 0 Wanderers 1 @ Vincent Sq.

Season	Apps	Goals	Season	Apps	Goals
1871/72	1	0	1872/73	3	0
1873/74	0	0	1874/75	0	0
1875/76	2	1	1876/77	4	0
1877/78	14	8	1878/79	6	0
1879/80	11	3	Total	41	12

'A fast wing player, and did good service for the Wanderers in some of the cup ties; not a good shot at goal.'
Football Annual 1878

Charles Ashpitel Denton attended Bradfield College from 1862 to 1872 and later progressed to Trinity College, Oxford University. On leaving education Denton became a Solicitor in 1880 and became Assistant Secretary of the Union Bank of London which was part of the London Assurance Corporation.

Denton played for the Wanderers on and off for nearly ten years. It was not until 1877 that he began to feature regularly and appeared in the 1877 and 1878 F.A. Cup finals as a result. He was one of the few players to continue after 1878 and of those he certainly made the largest contribution in this troubled period of the club's history.

T. C. Hooman

Date of Birth	28th December 1850
Died	22nd September 1938
Place of Birth	Kidderminster
School	Charterhouse School
Position	Forward
Other Clubs	Old Carthusians
Debut	19th December 1868 Wanderers 3 Crusaders 0 @ Vincent Sq.
Last Game	9th November 1872 Wanderers 1 Gitanos 1 @ Oval

Season	Apps	Goals	Season	Apps	Goals
1868/69	7	3	1869/70	4	0
1870/71	16	6	1871/72	11	1
1872/73	2	0	Total	40	10

'Perhaps the fastest forward of the day, and an accomplished performer in all branches of the game. Is highly appreciated in Sheffield.'
Football Annual 1873

Thomas Hooman attended Charterhouse as a day pupil from 1863 to 1868. By 1891 Hooman was in the manufacturing industry where he was listed as an employer in making Portland Cement.

Hooman appears to have joined the Wanderers straight from school, where he was no doubt spotted in the frequent matches between the two organizations at this time. He gained two unofficial caps in the pseudo internationals of 1870 and 1871, and then gained an F.A. Cup winners medal in 1872. Hooman also represented the north of England versus the south in 1870 and also gained further honours appearing for Middlesex versus Surrey in 1872 and 1873, and also in the three London versus Sheffield games which occurred in 1872. There is no record of Hooman playing after the 1872/73 season and it seems he retired from the game at a very early age. His obituary tends to focus on his early football rather than anything else; although it is known he represented Charterhouse at Cricket and headed their batting average for two years. He later moved to Torquay and then Hythe where he died in 1938.

H. Wace

Date of Birth	**21st September 1853**
Died	**5th November 1947**
Place of Birth	**Shrewsbury**
School	**Shrewsbury School & Cambridge University**
Position	**Forward**
Other Clubs	**Cambridge University, Clapham Rovers, Shropshire Wanderers**
Debut	**18th March 1871 Wanderers 2 Forest Club 0 @ Oval**
Last Game	**23rd October 1880 Wanderers 0 Upton Park 2 @ Oval**

Season	Apps	Goals	Season	Apps	Goals
1870/71	1	0	1876/77	15	7
1877/78	13	9	1878/79	3	0
1879/80	4	2	1880/81	2	0
			Total	**38**	**18**

'A very good and dangerous 'centre' plays pluckily and sticks to the ball; at times gets a little too forward.'
Football Annual 1875

Henry Wace attended Shrewsbury School before progressing to St. John's College, Cambridge University. He took an active part in the Wanderers from the 1876/77 season and collected two F.A. Cup winners' medals in 1877 and 1878. During his time with Wanderers he also won three England caps during 1878 and 1879. He also appeared for London against both, Sheffield and Birmingham.

Wace has the distinction of scoring the Wanderers last ever F.A. Cup goal, against the Old Etonians in 1880. He is also known to have played Rugby for Cambridge against Oxford in 1873 and 1874.

Date of Birth	14th March 1850
Died	1st August 1910
Place of Birth	Chorlton, Manchester
School	Winchester College & University College, Oxford University
Position	Half Back
Other Clubs	Oxford University, Middlesex, Old Wykehamists
Debut	21st October 1873 Forest School 2 Wanderers 2 @ Snaresbrook
Last Game	24th March 1877 Wanderers 2 Oxford University 1 @ Oval F.A. Cup Final

Season	Apps	Goals	Season	Apps	Goals
1873/74	4	0	1874/75	8	0
1875/76	10	1	1876/77	10	0
			Total	32	1

'A very fine half-back, kicking well with either foot and very difficult to pass; plays the game thoroughly,'
Football Annual 1875

Francis Hornby Birley was born in Chorlton, Manchester in 1850. At the age of 13 he started at Winchester College where he stayed until 1868. He was an all round sportsman who appeared for the Commoner XI at Cricket in 1866, and the football side in the same year. He later played fives and continued to represent the school at cricket and football. In 1868 he became the steward for athletic sports and took part in throwing the ball and throwing the hammer; he won the high jump with pole at nine foot and also won the standard high jump. In his time at Oxford he threw the Hammer against Cambridge in 1872 and represented the University at football in 1874.

In 1873 he got his B.A. from Oxford University and became a Barrister in the Inner Temple in 1876. He later worked on the Northern Circuit and became a Justice of the Peace in Surrey.

Birley was to win three F.A. Cup winners medals, in 1874 for Oxford University a year after getting his degree, and in later years two with the Wanderers in 1876 and 1877. He was also a runner up at the hands of the Wanderers in 1873. He was to gain two caps for England in 1874 and 1875 whilst with the Wanderers and also represented London and Middlesex. In all his games for the Wanderers he only scored one goal: it was a vital one however in the F.A. Cup semi final against Swifts in 1876.

Birley also had a long association with first class Cricket at Lancashire and Surrey between 1870 and 1879. In five matches and eight innings he scored 65 runs, whilst he took four wickets in the matches he bowled in. In 1910 Birley died at Dormans Land, Surrey.

C. L. Huggins

Date of Birth	Unknown
Died	Unknown
Place of Birth	Unknown
School	Possibly Forest School
Position	Forward
Other Clubs	Clapham Rovers
Debut	21st November 1868 Upton Park 1 Wanderers 0 @ Upton Park
Last Game	2nd December 1873 Wanderers 4 Civil Service 0 @ Lille Bridge

Season	Apps	Goals	Season	Apps	Goals
1868/69	6	0	1869/70	8	4
1870/71	8	2	1871/72	8	4
1872/73	0	0	1873/74	2	0
			Total	32	10

C.L. Huggins possibly attended Forest School and little else is known about the player except that he also played for Clapham Rovers. He did have a reasonable scoring record, his best effort being a brace against Civil Service in December 1869. He also hit a goal in three consecutive games at the start of 1871/72 season against Civil Service, Gitanos and Forest School.

Q. Hogg

Date of Birth	14th February 1845
Died	17th January 1903
Place of Birth	Unknown
School	Eton College
Position	
Other Clubs	Crusaders, Gitanos, Old Etonians, Hanover United
Debut	3rd February 1866 Harrow School 0 Wanderers 2 @ Harrow
Last Game	25th March 1871 Wanderers 1 The World 1 @ Oval

Season	Apps	Goals	Season	Apps	Goals
1865/66	1	0	1866/67	2	0
1867/68	2	0	1868/69	0	0
1869/70	7	0	1870/71	19	1
			Total	31	1

Quinton Hogg was one of the more famous names associated with the Wanderers Football Club. He was prominent in his own right but the name lived on as he was Grandfather and Father of Lord Chancellors of the same family name.

He attended Eton College where he was a member of the Wall and Field XI's in 1863. In the same year he won the Eton fives, was keeper of fives and in the shooting XI. After leaving Eton he founded Polytechnic Institute and was a senior partner in Hogg, Curtis, Campbell & co. He was also a Member of Parliament.

Hogg played all of his games for the Wanderers prior to the commencement of competitive football, but he did receive recognition in that he represented Scotland versus in England twice in the pseudo internationals in 1870 and 1871. He also appeared in the north versus south fixture of 1870. His only known goal came in his last season against Civil Service. He was also captain of Old Etonians for seven years where it is said he never sustained a defeat during this period.

C. J. Chenery

Date of Birth	1st January 1850
Died	Unknown
Place of Birth	Lambourn, Berkshire
School	Unknown
Position	Forward
Other Clubs	Crystal Palace, Surrey
Debut	16th November 1870 Westminster School 0 Wanderers 0 @Vincent Sq.
Last Game	21st February 1877 Westminster School 0 Wanderers 1 @ Vincent Sq.

Season	Apps	Goals	Season	Apps	Goals
1870/71	11	1	1871/72	2	0
1872/73	2	0	1873/74	7	1
1874/75	4	2	1875/76	0	0
1876/77	4	1	Total	30	5

'An excellent dribbler, never far from the ball, and always playing the game thoroughly.'
Football Annual 1873

'A very hard working forward, playing up pluckily until the last, and always for his side.'
Football Annual 1875

Charles John Chenery was an accomplished all round sportsman, although little is known about his back ground and professional life. He won three caps for England scoring one goal and from the Football Annual's description of him. Chenery was obviously greatly admired and respected and gained representative honours appearing for London and Surrey.

From 1872 to 1873, Chenery enjoyed a spell playing first class cricket for Surrey, playing in 13 matches and in 24 innings he scored 309 runs. Chenery was a stalwart of the Crystal Palace Football Club for many years.

M. P. Betts

Date of Birth	30th August 1847
Died	19th April 1914
Place of Birth	Bloomsbury
School	Harrow
Position	Full Back/ Forward
Other Clubs	Old Harrovians, Kent, Harrow Pilgrims, West Kent, Harrow Chequers
Debut	25th October 1870 Forest School 1 Wanderers 4 @Walthamstow
Last Game	19th December 1882 Wanderers 1 Harrow School 1 @ Oval

Season	Apps	Goals	Season	Apps	Goals
1870/71	8	0	1871/72	10	1
1872/73	3	2	1876/77	7	3
1882/83	1	0	Total	29	6

'An invaluable man in any position; a most effective dribbler, and good back. Is now abroad.'
Football Annual 1873

Morton Peto Betts is sometimes better known be his pseudonym A.H. Chequer. This is how he was listed after the first F.A. Cup final when he scored the winning goal. It is a reference to 'A Harrow Chequer' the side he may well have played for had they not scratched from the inaugural competition.

M.P. Betts

Betts was certainly one of the more colourful characters associated with the Wanderers Football Club, and was a well travelled man of the world. He grew up in Kent and attended Harrow School; later he became a Civil Engineer. In 1870 he became the first Honorary Secretary of the Old Harrovians a position he would hold until 1873 when he moved to South America.

On his return to England Betts immediately started playing for the Wanderers again and featured in seven games during the 1876/77 season and also won his only cap for England in March 1877; he had previously featured in one of the pseudo internationals in 1871. By 1878 he was off on his travels again this time spending two years in Copenhagen. Betts also represented London versus Sheffield in 1872 and 1873 and served on the F.A. Committee from 1871-1873 and 1881-1891; the last season of which he was Vice President.

Betts was also a keen Cricketer and played once for Middlesex in 1872 and Essex before they were awarded first class status. He also played twice for Kent between 1872 and 1881 scoring 44 runs and became Secretary of Essex County Cricket Club, whilst being a F.A. Councillor for twenty years.

He retired to France in 1911 and he died there three years later just four months prior to the outbreak of the First World War.

A. Borwick

Date of Birth	Unknown
Died	Unknown
Place of Birth	Unknown
School	Unknown
Position	Forward
Other Clubs	Crystal Palace
Debut	28th October 1868 Westminster School 0 Wanderers 1 @ Vincent Sq.
Last Game	15th December 1873 Wanderers 2 Cambridge University 1 @ Oval

Season	Apps	Goals	Season	Apps	Goals
1868/69	6	0	1869/70	7	1
1870/71	5	3	1871/72	0	0
1872/73	4	0	1873/74	4	1
			Total	26	5

A. Borwick is another player of whom little is known, apart from that he played for Crystal Palace. There is no trace of any representative honours. He played semi regularly for the Wanderers scoring several goals, but he seems to have stopped playing after the 1873/74 season.

F. B. Maddison

Date of Birth	1850
Died	25th September 1907
Place of Birth	Unknown
School	Brasenose College, Oxford University
Position	Full Back/ Forward
Other Clubs	Oxford University, Crystal Palace
Debut	21st November 1874 Wanderers 5 Barnes 0 @ Oval – F.A. Cup
Last Game	15th November 1879 Rochester 0 Wanderers 6 @ Bat & Ball Ground F.A. Cup 1st round

Season	Apps	Goals	Season	Apps	Goals
1874/75	5	1	1875/76	9	5
1876/77	10	2	1877/78	0	0
1878/79	1	0	1879/80	1	0
			Total	26	8

'A hard worker and very useful either forward or back.'
Football Annual 1875

It is said that Frederick Brunning Maddison attended Marlborough College, but while he was there he was known as Frederick Patey Chappell; this was changed in 1873. He went onto attend Brasenose College, Oxford University and later became a Solicitor. It was while at Oxford University that he won his first F.A. Cup winners medal in 1874. The previous season he had been a runner-up against the Wanderers. His second F.A. Cup winners' medal came in 1876 whilst playing for the Wanderers. He also won one England cap while still at University in 1872 having previously represented Scotland in a pseudo international in 1871.

Maddison's best scoring achievement while with the Wanderers was a hat trick scored against Cricklewood during the 1875/76 season. Maddison also represented London three times against Sheffield.

Rev. R. W. S. Vidal

Date of Birth	3rd September 1853
Died	5th November 1914
Place of Birth	Cornborough nr. Bideford
School	Westminster School, Christ College, Oxford University
Position	Forward
Other Clubs	Oxford University, Old Westminsters
Debut	23rd October 1869 Wanderers 0 Old Etonians 2 @ Oval
Last Game	15th December 1876 Wanderers 2 Cambridge University 0 @ Oval

Season	Apps	Goals	Season	Apps	Goals
1869/70	4	0	1870/71	10	2
1871/72	6	2	1872/73	2	3
1873/74	2	0	1876/77	1	0
			Total	25	7

'One of the fastest and best dribblers of the day, and well known for his marvellous side shots at goal.'
Football Annual 1873

Robert Walpole Sealy Vidal or the 'Prince of Dribblers' as he was affectionately named, was born in Cornborough in 1853. He started his senior education in 1867 at Westminster School and made his Wanderers debut just two years later aged 16 years.

He was one of the most exciting players of his day and won his first F.A. Cup winners medal in 1872 aged just 18 years. In 1872 Vidal was to further his education by moving to Oxford University and as a result Wanderers lost his services in competitive matches from that moment forward.

Vidal faced the Wanderers in the 1873 final, which Oxford lost, but he gained his revenge by setting up the goal in Wanderers first defeat in the competition in 1874. That season he went on to collect his second winner's medal when Oxford University beat Royal Engineers in the final. His football career seems to have more or less ended after this second victory as he was missing from the Oxford team when they beat Wanderers again in 1874/75 and from their cup winning side of 1877. He did make a brief appearance for Wanderers against Cambridge University in December 1876. Vidal's only England cap came in 1873 against Scotland, although he did feature in all five pseudo internationals.

Vidal also gained honours playing for London versus Sheffield and played as a forward in the Oxford versus Cambridge Rugby match of February 1873. Vidal also was on the F.A. Committee from 1872 to 1873 and from 1874 to 1875.

84

In 1877 Vidal was ordained by the Church of England and became Curate of St Edmunds in the same year. Between 1878 and 1881 he was vice principal of Ely College and from 1880 to 1881 was Curate at Holy Trinity, Ely. In 1881, Vidal became Vicar of Abbotsham in Devon where he was to remain until his death in 1914.

W. Lindsay

Date of Birth	3rd August 1847
Died	15th February 1923
Place of Birth	India
School	Winchester College
Position	Full Back/ Forward
Other Clubs	Old Wykehamists, Surrey, Crystal Palace, Civil Service, Gitanos, South Norwood
Debut	2nd October 1875 Clapham Rovers 0 Wanderers 0 @ Balham
Last Game	24th January 1880 Wanderers 1 Old Etonians 3 @ Oval F.A. Cup 3rd Round

Season	Apps	Goals	Season	Apps	Goals
1875/76	8	0	1876/77	7	1
1877/78	5	0	1878/79	2	0
1879/80	2	0	Total	24	1

'A very good half-back, being a remarkably sure kick, and never 'funks;' plays well too for his side.'
Football Annual 1875

William Lindsay was born in India 1847, the son of Major William Lindsay, 10th Regiment. Unfortunately his father and most of his family were murdered at Cawnpore in 1857 during the Indian Mutiny. He was admitted as a commoner to Winchester in 1858 where he stayed until 1865.

He was a keen sportsman while at school and played cricket for the Commoner XI between 1862 and 1864, and the football team during the same period. Other successes included winning the wide jump in 1860 and in the same year he came second in the 100 yards. He later won the high jump and wide jump in 1863, the high jump with pole in 1864 and the sack race no less, in 1865.

Lindsay joined the Wanderers quite late on his football career and was about 28 when he made his debut against Clapham Rovers in 1875. He proved a good acquisition and in his first three seasons he collected three F.A. Cup winners' medals. In the 1877 final Lindsay scored his only goal for the club as Wanderers defeated Oxford University 2-1 in extra time. Lindsay proved a loyal servant to the club and played up until 1880 when he was in the side that lost 1-3 to Old Etonians in Wanderers last ever competitive match.

In 1867 Lindsay began work as a junior clerk at the store department of the India Office. He became private secretary to the Parliamentary Under Secretary of State in 1877 and by 1882 had become the senior clerk and private secretary to Lord George Hamilton. Lindsay retired in 1900 and lived for another 23 years.

A. Morten

Date of Birth	1831 or 1832
Died	16th September 1916
Place of Birth	Middlesex
School	Unknown
Position	Goal Keeper
Other Clubs	Crystal Palace, Middlesex
Debut	16th December 1865 Reigate Club 1 Wanderers 3 @ Reigate
Last Game	24th October 1874 Wanderers 0 Royal Engineers 2 @ Oval

Season	Apps	Goals	Season	Apps	Goals
1865/66	1	0	1866/67	2	0
1867/68	0	0	1868/69	0	0
1869/70	6	0	1870/71	7	0
1871/72	4	0	1872/73	2	0
1873/74	1	0	1874/75	1	0
			Total	24	0

''Toujours pret' is his motto when between the posts, in which position he is without a rival, never losing his head, even under the most trying circumstances. Has for many years rendered good service to the cause of the Association game.'
Football Annual 1873

It has been suggested that Alexander Morten was born in Middlesex in either 1831 or 1832 which certainly would make him one of the oldest players to make his debut for England when he played in 1873. Strangely he played on behalf of Scotland in the pseudo international of March 1870. Morten also played for both London and Middlesex at representative level. Morten later served on the F.A. Committee between 1874 and 1875; he died in New York in 1916.

H. Emmanuel

Date of Birth	Unknown
Died	Unknown
Place of Birth	Unknown
School	Unknown
Position	
Other Clubs	No Names
Debut	3rd November 1866 Forest School 2 Wanderers 0 @ Walthamstow
Last Game	1st January 1874 Wanderers 2 Harrow Chequers 1 @ Oval

Season	Apps	Goals	Season	Apps	Goals
1866/67	3	0	1867/68	4	1
1868/69	3	0	1869/70	7	1
1870/71	1	0	1871/72	3	0
1872/73	1	1	1873/74	2	0
			Total	24	3

There is little known about H. Emmanuel or Emanuel as it was sometimes written. It appears that he was never what you would call a regular player; only in 1869/70 did he make more than four appearances. There is no description of his style of play in the Football Annual, so it appears he was not held in the same high regard as some of his contemporaries. What is known is that he represented Surrey in 1875, London in 1875 and 1878 and Middlesex in 1867.

W. D. O. Greig

Date of Birth	1858 (approximately)
Died	Unknown
Place of Birth	Unknown
School	Farningham School
Position	Goal Keeper
Other Clubs	Hertfordshire Rangers, Farningham
Debut	17th January 1874 Upton Park 2 Wanderers 1 @ Upton Park
Last Game	25th November 1876 Upton Park 0 Wanderers 0 @ Plaistow

Season	Apps	Goals	Season	Apps	Goals
1873/74	1	0	1874/75	2	2
1875/76	15	0	1876//77	5	0
			Total	23	2

W.D.O. Greig's story is unique. He was in goal for Farningham during their brief F.A. Cup journey of 1874/75. It was a remarkably brief venture as Wanderers demolished them 16-0 in the first round. Greig must have impressed the Wanderers players as he became a regular the following season, (although he had made his debut the previous year) when he was their goal keeper in their 1876 success. Is there another player to go from losing 16-0 one season to being a winner the next?

Greig even scored two goals against Civil Service in 1874 during a rare appearance as an outfield player. He was selected for the London versus Sheffield fixture in 1874 and 1876. The only other facts that are known of Grieg is that he attended Farningham School and appeared for Hertfordshire Rangers.

W. P. Crake

Date of Birth	1852
Died	1st December 1921
Place of Birth	Madras, India
School	Harrow
Position	
Other Clubs	Barnes, Harrow Chequers
Debut	5th January 1870 Crystal Palace 0 Wanderers 1 @ Crystal Palace
Last Game	21st October 1874 Wanderers 1 Uxbridge 1 @ Oval

Season	Apps	Goals	Season	Apps	Goals
1869/70	2	0	1870/71	9	2
1871/72	6	0	1872/73	3	1
1873/74	2	0	1874/75	1	0
			Total	23	3

'A very neat dribbler, slow but certain; very useful on the side.'
Football Annual 1873

William Crake was probably introduced to the Wanderers by E.E. Bowen having attended Harrow School between 1866 and 1870. In later life he went back to his roots in India, where he became a merchant. He returned to England later dying at home near Hyde Park in 1921.

Crake enjoyed a brief but successful playing career, appearing in two pseudo internationals, the South v North fixture in 1870 and also three times for Middlesex. In 1872 he was part of the Wanderers side which won the first F.A. Cup.

W. J. Dixon

Date of Birth	**24th March 1848**
Died	**20th October 1879**
Place of Birth	**Unknown**
School	**Westminster School**
Position	
Other Clubs	
Debut	**22nd December 1866 Wanderers 1 Harrow Chequers 1 @ Battersea Park**
Last Game	**23rd February 1870 Westminster School 1 Wanderers 0 @ Vincent Square**

Season	Apps	Goals	Season	Apps	Goals
1866/67	1	0	1867/68	8	2
1868/69	8	1	1869/70	5	0
			Total	22	3

W.J. Dixon went to Westminster School, but his life was to be a short and tragic one. Less than a month after making his Wanderers debut, Dixon helped to save lives during the terrible ice accident in Regents Park on 15th January 1867. In the process of this heroic act, he caught a severe chill which for the rest of his life caused him a great many problems. His playing record reflected this as following his debut he did not play again until the following season. Dixon also gained honours playing for Middlesex and London.

He died at the age of 31 in 1879, having finally ended his football with the Wanderers in 1870. Dixon also served on the F.A. Committee from 1869 to 1871.

E. H. M. Elliot

Date of Birth	30th November 1852
Died	1921
Place of Birth	Hawick (possibly)
School	Harrow School
Position	
Other Clubs	
Debut	28th November 1871 Wanderers 5 Forest School 0 @ Oval
Last Game	22nd March 1873 Upton Park 1 Wanderers 1 @ Upton Park

Season	Apps	Goals	Season	Apps	Goals
1871/72	10	0	1872/73	12	0
			Total	22	0

'Oh, would that this too solid flesh could melt,' might well be the exclamation of those whom he comes into contact. A truly ponderous player but successful as a dribbler withal; has been known to kick a goal.'
Football Annual 1873

Edward Hay Mackenzie Elliot started at Harrow School in January 1867 and stayed until Easter 1870. He was the son of Sir Walter Elliott, KCSI of Wolfelee, Hawick, Scotland. Elliot played for the Wanderers for two seasons making a valuable contribution to the club and represented London in 1872. In 1874 he joined the 82 Regiment which may be the reason why he stopped playing for the Wanderers in 1873. By 1888 Elliot had transferred to the South Lancashire Regiment and when he retired in 1899 had reached the rank of Major. Elliot's greatest honour in football came when he appeared for Scotland in the 1871 and 1872 pseudo internationals.

From 1892 to 1897 Elliot was Private Secretary to Lord Glasgow while he was Governor of New Zealand. Elliot was also a Commandant of Prisoners of War during the Second Boer War. His other activities included being a Justice of the Peace for Roxburgh.

E. Lubbock

Date of Birth	22nd February 1847
Died	9th September 1907
Place of Birth	London
School	Eton College
Position	Back/ Half Back
Other Clubs	West Kent, Crusaders, Gitanos, Old Etonians
Debut	22nd Dec 1866 Wanderers 1 Harrow Chequers 1 @ Battersea Pk
Last Game	24th October 1874 Wanderers 0 Royal Engineers 2 @ Oval

Season	Apps	Goals	Season	Apps	Goals
1866/67	1	0	1867/68	1	0
1868/69	3	2	1869/70	7	0
1870/71	1	0	1871/72	5	0
1872/73	0	0	1873/74	3	0
1874/75	1	0	Total	22	2

'Still unrivalled as a back, and no English Eleven can be complete without him; very accurate in his kicking'
Football Annual 1875

Edgar Lubbock attended Eton College where he a member of the Eton XI between 1864 and 1866, becoming captain in his last year. He was also part of the mixed Wall team between 1863 and 1865.

Lubbock was a good all round sports man and won his first F.A. Cup winner's medal with the Wanderers in 1872. From here he went off on the Fitzgerald North America Tour in the summer of the same year. Lubbock was more noted as an Old Etonian and featured in the 1875 and 1876 F.A. Cup finals for that team and played in both games in 1875 when the Old Etonians lost to Royal Engineers and the first game which was drawn against Wanderers in 1876.

Geoffrey Green recalls a story about Lubbock and Alcock:
'....the famous story about a match between the Wanderers, the Champions of early football, and the Old Etonians at Kennington Oval. Alcock, the Wanderers' captain, tried out a special charge of his own against 'Quintus' Lubbock, one of the great half backs of the day. 'By heaven! Alcock,' cried out the towering Lubbock. 'If you do that again I'll hack your legs off!'[5]

Further recognition came to Lubbock in the form of being selected for all five of the pseudo internationals at football and also representing Kent, London and Middlesex. He also played for Kent County Cricket Club and the Gentlemen of Kent. He was noted as being a left arm fast underarm bowler.

Lubbock's professional career saw him become a partner in the Whitbread Brewery in 1875 and a Director of the Bank of England from 1891. He was also a Master of the Blankney Foxhounds. Lubbock died in Knightsbridge in 1907.

P. Rhodes

Date of Birth	Unknown
Died	7th April 1883
Place of Birth	Unknown
School	Harrow School
Position	
Other Clubs	Barnes, Crusaders
Debut	6th January 1866 Crystal Palace 0 Wanderers 3 @ Penge
Last Game	11th February 1871 Wanderers 2 Gitanos 0 @ Oval

Season	Apps	Goals	Season	Apps	Goals
1865/66	1	0	1866/67	5	0
1867/68	3	1	1868/69	6	0
1869/70	4	0	1870/71	3	0
			Total	22	1

P. Rhodes played most of his football in the early days. He was educated at Harrow School and again could have been one of E.E. Bowen's recruits. Rhodes scored just one goal for the Wanderers against C.C.C. on the opening day of the 1867/68 season. He represented Surrey three times between 1867 and 1868. In later life Rhodes went into business in Hong Kong before dying at an early age in 1883.

J. H. Giffard

Date of Birth	1847
Died	Unknown
Place of Birth	Unknown
School	Unknown
Position	
Other Clubs	Civil Service, Gitanos
Debut	19th January 1869 Wanderers 4 Bedouins 0 @ Middlesex County Cricket Ground
Last Game	14th December 1875 Wanderers 2 Harrow School 2 @ Oval

Season	Apps	Goals	Season	Apps	Goals
1868/69	2	0	1869/70	2	0
1870/71	0	0	1871/72	5	2
1872/73	5	0	1873/74	5	0
1874/75	1	0	1875/76	2	1
			Total	22	3

John Hardinge Giffard enjoyed a career in the Civil Service at the Admiralty and played for the Civil Service club. He appeared for the Wanderers on and off over a six year period scoring three goals, against Forest School and Upton Park in 1871/72, and against Westminster School in the 1875/76 season; he later served on the F.A. Committee from 1871 to 1877.

J. B. Martin

Date of Birth	10th June 1841
Died	20th March 1897
Place of Birth	Worcestershire (probably)
School	Harrow School & Exeter College, Oxford University
Position	
Other Clubs	West Kent, Crusaders
Debut	28th October 1865 Civil Service 0 Wanderers 5 @Battersea Park
Last Game	9th February 1870 Wanderers 0 Crystal Palace 2 @ Oval

Season	Apps	Goals	Season	Apps	Goals
1865/66	11	7	1866/67	0	0
1867/68	3	2	1868/69	3	1
1869/70	4	1	Total	21	11

John Biddulph Martin was educated at Harrow School and from there he progressed to Exeter College, Oxford. On leaving education he became treasurer at the Institute of Bankers and also treasurer of Charing Cross Hospital.

Martin made an immediate impact for the Wanderers, scoring on his debut against Civil Service, before finishing the 1865/66 season as top scorer with seven goals. His best tally was a brace against Westminster School during that first season. He certainly enjoyed playing against Westminster, as he scored two in two games during the 1867/68 season as well. Martin represented London against Sheffield in the March 1866 game and also Middlesex versus Surrey & Kent in 1867.

Martin died in Las Palmas, Gran Canaria in 1897.

J. G. Wylie

Date of Birth	1854
Died	30th July 1924
Place of Birth	Unknown
School	Shrewsbury School
Position	Forward
Other Clubs	Sheffield F.C., Sheffield F.A., Shropshire Wanderers
Debut	19th January 1875 Wanderers 1 Gitanos 1 @ Oval
Last Game	28th November 1879 Oxford University 2 Wanderers 1 @ Oxford

Season	Apps	Goals	Season	Apps	Goals
1874/75	1	0	1875/76	0	0
1876/77	1	0	1877/78	11	9
1878/79	4	0	1879/80	4	0
			Total	21	9

'A good centre, with pace and strength; should play for his side more.'
Football Annual 1879

John George Wylie was a pupil at Shrewsbury School from 1869 to 1872 and became a Solicitor in 1878 after leaving school. The Shrewsbury School register says he lived in Putney.

Wylie won one F.A. Cup winners medal in 1878, which was the only season where Wylie made a big contribution to the Wanderers, although he did feature in four other seasons and stayed with the club as late as the 1879/80 season. Wylie scored six of his nine goals in the F.A. Cup during the 1877/78 campaign. He gained one England cap in 1878, a 2-7 defeat at the hands of Scotland and scored one of the goals. He was also borrowed by London from Sheffield in 1874 for the London versus Sheffield fixture.

T. B. Hughes

Date of Birth	17th September 1851
Died	Unknown
Place of Birth	Unknown
School	Winchester College, Oxford University
Position	Forward
Other Clubs	Oxford University, Swifts, Old Wykehamists
Debut	29th January 1876 Wanderers 3 Sheffield 0 @ Oval F.A. Cup 3
Last Game	19th December 1882 Wanderers 1 Harrow School 1 @ Oval

Season	Apps	Goals	Season	Apps	Goals
1875/76	5	2	1876/77	3	0
1877/78	0	0	1878/79	0	0
1879/80	6	0	1880/81	5	2
1881/82	0	0	1882/83	1	0
			Total	20	4

'A hardworking forward, and good shot at goal.'
Football Annual 1876

T.B Hughes attended Winchester College between 1863 and 1870 and excelled academically. He was top of the highest class for three consecutive years between 1867 and 1870, but there seems to have been some problems with him gaining a scholarship to New College, Oxford. This took him three years before he was successful. His other activities at Winchester included being a prefect and in 1869/70 he was Prefect of Hall which was effectively head boy; he was also a keen Cricketer represented the school from 1868 to 1870, and played fives.

In 1876 Hughes studied at the Inner Temple, before becoming a school master at Repton from April to December 1878, and then at Brighton College from January to July 1879. This explains Hughes's absence from the team for two years. Hughes finally settled at Evelyn's in Hillingdon where he remained until at least 1907.

Hughes won F.A. Cup winners medals in both 1876 and 1877 and was probably robbed of a third through his work commitments. He stayed with the club until almost the end and played in the penultimate game in 1882. Hughes also played for Oxford University against Cambridge in March 1874.

A. M. Tebbut

Date of Birth	Unknown
Died	Unknown
Place of Birth	Unknown
School	Unknown
Position	
Other Clubs	No Names
Debut	15th March 1862 Forest 1 Crystal Palace 0 @ Leytonstone
Last Game	3rd November 1866 Forest School 2 Wanderers 0

Season	Apps	Goals	Season	Apps	Goals
1861/62	2	0	1862/63	0	0
1863/64	7	2	1864/65	2	1
1865/66	8	0	1866/67	1	0
			Total	20	3

A.M. Tebbut's life is a mystery, although like his brother it has been suggested he was educated locally. Despite this he had written himself into the history of the Wanderers Football Club, by being the scorer of the first ever goal after the club evolved from Forest F.C. The game in April 1864 was away at No Names, a club he also played for and Tebbut's goal meant the newly named club got off to a winning start.

Tebbut was not a prolific goal scorer, but did score for Forest during the 1863/64 season against Richmond and also in the Wanderers first game of the 1864/65 season against The Officers. Tebbut played in the opening game of the 1866/67 season but the report states he was disabled. It is not known how serious the injury was, but he did not appear for the Wanderers again.

R.C. Barker

Date of Birth	19th June 1847
Died	11th November 1915
Place of Birth	Rickmansworth
School	Marlborough College
Position	Forward/ Back
Other Clubs	Hertfordshire Rangers, Middlesex, Kent
Debut	5th October 1872 Wanderers 4 Clapham Rovers 0 @ Oval
Last Game	2nd October 1880 Wanderers 6 Old Harrovians 2 @ Oval

Season	Apps	Goals	Season	Apps	Goals
1872/73	4	0	1873/74	4	0
1874/75	5	1	1875/76	0	0
1876/77	3	0	1877/78	1	0
1878/79	0	0	1879/80	2	0
1880/81	1	1	Total	20	2

'An excellent player; slow but a hard and honest forward; can play back well, if required.'
Football Annual 1875

Robert Barker was a pupil at Marlborough College between 1858 and 1862. His career saw him take the path of an engineer and he later became Chief Assistant Engineer to the South Eastern Railway.

Barker appeared for the Wanderers over many years, although his primary club can be regarded as the Hertfordshire Rangers. It was while with this club that he was capped for England in 1872, against Scotland and became the first ever England goal keeper in the process. Barker also represented London on numerous occasions.

Date of Birth	1850
Died	Unknown
Place of Birth	Unknown
School	Mill Hill School
Position	Forward
Other Clubs	Uxbridge, Swifts, Windsor
Debut	3rd October 1874 Wanderers 5 Clapham Rovers 0 @ Oval
Last Game	13th February 1878 Westminster School 2 Wanderers 5 @ Vincent Sq.

Season	Apps	Goals	Season	Apps	Goals
1874/75	3	1	1875/76	10	4
1876/77	1	0	1877/78	5	0
			Total	19	5

'Played in most of the principle matches of the year and is always useful. Dribbles well, but is rather too light.'
Football Annual 1875

Frank Heron attended Mill Hill School and was the elder brother of the Hubert who is mentioned previously. Frank and Hubert were the first brothers to play together for England in 1876. It was the only cap that Frank Heron gained, and ended in a 0-3 defeat by Scotland. Frank collected a F.A. Cup winner's medal in 1876 and scored two crucial goals against Sheffield F.C. in the third round. Heron's other honours include representing Middlesex and London.

C. W. Stephenson

Date of Birth	27th February 1853
Died	22nd April 1924
Place of Birth	Unknown
School	Westminster School
Position	Back
Other Clubs	Westminster School, Barnes
Debut	23rd October 1869 Wanderers 0 Old Etonians 2 @ Oval
Last Game	6th November 1872 Westminster School 0 Wanderers 2 @ Vincent Sq.

Season	Apps	Goals	Season	Apps	Goals
1869/70	6	0	1870/71	3	0
1871/72	9	0	1872/73	1	0
			Total	19	0

'...was as usual a most efficient back.'
Sportsman 17.10.1871

Stephenson was a highly regarded player, but retired early at the age of 20 as far as can be established. After leaving Westminster School, Stephenson worked as a surveyor in Parliament Street. He was selected for the November 1871 pseudo international, but had all but given up playing by the time the first official international games were played. Stephenson played in the first two Wanderers F.A. Cup matches but was missing in the semi final and final ties. He also appeared for London versus Sheffield in 1871 and 1872 and served on the F.A. Committee from 1871 to 1873.

Hon. T. H. W. Pelham

Date of Birth	21st December 1847
Died	23rd December 1916
Place of Birth	Unknown
School	Eton College & Cambridge University
Position	Forward
Other Clubs	Gitanos
Debut	20th February 1868 Hitchin Club 0 Wanderers 2 @ Hitchin
Last Game	18th December 1872 Wanderers 5 Crystal Palace 2 @ Oval

Season	Apps	Goals	Season	Apps	Goals
1867/68	1	0	1868/69	1	0
1870/71	8	4	1871/72	6	2
1872/73	3	0	Total	19	6

Thomas Henry William Pelham was the third son of Henry Thomas Pelham, the third Earl of Chichester. He attended Eton College between 1861 and 1866 where he appeared for the Eton XI and then progressed to Cambridge University. Pelham became a barrister and did work for the War Office and the Charity Commission.

Pelham had a reasonable goal scoring record, although he enjoyed a purple patch in February-March 1871 when he scored four goals in three games against Hampstead Heathens, Westminster School and Charterhouse School. Pelham's most important and famous goal came against Clapham Rovers in Wanderers first ever F.A. Cup tie in 1871.

A. G. Bonsor

Date of Birth	1850 (approximately)
Died	17th August 1907
Place of Birth	Unknown
School	Eton College
Position	Forward
Other Clubs	Old Etonians, Surrey, Gitanos
Debut	18th February 1871 Wanderers 2 Hampstead Heathens 0 @ Oval
Last Game	29th March 1873 Wanderers 2 Oxford University 0 @ Lille Bridge – F.A. Cup Final

Season	Apps	Goals	Season	Apps	Goals
1870/71	2	0	1871/72	11	6
1872/73	5	1	Total	18	7

'An indefatigable forward with weight and pace; plays hard and close on the ball, though rather apt to tire towards the finish.'
Football Annual 1875

Alexander George Bonsor has been described as a Victorian gentleman, and appropriately in view of this he attended Eton College from 1865 until 1868. Bonsor joined the Wanderers in 1871 and in the two subsequent years he collected two F.A. Cup winners' medals. After the 1873 final, Bonsor left to join the Old Etonians and he made two further appearances in the final losing in 1875 and 1876. He also gained two England caps in 1873 and 1875, scoring one goal in his first appearance and also represented London and Surrey.

Bonsor was a brother of the Chairman of Watney's and a shareholder in Combe, Delafield & Co., (which later became part of Watney, Coombe Reid) to the tune of £30,000. When he died in 1907 his estate was worth just £5. Prior to his death he moved to Belgium briefly before moving back to England and was listed as a brewer in Charing Cross by 1881.

R. K. Kingsford

Date of Birth	23rd December 1849
Died	14th October 1895
Place of Birth	Sydenham Hill
School	Marlborough College
Position	Forward
Other Clubs	Surrey, Crystal Palace
Debut	30th November 1872 Wanderers 0 Royal Engineers 2 @ Oval
Last Game	30th January 1875 Wanderers 1 Oxford University 2 @ Oval F.A. Cup 3rd Round

Season	Apps	Goals	Season	Apps	Goals
1872/73	7	1	1873/74	6	4
1874/75	5	5	Total	18	10

'A fast and invaluable forward.'
Football Annual 1873

Robert Kennett Kingsford was a pupil at Marlborough College from 1863 to 1868 and was a member of Preshute Boarding House.

Kingsford joined the Wanderers in 1872 and helped the club to win the F.A. Cup the following year. In 1874/75 he set the Wanderers scoring record for goals in one match when he scored five against Farningham. He was also capped for England against Scotland in 1874, when he scored a goal in a 1-2 defeat and represented London versus Sheffield and Nottinhamshire.

Between 1872 and 1874 Kingsford played a number of first class cricket games for Surrey and scored 80 runs in five innings during that period. He also kept wicket for them. Kingsford later immigrated to Australia, where he died in Adelaide in 1895.

T. N. Tyndale

Date of Birth	Unknown
Died	Unknown
Place of Birth	Unknown
School	Brighton College
Position	
Other Clubs	Barnes
Debut	13th Feb 1878 Westminster School 2 Wanderers 5 @ Vincent Sq.
Last Game	23rd October 1880 Wanderers 0 Upton Park 2 @ Oval

Season	Apps	Goals	Season	Apps	Goals
1877/78	1	1	1878/79	6	0
1879/80	8	1	1880/81	3	0
			Total	18	2

'A fast forward, and occasionally plays brilliantly; a little uncertain.'
Football Annual 1879

T.N. Tyndale joined the Wanderers very late in the club's history and so did not really feature in the glory days apart from a brief appearance in the 1877/78 season when he scored on his debut against Westminster School. He continued to play for Wanderers right through the decline until 1880 when he left after a 0-2 defeat by Upton Park. He also represented Surrey in 1877 and featured in the England trial match in 1878. The other information that is known about Tyndale is that he attended Brighton College.

J. M. Yates

Date of Birth	19th June 1844
Died	17th April 1916
Place of Birth	Chorlton cum Hardy, Lancashire
School	Westminster School & Cambridge University
Position	
Other Clubs	
Debut	13th November 1867 Westminster School 0 Wanderers 1 @ Vincent Sq.
Last Game	27th March 1869 Forest Club 0 Wanderers 0 @ Woodford

Season	Apps	Goals	Season	Apps	Goals
1867/68	8	0	1868/69	9	1
			Total	17	1

Joseph Maghull Yates was a regular player for the Wanderers for two seasons in the late 1860's having been discovered playing for Westminster School. Whilst at Westminster, Yates rowed for the school against Eton College. He went on to study at Trinity College, Cambridge, before entering the legal profession.

From 1889 to 1904, Yates was Recorder of Salford and was Chairman of the Quarter Sessions, Salford Hundred and Stipendiary Magistrate, Manchester Division of Lancashire from 1894.

During his time at Cambridge University, Yates featured in his only first class cricket match scoring ten runs. He also represented Middlesex versus Surrey at football in 1868.

F. Stileman

Date of Birth	Unknown
Died	Unknown
Place of Birth	Unknown
School	Harrow School
Position	
Other Clubs	Harrow Pilgrims
Debut	23rd January 1869 Forest Club 0 Wanderers 3 @ Woodford
Last Game	4th March 1871 Wanderers 0 Clapham Rovers 1 @ Oval

Season	Apps	Goals	Season	Apps	Goals
1868/69	2	0	1869/70	0	0
1870/71	15	0	Total	17	0

F. Stileman attended Harrow School and went on to become a consulting engineer. Stileman had two spells at the Wanderers the first a somewhat brief spell in 1868/69, the second where he played in nearly half the games played that season. No evidence of any representative honours has been found for this player.

Rev. H. H. Stewart

Date of Birth	8th November 1847
Died	20th March 1937
Place of Birth	Unknown
School	Repton School & Trinity College, Cambridge University
Position	
Other Clubs	
Debut	4th March 1872 Wanderers 0 Queens Park 0 @ Oval F.A. Cup semi final
Last Game	15th December 1873 Wanderers 2 Cambridge University 1 @ Oval

Season	Apps	Goals	Season	Apps	Goals
1871/72	1	0	1872/73	8	0
1873/74	3	0	Total	12	0

'Keeps well on the ball and never flags.'
Football Annual 1873

Rev. Henry Holmes Stewart attended Repton School; from there he went to Cambridge University, later becoming a vicar. He gained recognition when picked to represent Scotland in the 1872 pseudo international. Stewart gained his only F.A. Cup winners medal in the 1873 final.

Stewart was Vicar of East Witton from 1874 to 1878 and then Rector of Brighton until 1898. In 1898 he relocated and became Rector of Barry and Porthkerry in South Wales until in 1914 becoming Vicar of St. Lythan's. Stewart finished his career in the church by being the Rector of Michaelston le Pit between 1925 and 1934.

C. M. Thompson

Date of Birth	5th December 1849
Died	12th September 1881
Place of Birth	Unknown
School	Eton College, Trinity College, Cambridge University
Position	
Other Clubs	Old Etonians
Debut	14th February 1872 Wanderers 6 Civil Service 1 @ Oval
Last Game	12th November 1873 Wanderers 0 Swifts 5 @ Oval

Season	Apps	Goals	Season	Apps	Goals
1871/72	1	0	1872/73	2	0
1873/74	4	0	Total	7	0

Charles Moude Thompson was another player who seems to have been drafted in for the 1873 final which Wanderers won against Oxford University, possibly due to the fact that he was the younger brother of A.C. Thompson. Thompson was picked to represent Scotland in the 1872 pseudo international.

Thompson gained an M.A. from Cambridge in 1875 and was Rector of Claydon, Buckinghamshire from 1870 to 1879. He represented Cambridge versus Oxford in 1872 in the Hammer event.

J. R. Sturgis

Date of Birth	21st October 1848
Died	13th April 1904
Place of Birth	Boston, U.S.A.
School	Eton College & Balliol College, Oxford University
Position	
Other Clubs	
Debut	30th November 1872 Wanderers 0 Royal Engineers 2 @ Oval
Last Game	3rd November 1875 Westminster School 2 Wanderers 3 @ Vincent Square

Season	Apps	Goals	Season	Apps	Goals
1872/73	5	0	1873/74	1	0
1875/76	1	0	Total	7	0

Julian Russell Sturgis came to England when he was seven months old and was a pupil at Eton College. In his time there he played an active role and participated in the mixed Wall and Field XI's in 1867, was Keeper of the Field in 1867 and edited the Eton College Chronicle. Whilst at Oxford

100

he rowed for three years in the Balliol College eight. On leaving Eton he became a barrister-at-law and a British subject.

Sturgis was a well known novelist at the time and also travelled to the Levant in 1878 and visited the Turkish and Russian armies before Constantinople in the same year.

Sturgis was a member of the 1873 F.A. Cup final side which beat Oxford University and as such was the first American to play in the final. It is usually claimed that it was John Harkes for Sheffield Wednesday in the 1993 final.

W. S. Kenyon-Slaney

Date of Birth	24th August 1847
Died	24th April 1908
Place of Birth	Rajkot, Gujarat, India
School	Eton College & Christ Church, Oxford University
Position	Forward
Other Clubs	Old Etonians, Oxford University
Debut	5th March 1873 Westminster School 4 Wanderers 2 @ Vincent Square
Last Game	17th January 1874 Wanderers 0 Gitanos 1 @ Oval

Season	Apps	Goals	Season	Apps	Goals
1872/73	2	1	1873/74	1	0
			Total	3	1

'Earned for himself, during the last few weeks of the season, the reputation of being the most successful forward of the year.'
Football Annual 1873

William Slayney Kenyon-Slaney certainly had an illustrious military career after leaving Eton College. He joined the Household Brigade and by 1867 he was an Ensign. He was promoted to Captain in 1870 and Lieutenant Colonel in 1878. At some point he switched to 2nd Battalion of the Grenadier Guards where he served in the Egyptian War of 1882. In 1883 Kenyon-Slaney, was promoted to Major and finally in 1887 he became a Colonel.

Slaney was also a Member of Parliament for Newport North Division of Shropshire from 1886 to 1908 when he died at Hatton Grange, Shifnal in Shropshire.

Kenyon-Slaney's sporting prowess led to him appearing in three F.A. Cup finals winning in 1873 with the Wanderers and then being runners up twice with Old Etonians. Kenyon-Slaney was also capped once for England, and scored two goals in a 4-2 victory against Scotland. He was also a regular for the M.C.C. from 1869 to 1880 and played in eleven matches during this time scoring 145 runs; also served on the M.C.C. Committee.

101

J. H. Edwards

Date of Birth	1850
Died	14th January 1893
Place of Birth	Shrewsbury
School	Unknown
Position	Forward
Other Clubs	Shropshire Wanderers, Shrewsbury
Debut	4th March 1874 Westminster School 0 Wanderers 4 @ Vincent Square
Last Game	18th March 1876 Wanderers 3 Old Etonians 0 @ Oval F.A. Cup Final replay

Season	Apps	Goals	Season	Apps	Goals
1873/74	1	1	1875/76	2	1
			Total	3	2

'A useful man; being a hard worker, a strong dribbler, and unselfish player'
Football Annual 1875

John Hawley Edwards is interesting in that he gained international recognition by both England and Wales. He was capped by England in 1874 against Scotland and then on the formation of the Welsh F.A. he was capped by Wales against Scotland in 1876.

Edwards also became the first Secretary of the newly formed Football Association of Wales in 1876. He gained one F.A. Cup winners medal in the 1876 final, when his goal helped ensure the first game ended in a 1-1 draw. Wanderers comfortably won the replay. From 1874 to 1893. Edwards was a clerk to the Shrewsbury Magistrates.

L. S. Howell

Date of Birth	6th August 1848
Died	7th September 1895
Place of Birth	Herne Hill
School	Winchester College
Position	Half Back
Other Clubs	Surrey
Debut	29th March 1873 Wanderers 2 Oxford University 0 @ Lille Bridge F.A. Cup Final
Last Game	6th December 1873 Wanderers 1 Oxford University 1 @ Oval F.A. Cup 3rd Round

Season	Apps	Goals	Season	Apps	Goals
1872/73	1	0	1873/74	1	0
			Total	2	0

'Is perhaps better known to fame as a member of the Surrey Cricket Eleven. At the winter game he excels as a half-back; and his kicking not unfrequently 'brings down the house.''
Football Annual 1873

Leonard Sidgwick Howell attended Winchester College from 1861 as a commoner and represented the school at Cricket from 1864 to 1866. In the last year he was captain. Howell was also a good athlete and won the 100 yards, 300 yards and the 110 yards hurdles in 1866.

Howell played for Surrey County Cricket Club from 1869 to 1880 and in nineteen matches he scored 519 runs. He gained one F.A. Cup winners medal, in 1873, during his brief stay at the Wanderers and was capped by England in the same year. Howell must be one of the few players to have made his debut in a F.A. Cup final.

Howell became a Malt Factor when he left Winchester and died in Switzerland in 1895.

References

1   Green *A History of the Football Association* p159
2   MacDonald *Soccer a Pictorial History* p16
3   *Alpine Journal* November 1926
4   Bailey, Thorn, Wynne-Thomas *Who's Who of Cricketers* p1000
5   Green *Association Football* vol 3 p8

Other Interesting Players

Absolom C. born 7th June 1846   died 30th July 1889
Absolom was capped for England versus Australia at Cricket in 1878/79 and played for Kent County Cricket Club 57 times. In the last ten years of his life he travelled around America spending much time with the Red Indians. He died whilst being employed as a purser on a ship when a crane loading sugar cane collapsed and crushed him.

Alcock J.F. born 14th April 1841 died 13th March 1910
John Alcock was the brother of the more prominent Charles and was present at the founding meeting of the Football Association. He served on the F.A. Committee from 1863 to 1866.

Alington E.H.
Alington was a F.A. Cup runner up with Oxford University in 1877.

Almond H.J.
Almond was a civil engineer in Venezuela and Costa Rica where he helped build the railways.

Anderson W.J.
Anderson was on the original committee of the Corinthians and collected a F.A. Cup winners' medal with Old Etonians in 1882, having been a runner up the previous year. Anderson played in the England trial match when the South played the North in 1882.

Bailey N.C. born 23rd July 1857 died 13th January 1923
One of the finest half backs of his day, representing England against Scotland from 1878 to 1887 and gaining additional caps versus Wales in 1879 and from 1882 to 1887 and against Ireland 1884 to 1885. Played for Clapham Rovers and Swifts and was also a founder member of the Corinthians. He later became vice-president of the Football Association having served on the F.A. Committee from 1882 to 1885.

Bain F.W. born 1863 died 3rd March 1940
Bain played in the last Wanderers match in 1883 and went onto become Principal Professor of History and Political Economy at Deacon College, Poona, India. Bain also made two appearances for Corinthians' between 1886 and 1887.

Bastard S.R. born 1853 died 20th March 1921
Bastard was capped for England in 1880 and served on the F.A. Committee from 1877 to 1883; he also played for Corinthians and refereed the 1878 F.A. Cup final. Later he became a racehorse owner.

Bartholomew A.C. born 21st February 1846 died 29th March 1940
Bartholomew enjoyed a first class cricket career with Devonshire playing in eight matches scoring 158 runs. Professionally he owned a private school in Reading; he also played for Marlow and Reading.

Benson R.H. born 24th September 1850   died 7th April 1929
Benson played for Oxford University in their F.A. Cup winning team of 1874 and was a runner up the following year with Old Etonians.

Brockbank J.   born 22nd August 1848   died 29th January 1904
Brockbank was an actor by profession and was also capped on one occasion by England.

Buchanan W.S.   born 1st June 1855
Buchanan was capped by England in 1876.

Buller C.F.   born 26th May 1846   died 22nd November 1906
A distinguished Cricket player, who played for Middlesex, scoring 3140 runs in 158 innings.

Cloete W.B,   born 1851   died 7th May 1915
Cloete was a landed proprietor and owned large estates in Mexico; he also won the 2000 Guineas in 1885 and The Oaks in 1911.

Cotterill J.M.   born 23rd November 1851   died 30th December 1933
Cotterill was one of the best known surgeons of his day and was President of the Royal College of Surgeons Edinburgh; he also played 27 cricket matches for Sussex between 1870 and 1888. Cotterill was also famous for throwing a cricket ball 121 yards in 1875.

Crawford R.E.W.   born 5th Septmeber 1852 died 23rd May 1894
Crawford gained an unofficial Scottish cap in 1870. He joined the 60th Rifles where he served in the Afghan War from 1878 to 1879 with Sir F. Roberts on the march to Candahar. He also commanded the Sierra Leone Frontier Police, later becoming known as Copland-Crawford in 1872. Appeared three times for the M.C.C. between 1872 and 1873.

Currie F.A.   born 23rd September 1851 died 13th June 1902
Currie joined the 9th Norfolk Regiment and retired as a Lieutenant Colonel. He served in the Jowaki campaign and in the Afghan War being present at the capture of Ali Musjid. Also played one cricket match for the M.C.C. in 1894.

Curteis H.   born 14th April 1849 died 28th October 1919
Curties played one match for Sussex County Cricket Club in 1873.

Curteis R. born 12th October 1851 died 21st January 1927
Curteis played for Cricket for Sussex from 1873 to 1878 and also the M.C.C. in 1881.

Cutbill W.J.
An early player for Wanderers F.C.; his regular club was however Crystal Palace. He also served on the F.A. Committee from 1864 to 1871.

Dixon H.B.   born 11th August 1852   died 18th September 1930
Dixon was a scientist working for various government bodies advising about chemicals and explosives.

Ewing C.L.O.   born 8th September 1860 died 24th December 1903
Ewing was an M.P. for Ayr District from 1895 to 1903; he was also a Justice of the Peace for Dumbarton. He also was a Captain in the 3rd Battalion Argyll and Sutherland Highlanders from 1880 to 1889.

Field E.   born 29th July 1854 died 11th January 1934
Field was capped twice by England in 1876 and 1881 and was an F.A. Cup runner up with Clapham Rovers in 1879 and a winner the following year.

Fitzmaurice Lord E. born 19th June 1846 died 21st June 1935
Fitzmaurice was a M.P. for Calne from 1869 to 1885 and for Cricklade, Wiltshire from 1898 to 1905. He was under Secretary of State for Foreign Affairs from 1882 to 1885 and 1905 whilst also being a trustee of the National Portrait Gallery. Fitzmaurice served on the F.A. Committee from 1869 to 1871.

Fryer F.E.R. born 7th January 1849   died 1st October 1917
Fryer was a noted golfer and played cricket for Suffolk County Cricket Club. In 58 matches he scored 2149 runs and took 39 wickets.

Geaves R.L. born 1854 died 21st March 1935
Geaves was born in Mexico and became a captain in the Prince of Wales Yorkshire Regiment; he played for Clapham Rovers and Old Harrovians and gained one England cap in 1875.

Gibson E.C.S. born 23rd January 1848   died 8th March 1924
Gibson was Bishop of Gloucester from 1905 to 1922 and was the author of many theological works.

Giles C.T. born 2nd February 1850   died 16th January 1940
Giles became a Kings Counsel and was M.P. in Cambridgeshire from 1895 to 1900.

Gladstone W.H. born 3rd June 1840 died 4th July 1891
Son of the Prime Minister and went onto be M.P. for Chester from 1865 to 1868 and M.P. for Whitby between 1868 and 1886. From 1869 to 1874 he was a Lord of the Treasury. Gladstone also played for Scotland in the 1870 and 1871, pseudo internationals.

Goldney J.T. born 15th June 1846 died 11th April 1920
After leaving Trinity College, Cambridge, Goldney went on to be a Judge of the Supreme Court, a Chief Justice of Trinidad from 1892 to 1902 and was Knighted in 1893; also a Director of the Capital and Counties Bank.

 W.G. Grace

Grace W.G. born 18th July 1848 died 23rd October 1915
A Cricketing legend who scored 54,000 runs in a career spanning 44 years from 1865 to 1908 where he played for England in 22 test matches, Gloucestershire and London County. A doctor by profession, although it took him eleven years to qualify, it has been suggested, as a result of his

106

Cricket career. It has been said that his most conspicuous act as a doctor is thought to have occurred when an unfortunate fieldsman impaled himself on the boundary fence at Old Trafford.

Greaves T.W. died 21st January 1878
Greaves became a Superintendent of the Nowgong Tea Gardens under the Upper Assam Tea Company.

Grey A.H.G. born 28th November 1851 died 29th August 1917
Grey was a Liberal M.P. for South Northumberland from 1880 to 1885 and then Tyneside from 1885 to 1886. In 1894 he succeeded his uncle and became the 4th Earl Grey and in the same year became Administrator of Rhodesia a post he held until 1897. From 1904 to 1911 he was Governor General and Commander in Chief of Canada.

Gurdon-Rebow H.J. born 11th September 1846
Gurdon-Rebow was Mayor of Colchester from 1884 to 1885 and was High Sheriff of Essex in 1882.

Hamilton W.A.B. born 6th September 1844 died 6th July 1920
Hamilton appeared twice for Scotland in the pseudo internationals for Scotland.

Hammans A.W. born 31st August 1846 died 13th June 1916
Hammans was a Major in the army and served in Burma from 1892 to 1893; he died from overworking in the recruitment office during World War One.

Hammick E.A. born 3rd January 1850 died 2nd September 1920
Hammick was Archdeacon of Zululand from 1886 to 1889 and later Durban from 1899 to 1907. Later moved to Queensland Australia where he was Incumbant for Blackall Rockhampton and Pitsworth Brisbane.

Hammond C.E. born 6th December 1856 died 9th December 1933
Hammond was a partner in Hammond & Co. from 1883; this was sold to Barclays & Co. in 1905; he was also a Justice of the Peace for Suffolk and Cambridge.

Hargreaves F.M. born around 1858
Hargreaves rowed for Oxford in the Boat Race of 1880.

Haygarth E.B. born 26th April 1854 died 14th April 1915
Haygarth played Cricket for both Hampshire and Gloucestershire.

Hewlett W.O. born 30th March 1845 died 2nd March 1912
Hewlett was a Solicitor and Master of the Supreme Court.

Hills A.F. born 12th March 1857 died 7th March 1927
Hills was the founder of Thames Ironworks F.C. and later West ham United F.C.; he had previously been a runner up in the F.A. Cup with Oxford University in 1877 and was capped by England in 1879. He was also the Amateur Athletics' Association One Mile Champion in 1878.

A.F. Hills

Hoare W. born 15th September 1847 died 22nd July 1925
Hoare was a Director of Hoare & Co's Brewery; he also played cricket for the Gentlemen of Kent in 1879.

Holden-White C. died 14th July 1948
Holden-White was capped twice by England and played for Corinthians from 1882 to 1891, being their first captain and also served on their committee; he played for Middlesex at football between 1883 and 1886.

Hotham F.W. born 17th January 1844 died 23rd June 1908
Hotham played one game for Somerset County Cricket Club in 1882 and one match for the M.C.C. in 1883. He later appeared for Hertfordshire.

Huxley T.C. born 8th March 1850 died 12th April 1934
Huxley was a Tea Planter in Ceylon.

Inglis J.F. born 16th July 1853 died 27th February 1923
Inglis played once for Kent County Cricket Club; also appeared for Scotland in the February 1871 pseudo international.

Jarrett B.G. born 18th July 1855 died 11th April 1905
Jarrett was capped three times by England between 1876 and 1878 and served on the F.A. Committee between 1876 and 1879.

Law W. born 9th April 1851 died 20th December 1892
Law was Vicar of Rotherham; he also played for cricket for Yorkshire and Gentlemen of England.

Longman C.J. born 14th April 1852 died 17th April 1934
Longman was the Champion of England at Archery in 1883 and was a runner up with Oxford University in the 1873 F.A. Cup final.

Lubbock A. born 31st October 1845 died 17th July 1916
Lubbock was a Wine Merchant by trade.

Lyttleton A. born 7th February 1857 died 4th July 1913
Lyttleton gained one cap for England at football in 1877 and also played in four England cricket test matches. In a ten year career for Middlesex County Cricket Club he scored 4429 runs in 171 innings over 101 matches; he also appeared in the F.A. Cup final for Old Etonians.

Mackenzie H.M. born 2nd April 1850 died 20th January 1889
Mackenzie joined the army and served in the Sudan in 1885; he was also a first class polo player.

Mackenzie K.A.M. born 26th June 1845 died 22nd May 1930
Served on the F.A. Committee from 1869 to 1870 and in 1915 became Baron Muir Mackenzie.

Mackenzie M.J.M. born 29th September 1847   died 18th April 1919
Mackenzie was a Barrister and was Secretary to Lord Chief Justice Coleridge from 1873 to 1877; he was later Recorder of Deal in 1892 and later Recorder of Sandwich and Bencher of the Middle Temple from 1894 to 1905.

Maynard W.J. born 18th March 1853
Maynard was capped twice by England against Scotland in 1872 and 1876.

Metcalfe C.H.T. born 8th September 1853 died 29th December 1928
Metcalfe succeeded his father in 1883 as the 6th Baronet.

Moncrieff R.C. born 24th August 1843 died 14th May 1913
Moncrieff was a Vicar, before in 1909 he succeeded his brother as the 3rd Baron Moncrieff.

Money W.B. born 27th July 1848 died 1st March 1924
Money was a talented cricketer and played in 29 matches for Suffolk scoring 1154 runs, before entering the church and retiring from serious cricket.

Montgomery H.H. born 3rd October 1847 died 25th November 1932
Montgomery's third son was Bernard Law Montgomery who following his successes in World War Two became 1st Viscount Montgomery of Alamein.

 H.H Montgomery

Morgan D.J. born 1844 died 28th February 1918
Morgan was a businessman in Russian Trade and also a M.P. for Walthamstow.

Morgan J.H. born 19th August 1847 died 11th October 1924
Morgan attended Trinity College, Oxford and was President of the O.U.A.C.. He later became a surgeon and lecturer at Charing Cross Hospital and a Knight of St. John of Jerusalem.

Morice C.J. born 27th May 1850 died 17th June 1932
Morice enjoyed a career working at the Stock Exchange; he gained one England cap in 1875 and served on the F.A. Committee from 1873 to 1878.

Nepean C.E.B. born 5th February 1851 died 26th March 1903
Nepean played two cricket matches for Middlesex and also appeared for Dorset; he was later on the committee for Kent County Cricket Club.

Newman E.H.A. born 21st January 1862 died 29th October 1915
Newman was a Solicitor and was killed on the railway in a fog at Edmonton, Middlesex, while acting as a Special Constable.

Nickisson J.L. born 25th March 1861
Played in the last Wanderers F.C. game in 1883; he also played for the Corinthians from 1884 to 1889 and was Joint Master of the Old Berks Hounds. Nickisson was Secretary of the Essexx County F.A. from 1883-85 and then joint Honorary Secretary from 1885-86 and also played for Brentwood F.C. and represented Essex at football during 1883/84.

Norman E. born 3rd July 1847 died February 1923
Norman was a Clerk in the House of Commons from 1870 to 1881 and then became a banker at Martin's Bank becoming Chairman in 1916. He was also Chairman of Public Works Loan Commission in 1908, Director of Guardian Assurance Co. Ltd and the Buenos Aires Pacific Railway Co. Ltd and Chairman of the Commercial Bank of Spanish America Ltd.

Norman P. born 9th July 1842 died 17th May 1931
Norman was a Director of the Bank of England; he also had paintings exhibited at the Royal Academy and had various books and articles published.

Ogden L. born 12th April 1847 died 26th April 1915
Ogden settled in Toronto and worked on Stock Exchange. He also represented Canada verses Australia at Cricket in 1878.

Otter H.S.
Otter was a runner up with Oxford University in the 1877 F.A. Cup final.

Pardoe J. born 1st April 1839 died 23rd April 1892
Founding member of Forest F.C.; he was Rector of Gravely in Hertfordshire.

Parry C.H.H. born 27th February 1848 died 7th October 1918
Parry was a Director of the Royal College of Music from 1895, and a Professor of Music at Oxford University from 1899.

Parry E.H. born 24th April 1855 died 19th July 1931
Parry was a F.A. Cup winner with Old Carthusians in 1881 and a runner up with Oxford University in 1877; he was also capped three times by England and served on the F.A. Committee from 1881 to 1882. Parry scored four goals in the last ever Wanderers F.C. match.

Paton W.B. born around 1853
Paton played for Oxford University and was a runner up in 1873, before going one better in 1874.

Pelham F.G. born 18th October 1844 died 21st April 1905
Pelham was 2nd son of Henry Thomas, 3rd Earl of Chichester and brother of Walter John 4th Earl of Chichester and related to T.H.W. Pelham who also played for the club. He became a vicar. Pelham played regularly for Sussex County Cricket Club between 1864 and 1868.

Pember A.
Arthur Pember was the first F.A. President form 1863 to 1867. His playing career saw him captain No Names, Kilburn.

Phipps H.G. born 8th August 1845 died 19th October 1899
Phipps was a merchant in China and died at Tiensin; he played two cricket matches for the M.C.C.

Philpot R. born 30th December 1849 died 9th December 1913
Philpot featured in Old Etonians F.A. Cup run of 1874/75, but was not selected for the cup final.

Pidcock C.A. born 27th August 1850 died 28th October 1901
Pidcock was a Magistrate and Civil Commissioner for the Tuli District in Matabeleland, Rhodesia; he also played for an England cricket XI in 1872 scoring 12 runs.

Rawlinson J.F.P. born 21st December 1860 died 14th January 1926
Rawlinson represented the Treasury in the inquiry held in South Africa as to the circumstances connected with the Jameson Raid in 1896; he was also Unionist M.P. for Cambridge University from 1906 to 1926. In 1882 he was capped by England and served on the F.A. Committee from 1885 to 1886.

Rawson W.S. born 14th October 1854 died 4th November 1932
Rawson was capped twice for England in 1875 and 1877; he was on the F.A. Committee from 1876 to 1878 and again in 1879 to 1880.

Rees-Mogg W.W. born 21st November 1848 died 16th September 1913
Rees-Mogg's son was grandfather of William, Baron Rees-Mogg who was editor of 'The Times' and Vice Chairman of the Board of Governors of the B.B.C. from 1981 to 1986.

Reeve C.A. born December 1857 died 23rd April 1936
Reeve was the City Editor of the 'Daily Telegraph' from 1901.

Renshaw A.G. born 8th September 1844 died 14th July 1897
Renshaw played one match for the M.C.C. and was out for a duck.

Rivett-Carnac J. born 27th June 1846 died 4th June 1909
Rivett-Carnac served in the 73rd regiment from 1865 to 1867 and then worked in the Inland Revenue. He succeeded as the 3rd Baronet in 1883 and became known as Sir James H.S. Rivett-Carnac, Bart., River Dene, Weybridge.

Rivett-Carnac L.W.G. born 1854 died 7th May 1904
Rivett-Carnac was the Administrator General of Bombay.

Rivett-Carnac P.T. born 12th January 1852 died 1932
Rivett-Carnac was a Sub-Lieutenant in the 43rd Light Infantry from 1872. He was Captain of the 2nd Duke of Wellington's regiment in 1883 and served in the Sudan War gaining a medal and Khedive's Star in 1884 before becoming a Major in 1892.

Roberts S. born 30th April 1852   died 19th June 1926
Roberts was M.P. for Ecclesall Division of Sheffield from 1902 to 1923; he was later made a Baronet.

Rodwell W.H. born 18th April 1850 died 3rd August 1929
Rodwell played one cricket match for the M.C.C. and also appeared for Suffolk and Essex.

Round F.R. born 22nd January 1845   died 24th November 1920
Round was Private Secretary to the Secretary of State for the Colonies from 1878 to 1880; he was later Acting Colonial Secretary in Mauritius from 1886 to 1887.

Shaw V.K. born 14th January 1854   died 18th December 1905
Shaw went to Caius College, Cambridge. He later became a breeder and exhibitor and judge of horses, dogs and poultry. Shaw was also an author and journalist on the 'Morning Advertiser', 'Tribune', 'Illustrated Sporting and Dramatic News' and 'Field'. Shaw also played 25 cricket matches for Kent scoring 560 runs in 56 innings, whilst gaining 38 wickets as a bowler.

Shearman M. born 7th April 1857   died 6th January 1930
Shearman was a Judge of the High Court of Justice from 1914; he was also joint author of 'Football: It's History for Five Centuries.'

Smith C.E. born 1850 died 10th January 1917
Smith was the cousin of the famous Corinthian, G.O. Smith and was born in Colombo, Ceylon; he was capped for England in 1876 and was on the F.A. Committee between 1875 and 1877.

Soden F.B. born 30th March 1846   died 13th April 1877
Soden played cricket for Surrey between 1870 and 1871 featuring in three matches.

Sparks F.J. born 4th July 1855   died 13th February 1934
Sparks gained a F.A. Cup winners medal with Clapham Rovers in 1880 and was capped three times by England; he served on the F.A. Committee from 1878 to 1881.

Spiro D.G. born 21st December 1863   died 16th January 1935
Spiro was a member of the Corinthians and also played cricket for the M.C.C.

Stair A.
Alfred Stair refereed the first F.A. Cup final and served on the F.A. Committee from 1871 to 1877.

Stanley A.J.
Stanley was a regular for Clapham Rovers with whom he collected a F.A. Cup winners' medal in 1880 having been a runner up the year before.

Street F.E.   born 16th February 1851   died 4th June 1928
Street played four matches for Kent County Cricket Club.

Strutt C.H. born 18th April 1849   died 19th December 1926
Strutt was Chairman of the Rock Life Assurance Co. and the New London Borneo Tobacco Co.; he was also Conservative M.P. for East Essex 1883 to 1885 and Maldon 1895-1906.

Tabor A.   born 24th February 1850   died 16th December 1925
Tabor played one cricket match for Middlesex and later moved to Ceylon where he captained their cricket team.

Tayloe J.E.   born 1st January 1848 died 19th January 1919
Tayloe became a broker in Calcutta then moved to South Africa.

Templar F.G.   born 12th June 1849 died 28th August 1918
Templar was a barrister and became a District Judge in Cyprus and also Judge of Durham and York County Court.

Thompson H.M.   born 30th August 1845   died 3rd March 1929
Thompson attended Eton College and then Trinity College, Cambridge and went on to be an M.P. for Knaresborough in 1880, Brigg 1885-1886 and Handsworth 1892-1905. In 1905 he was created Baron Knaresborough.

Thornton P.M.   born 29th December 1841 died 8th January 1918
Thornton attended Jesus College, Cambridge. He became a M.P. for Clapham from 1892 to 1910 and was also an author and Honorary Secretary to Middlesex County Cricket Club.

Tupper C.L.
Tupper joined the Indian Civil Service and later became Vice Chancellor of the Punjab University.

Vidal H.S. born 5th November 1854 died 1st May 1905
Vidal like his brother became a Vicar and later moved to New South Wales.

Vincent J.E.   born 17th November 1857   died 18th July 1909
Author of several books on the Welsh Land and was joint author of 'Football: Its History for Five Centuries.'

Walker C.W. born 11th January 1851 died 2nd March 1915
Walker played one cricket match for the Gentlemen of the North; he later moved to Madras and then New Zealand.

Wallace W. born 18th October 1850 died 22nd August 1885
Wallace accidentally died in the River Thames.

Warner C. born 19th April 1852 died 10tH April 1890
Warner was capped once in goal for England, unfortunately for him it ended in a 2-7 defeat to Scotland. Died on a business trip to New York.

Webbe A.J. born 16th January 1855 died 19th February 1941
Webbe played 247 matched for Middlesex County Cricket Club between 1875 and 1900 and in 370 first class matches scored 14,465 runs, whilst taking 109 wickets. He was Captain of Middlesex from 1885 to 1898 and later became the club's President a post he held until 1937.

West S.H.   born 1848   died 2nd March 1920
West became a Physician and Lecturer at St. Bartholomew's Hospital.

Whitfeld H.   born 25th November 1858   died 6th May 1909
Whitfield played 39 matched for Sussex County Cricket Club scoring 2,400 runs; he was captain in 1883 and 1884. Whitfield played in the last ever Wanderers game in 1883.

Wotherspoon D.N.
Wotherspoon played for Queen's Park and was capped twice for Scotland against England.

Wylde E.W.   died 2nd April 1911
Wylde joined the Foreign Office and was the British representative to the Slave Trade Conference in 1889; he received the C.M.G. in 1891.

Appendix One

When ever possible every effort has been made to make sure the statistics are accurate. It is important to note the following.

The numbers above the statistics do not represent any positions and only reflect the order that they were listed in the newspapers. Number one is generally the Captain and it is impossible to differentiate between the positions.

There are a number of blanks spaces under numbers ten and eleven which indicates that the Wanderers did not field a full side.

All scorers are indicated by a number after their names.

The spellings of names are as stated in the newspapers and can lead to discrepancies.

Any major discrepancies have been recorded in the notes under the results grids.

Forest FC 1861/62

Date	Venue	Opponents	Res	Att	1	2	3	4
15-Mar	Leytonstone	Crystal Palace	1-0		Alcock.JF	Alcock.CW	Bigland.H	Bigland.C
05-Apr	Crystal Palace	Crystal Palace	4-0		Alcock.JF	Alcock.CW	Bigland.H	*Bigland.C 1*

Notes

15th March v Crystal Palace - 12 Savill M., 13 White J.E., 14 Woodward W.F., 15 Mackenzie A.W.

5th April v Crystal Palace - 12 Tebbut C., 13 Tebbut A., 14 Woodward W.F., 15 Mackenzie A.W.

Forest FC 1862/63

Date	Venue	Opponents	Res	Att	1	2	3	4
21-Feb	Barnes	Barnes	1-0		*Alcock C.W. 1*			
14-Mar	Leytonstone	Barnes	1-0		*Alcock C.W. 1*			
21-Mar	Leytonstone	Crystal Palace	2-1		*Alcock C.W. 2*			
?	Crystal Palace	Crystal Palace	?					

Forest FC 1863/64

Date	Venue	Opponents	Res	Att	1	2	3	4
07-Nov	Richmond Green	Richmond	3-0		*Pardoe 1*	*Morgan 1*	*Jackson 1*	
14-Nov	Barnes	Barnes	5-0		*Alcock C.W. 2*	*Pardoe 1*	*Morgan 1*	*Adams 1*
21-Nov	Leytonstone	Richmond	5-0		*Alcock J.F. 1*	*Alcock C.W. 1*	*Tebbut C. 1*	*Tebbut A. 1*
28-Nov	Leytonstone	N.N. (Kilburn)	4-0		*Alcock J.F. 2*	*Cotton 1*	*Absolom 1*	
12-Dec	Leytonstone	Barnes	1-0					
19-Dec	Leytonstone	Thompson's XI	4-0		Alcock J.F.	*Alcock C.W. 1*	*Adams F.C. 1*	*Absolom C 2*
23-Jan	Leytonstone	King's College	2-0		Alcock J.F.	Alcock C.W.	Adams F.C.	*Absolom C 1*
06-Feb	Harrow	Harrow School	0-0		Alcock J.F	Alcock C.W.	Adams F.C.	Absolom C
13-Feb	Leytonstone	Thompson's XI	2-2		Alcock J.F	*Alcock C.W 1*	Absolom C	Cotton R.
27-Feb	Kilburn	N.N. (Kilburn)	0-0		Alcock J.F.	Alcock C.W.	Mackenzie A.W.	Edmunds

$ listed as Edmonds in 'Field'

Wanderers F.C. 1864

Date	Venue	Opponents	Res	Att	1	2	3	4
02-Apr	Kilburn	N.N. (Kilburn)	1-0		Alcock C.W	Absolom C	Bigland C	Desborough F

Forest F.C. 1864/65

Date	Venue	Opponents	Res	Att	1	2	3	4
19-Nov	Penge	Crystal Palace	1-0		*Alcock C.W. 1*	Absolom C	Cotton R	Elliot J
26-Nov	Battersea Park	Civil Service	1-0		*Cotton R. 1*			
07-Jan	Leytonstone	Wanderers						
28-Jan	Leytonstone	Crystal Palace						
04-Feb	Leytonstone	N.N. (Kilburn)						
18-Feb	Leytonstone	Civil Service						
04-Mar	Leytonstone	Walthamstow Cl						

116

5	6	7	8	9	10	11
Jackson.C	MacKenzie.GW	Morgan.J	Pardoe.J	Robertson.J	Tebbut.C	Tebbut.A
Burness.AJ	Connery.FW	Jackson.CD	Morgan.DJ	*Pardoe.J 3*	Robertson.J	Standidge.WJB

5	6	7	8	9	10	11

5	6	7	8	9	10	11
Head H	Jackson C.D.	Jackson H.S.	Pardoe.J	Tabor B.D.	Tebbut C.M.	Tebbut A.M.
Burnett E.W.	Cotton R.	Finlay A.K.	Greaves T.W.	Gillespie D.	*Tebbut C.M. 1*	Tebbut A.M.
Burnett E.W.	Cotton R.	Finlay A.K.	Greaves T.W.	Gillespie D.	Tebbut C.M.	Tebbut A.M.
Cutbill	Edwards $	Gardiner	Jackson	*Pardoe 1*	Tebbut C.M.	Tebbut A.M.
Pardoe	Absolom C	Morley	Jackson	Head H	Tebbut C.M.	Tebbut A.M.

5	6	7	8	9	10	11
Edmunds GH	Greaves T.W.	Hillhouse J	*Tebbut AM 1*	Tebbut C.M.	Thompson A	----

5	6	7	8	9	10	11
Hamilton C	Jackson C.D	Tebbut A.M.	Tebbut C.M.	Thompson A.M.		

117

The Wanderers 1864/65

Date	Venue	Opponents	Res	Att	1	2	3
05-Nov	Aldershot	The Officers	1-0		Alcock C.W.	Baker W.F.	Cutbill W
12-Nov	Battersea Park	Civil Service	2-0		Alcock C.W.	Absolom C	Baker A
07-Jan	Leytonstone	Forest F.C.					
11-Feb	Battersea Park	Civil Service					
13-Feb	Charterhouse	Charterhouse					

Notes

12 Nov v Civil Service - 12 *Thompson W. 1*

The Wanderers 1865/66

Date	Venue	Opponents	Res	Att	1	2	3
28-Oct	Battersea Park	Civil Service	5-0		*Alcock C.W. 2*	Bowen E.E.	Green F.
08-Nov	Charterhouse	Charterhouse	1-0		Alcock C.W.	Burnett E.W.	Cutbill W.J.C.
11-Nov	Penge	Crystal Palace	1-1		Alcock C.W.	Baker W.F.	Carpingdale A.
18-Nov	Vincent Square	Westminster School	3-1		Alcock C.W.	Allfrey W.M.	Bowen E.E.
25-Nov	Epping	Forest School	2-0		*Alcock C.W. 1*	Elliot J.	Green F.
02-Dec	Kilburn	No Names, Kilburn	1-0		Alcock C.W.	Elphinstone R.D.	Green F.
09-Dec	Harrow	Harrow School	0-4		Alcock C.W.	Phipps H.G.	Reid C.F.
16-Dec	Reigate	Reigate Club	3-1		Alcock C.W.	*Elphinstone R.D. 2*	Green F.
03-Jan	?	A.F.Kinnaird's XI	0-0		Alcock C.W.	Barlow F. $	Cutbill W.J.C.
06-Jan	Penge	Crystal Palace	3-0		Alcock C.W.	*Barlow, Frank P. 1*	*Barlow, Fred P. 1*
03-Feb	Harrow	Harrow School	2-0		Alcock C.W.	*Boyson J.A. 1*	Broughton J.
06-Feb	Brompton	Crusaders	5-2		*Alcock C.W. 1*	Crompton A.	*Elphinstone R.D. 1*
10-Feb	Battersea Park	Civil Service	0-0		Buller C.F.	Burnett E.W.	Phipps H.G.
28-Feb	Vincent Square	Westminster School	1-1		*Alcock C.W. 1*	Boyson J.A.	Burnett E.W.
03-Mar	Charterhouse	Charterhouse	1-0		Alcock C.W.	Barlow F.B.	Boyson J.A.
10-Mar		Forest School	4-0		*Alcock C.W. 1*	*Elphinstone R.D. 1*	*Harper Syd. 1*

Notes

11th Nov v Crystal Palace - 12 Thompson A., 13 Thompson W., 14 Weber C.A.
18th Nov v Westminster School - 12 Thompson W.
6th Jan v Crystal Palace - 12 Thomspon A., 13 Thompson W., 14 Hammond A. *
3rd Mar v Charterhouse - 12 Thompson W.

* Report states (emergancy) after players name
$ Unclear whether Frank or Fred
$$ Unclear whether AM or CM
$$$ Unclear whether it is A or W

The Wanderers 1866/67

Date	Venue	Opponents	Res	Att	1	2	3
03-Nov	Walthamstow	Forest School	0-2		Alcock C.W.	Crompton A.	Emmanuel H.
10-Nov	Charterhouse	Charterhouse	0-1		Alcock C.W.	Forsyth H	Hogg Q
17-Nov	Vincent Square	Westminster School	1-0 **		Alcock C.W.	Tebbut C.M.	Norman E.
20-Nov	Battersea Park	Civil Service	1-0		Alcock C.W.	Berens A.	Emmanuel H.
24-Nov	Harrow	Harrow School	0-1		Alcock C.W.	Bowen E.E.	Cruikshank J.A.
01-Dec	Hitchin	Hitchin Club	5-0 %		Alcock C.W.	Allfrey W.M.	Beck J.
20-Dec	Battersea Park	Old Etonians	0-1		Alcock C.W.	Bowen E.E.	Crompton A.
22-Dec	Battersea Park	Harrow Chequers	1-1		Alcock C.W.	Dixon W.J.	*Forsyth H. 1*
29-Dec	Watford	Hertfordshire Rangers	0-0		Alcock C.W.	Baker A.	Emmanuel H.
10-Jan	Vincent Square	Westminster Hol. XI	2-1		*Alcock C.W. 2*	Hammans A.W.	Kennedy G.G.
02-Feb	Clapham Common	C.C.C.	0-1		Alcock C.W.	Alcock J.F.	Cutbill W.J.C.
09-Feb	Harrow	Harrow School	0-0		Alcock C.W.	Bowen E.E.	Crompton A.
16-Feb	Vincent Square	Westminster School	1-0		Alcock C.W.	*Butter J. 1*	Cutbill W.J.C.
16-Feb	The Parks,Oxford	Oxford	1-0		Kinnaird A.F.	Rigden J.	*Montgomery H.H. 1*
23-Feb	Charterhouse	Charterhouse	0-0		Alcock C.W.	Butter J.	Crompton A.
09-Mar	Clapham Common	C.C.C.	?				

Notes

22nd Dec v Harrow Chequers - 12 West S.H.

* Emergancy players
** unclear whether the scorers was Norman E. or Prior J.T.
% scorers unknown

4	5	6	7	8	9	10	11
Elliot F	Green F	Green H	Head H	Tebbut C.M.	*Tebbut A.M. 1*	Thompson A	2 others?
Baker W.F.	Burnett E.W.	*Green F 1*	Green Y	Head G	Head H	Phipps H.G.	Thompson A

4	5	6	7	8	9	10	11
Martin J.B. 1	Phipps H.G.	Reid C.F.	Tebbut C.M.	Tebbut A.M.	*Thompson A. 1*	Thompson W.	*Tupper C.L 1*
Green F.	*Herbert G. 1*	Martin J.B.	Reid C.F.	Tebbut A.M.	Tebbut C.M	Thompson A.	Thompson W.
Elliot J.	Harper S.	Head H.	Lucas J.	*Martin J.B. 1*	Reid C.F.	Tebbut A.M.	Tebbut C.M.
Green F.	Lucas J.	*Martin J.B. 2*	Burnett E.W.	*Phipps H.G 1*	Prior J.T.	Tayloe J.E.	Thompson A.
Green J.F.	*Harper S. 1*	Lock J.G.	Morley J.L	Parr C.C.	Tebbut A.M.	Tebbut C.M	Thompson A.
Head H.	Lucas J.	Lock J.C.	Martin J.B.	*Reid C.F. 1*	Thompson A.		
Allfrey W.M.	Green F or A?	Cater	Elphinstone R.D.	Martin J.B.	Smith *		
Head H.	Lucas J.	Mallock C.H.	*Martin J.B. 1*	Morten A.	Tebbut C.M.	Tebbut A.M.	Weber C.L.
Elphinstone R.D.	Green A.	Lucas F.	Lucas J.	Mackenzie M.J.M.	Martin J.B.	Tebbut A.M.	Tebbut C.M.
Boyson J.A.	Elphinstone R.D.	Harper S.	Lucas F.	Mackenzie M.J.M.	*Martin J.B.1*	Rhodes P.	Tebbut A.M.
Elphinstone R.D.	Hogg Q.	Martin J.B.	Noyes H.	Phipps H.G.	*J.Worsley 1*	Richardson H.	Thompson A.
Martin J.B. 1	Tebbut A.M.	Tebbut C.M.	*Thompson A. 2*	Thompson W.			
Elphinstone R.D.	Tebbut $$	Martin	Thompson $$$	Alcock C.W.			
Cruikshank Y.A.	Elphinstone R.D.	Lucas J	Phipps H.G.	Reid C.F.	Tebbut C.M.	Thompson A.	Randolph W.
Cruikshank J.A.	Elphinstone R.D.	*Forsyth H. 1*	Green F.	Haye A.	Hogg D.	Lucas J.	Thompson A.
Thompson A. 1							

4	5	6	7	8	9	10	11
Head H.	Rhodes P.	Parr C.C.	Tittey E. (sub)	Stow F.O. (sub)	Gascoign W *	Tebbut A.M.)	
Phipps H.G.	Tebbut C.M.	Thompson W.J.	Crompton A.	Thompson A.	Evans H.	Paulson F.G.	Almond H.J.
Forsyth H.	Butler J.	Nepean C.E.B.	Gibson E.C.S	Crompton A.	Thompson W.J.	Pryor J.T.	
Holland S.T.	Ball Rev. F.	Pember A.	*Phipps H.G. 1*	Reid C.F.	Tebbut C.M.		
Butler J.	Hewlett W.O.	Reid C.F.	Tebbut C.M.	Thompson W.J.	Thomas (sub)	Willis H.S.	Fryer F.E.R. *
Head H. 1	Holland S.T.	Lucas E.	Reid C.J.	Rhodes P.	Tebbut C.M.	Thompson W.J.	*Thornton PM 2*
Kennedy G.G.	Lucas F.	Mackenzie M.J.	Nepean C.E.B.	Holland S.T	Tebbut C.M.	Thompson W.J.	
Kinnaird A.F.	Lubbock A.	Lubbock E.	Lucas F.	Mackenzie M.J.	Nepean C.E.B.	Tebbut C.M.	Thompson A.
Pember A.	Rhodes P.	Reid C.F.	Tebbut C.M.	Holland S.T			
Kinnaird A.F.	Morten A.	Mackenzie M.J.	Tebbut C.M.	Tupper C.L.			
Finch W.	Forsyth H.	Kirkpatrick C.	Kirkpatrick J.	Morten A.	Townsend A. *	Tayloe E. *	
Elphinstone R.D.	Parr E.C.	Tebbut C.M.	Young J.S.	Shakespear H.H. *	Magor B. *	Carlisle A. *	Carlisle S. *
Elphinstone R.D.	Forsyth H.	Holland S.T.	Mammatt A.S.	Nepean C.E.B.	Reid C.F.	Rhodes P.	Tebbut C.M.
Noyes H.	Kennedy G.G.	Douglas C.	Richardson H.	Mason J.	Digby C.T.	Ainslie J.A.	Tatton R.R.G.
Elphinstone R.D.	Freeth E.	Hogg Q.	Kennedy G.G.	Miller F.	Rhodes P.	Green F (Taylor)	Dunn C.F.*

Date	Venue	Opponents	Res	Att	1	2	3	4
28-Sep	Clapham Com	C.C.C.	2-0		Alcock C.W.	Kennedy G.G.	Ker J.C.	Kirkpatrick J.
05-Oct	Battersea Park	Old Harrovians	2-2		Tebbut C.M.	Baker A.	Rivett Carnac J.	*Dixon W.J.* 1
12-Oct	Walthamstow	Forest School	1-1		Tebbut C.M.	Reid C.F.	Lloyd A.	Lloyd H.
26-Oct	Charterhouse	Charterhouse	1-0		*Alcock C.W. 1*	Baker A.	Bowen E.E.	Hewlett W.O.
28-Oct	Cambridge	Eton Club	0-0 $		Absolom C.A.	Alcock C.W.	Broughton F.R.	Mason S.
29-Oct	Cambridge	Harrow Club	0-1 $$		Alcock C.W.	Durnford W.	Fitzmaurice Lord E.	Kinnaird A.F.
30-Oct	Cambridge	St John's College	2-1		Alcock C.W.	Absolom C.A.	Montgomery HH	*Peel A. 1*
31-Oct	Trinity CC	King's College	0-1 $$$		Alcock C.W.	Holmes J.	Pelham Hon T.G.	Hoare W.
01-Nov	Parker's Piece	Cambridge University	0-3 $4		Alcock C.W.	Holmes J.	Pelham Hon T.G.	Peel T.E.
02-Nov	Watford	Hertfordshire Rangers	0-0		Bowen E.E.	Cruikshank J.A	Curteis H.	Curteis R.
07-Nov	Battersea Park	Civil Service	3-1		Kennedy G.G.	Rivett Carnac J	*Soden F.B. 1*	Baker A.
13-Nov	Vincent Sq	Westminster School	1-0		Alcock C.W.	Rivett Carnac W	Dixon W.J.	*Martin J.B. 1*
16-Nov	Upton Park	Upton Park XV	1-0		Rivett Carnac W	Charles W.F.	Emanuel H.	Foote J.A.
23-Nov	Harrow	Harrow School	1-3		Alcock C.W.	Baker A.	Rivett Carnac W	Bowen E.E.
27-Nov	Oxford	Harrow Chequers	0-1		Alcock C.W.	Bovill E.C.	Bickmore C.E.	Lucas F.
28-Nov	Oxford	Oxford University	0-1		Alcock C.W.	Bickmore C.E.	Henry E.	Richardson H.
30-Nov	Kilburn	No Name's (Kilburn)	0-1		Kennedy G.G.	Giles E.	Dixon W.J.	Yates J.M.
13-Dec	Battersea Park	Eton XI	0-0		Alcock C.W.	Baker A.	Dixon W.J.	Freeth E.
18-Dec	Brompton	Amateur Athletic Club	2-2 £		Alcock C.W.	Baker A.	*Dixon W.J. 1*	Henry E.
18-Jan	Chatham	Royal Engineers	2-0		*Alcock C.W. 1*	Baker A.	*Wylde E.W. 1*	West S.H.
01-Feb	Clapham	C.C.C.	1-2		Alcock C.W.	*Almond H.J. 1*	Boyle C.C.	Hammick E.A
20-Feb	Hitchin	Hitchin Club	2-0		*Alcock C.W. 1*	Elliot H.	*Emanuel H. 1*	Head H.
22-Feb	Harrow	Harrow School	1-4		Alcock C.W.	Barlow F.P.	Rivett Carnac W	Bowen E.E.
25-Feb	Chatham	Royal Engineers	0-2		Yates J.M.	Tebbut C.M.	Tayloe J.E.	Fanshawe J.
27-Feb	Vincent Sq	Westminster School	3-0		Alcock C.W.	*Baker A. 1*	Dixon W.J.	Hogg Q.
04-Mar	Middx CCC	Charterhouse School	0-0		Alcock C.W.	Baker A.	Dixon W.J.	Kirkpatrick J.
14-Mar	Upton Park	Upton Park XV	1-1		Rex G	Tebbut C.M.	Povah F.K.	Taylor J.W.
17-Mar	Walthamstow	Forest School	0-0		Alcock C.W.	Huggins J.T.	Hartung J.M.	Cutbill J.

*
Emergancies
** listed as absent in the report
$ Football Annual states lost by three touch downs
$$ states Wanderers defeated by one goal to one touch down (Radcliffe W.W.)
$$$ states King's won by one goal and one touch down to one touch down (Ogden L.)
$4 states Cambridge won by three goals and three touch downs to nothing
£ own goal

Notes
27th Nov v Harrow Chequers - 12 Johnson A.C.
30th Nov v No Names - 12 Collins J.D. *

Missing a CCC game - report in Feb says it's a return
Nov v Eton College - no report in Sportsman or Bells Life
Dec v Hitchin, Old Etonians & Harrow Chequers - no report in Sportsman or Bells Life
Jan v Westminster Holiday Team, Old Etonians & Harrow Chequers - no report in Sportsman or Bells Life

5	6	7	8	9	10	11
Reid C.F. 1	*Rhodes P. 1*	Tebbut C.M.	Thornton P.M.	Thornton R.C.	Thornton R.M.	Tupper C.N.
Holland S.T.	Kirkpatrick J.	Soden F.B.	*Tayloe J.E. 1*	Cutbill W.J.C. **	Lloyd A. **	Lloyd H. **
Kennedy G.G.	*Thornton R.M. 1*	Thornton R.C.	Rhodes P.	Worrall H.	Brown T.L.	Shelton E.H.S.J.
Kennedy G.G.	Norman E.	Norman P.	Reid C.F.	Tebbut C.M.	Thornton R.M.	Thornton P.M.
Money W.B.	Ogden L.	Peel T.E.	Peel A.	Russell J.	Templar F.G.	Walford O.S.
Ogden L.	Pelham Hon F.G.	Pulteney W.	Radcliffe E.	Gurdon Rebow H.	Thompdon A.C.	Walford O.S.
Kinnaird A.F.	*Gossett F. 1*	Holmes J.	Russell J.	Cuthell C.E.	Ogden L.	
Fitzmaurice Lord E	Kinnaird A.F.	Harvey E.	Ogden L.	Moncrieff R.C.	Walford O.S.	Lloyd E.W.M.
Fitzmaurice Lord E	Muir Mckenzie K.	Douglas S.K.	Radcliffe W.W.	Swainson E.R.		
Hewlett W.O.	Holland S.T.	Parr C.C.	Reid C.F.	Rivett Carnac J.	Tebbut C.M.	
Norman E. 1	*Berens E.O. 1*	Thornton W.P.	Thompson W.J.	Tebbut CM. (A Lemun)	Elphinstone R.D. **	Wylde E.W. **
Tebbut C.M.	Thompson W.J.	Thornton R.C.	Thornton R.M.	Wylde E.W.	Yates J.M.	Elphinstone R.D.
Holland S.T.	Kennedy G.G.	Lee G.H.	Smith J.C.	Tebbut C.M.	Thornton P.M.	*Venables E.E. 1*
Crompton A.	Cruikshank J.A.	*Kennedy G.G. 1*	Reid C.F.	Thornton R.C.	Thornton R.M.	Young J.M.
Holland S.T.	Henry E.	Douglas S.K.	Mackenzie K.A.M	Thomas J.	Wallace W.	West S.H.
Digby R.	Mackenzie K.A.M.	Pelham H.F.	Greenham E.	Bridges R.S.	Bovill E.C. **	Mackenzie M.J.M. **
Rivett Carnac W.	Thompson A.	Charles A.W.	Thornton R.C. **	Thornton R.M. **	Wylde E.W. **	Rhodes P. **
Henry F.	Hogg Q.	Lubbock E.	Martin J.B.	Other A.N.	Taylor J.E.	Yates J.M.
Holland S.T.	Norman P.	Norman E.	Wylde E.W.	Freeth H. **	Taylor J.E. **	
Yates J.M.	Purcell A.	Fellowes R.				
Kirkpatrick J.	Paulson F.G.	Yates J.M.	Ker R.	Tayloe E.		
Kinnaird A.F.	Ogden L.	Pelham Hon TW	Rigden W.	Tebbut C.M.		
Cruikshank J.A.	Elphinstone R.D.	Fairfield E.	Finlay A.K.	*Goldney J.T. 1*	Hewlett W.O.	Parsons J. *
Duthie W.	Turner P.V.	Dixon W.J.	Emanuel H.	Brown Lieut. *	Hewson Lieut. *	
Kennedy G.G.	*Martin J.B. 1*	*Norman P. 1*	Tebbut C.M.	Wylde E.W.	Yates J.M.	Tait C. **
Norman P.	Tebbut C.M.	Emanuel H.	Wylde E.W.	Yates J.M.	Povah F.K. *	
Hammick E.A.	Russell A.F.	*Paulson F.G. 1*	Almond H.G.	Sharland E.	Rhodes P.	
Soden F.B.	Tebbut C.M.	Cotton W.	Cutbill A.L.	Beauchamp E.B. *	Huggins M.V. *	Pownall L.E. *

F.A. Cup winners 1871/72 – 1882/83

Year	Winners	Runners Up	Result
1872	Wanderers	Royal Engineers	1-0
1873	Wanderers	Oxford University	2-0
1874	Oxford University	Royal Engineers	2-0
1875	Royal Engineers	Old Etonians	1-1 r 2-0
1876	Wanderers	Old Etonians	0-0 r 3-0
1877	Wanderers	Oxford University	2-1 aet
1878	Wanderers	Royal Engineers	3-1*
1879	Old Etonians	Clapham Rovers	1-0
1880	Clapham Rovers	Oxford University	1-0
1881	Old Carthusians	Old Etonians	3-0
1882	Old Etonians	Blackburn Rovers	1-0
1883	Blackburn Olympic	Old Etonians	2-1 aet

The Wanderers 1868/69

Date	Venue	Opponents	Res	Att	1	2	3
26-Sep	Clapham Common	C.C.C.	1-1		Alcock C.W. 1	Cutbill A.L.	Cutbill R.
17-Oct	Beaufort House	Amateur Athletic Club	2-0		Bowen E.E. 1	Dixon W.J.	Hewlett W.O.
28-Oct	Vincent Square	Westminster School	0-1		Thornton P.M.	Reid C.F.	Baker A.
04-Nov	Woolwich	Royal Military Ac.	0-2		Tebbut C.M.	Borwick A.	Cutbill R.
16-Nov	Cambridge	Eton Club	0-3 $		Shillitoe F.	Montgomery H.H.	Money W.B.
17-Nov	Trinity Col,Camb.	Harrow Club	0-0		Shillitoe F.	Emanuel H.	Broughton H.E.
21-Nov	Upton Park	Upton Park	0-1		Alcock C.W.	Emanuel H.	Huggins C.L.
21-Nov	Harrrow	Harrow School	0-2		Reid C.F.	Tabor A.	Rodwell W.H.
26-Nov	Hitchin	Hitchin	1-1		Alcock C.W. 1	Baker F.	Borwick A.
28-Nov	Crystal Palace	Crystal Palace	1-0		Alcock C.W.	Baker A. 1	Bayliff W.
01-Dec	Walthamstow	Forest School	2-1 £		Alcock C.W.	Tayloe E.	Nash A.
02-Dec	Middx County Gr.	Royal Engineers	1-1		Alcock C.W. 1	Baker A.	Kennedy G.G.
03-Dec	Oxford	Oxford Amalgation Cl.	3-1		Alcock C.W. 1	Hill H.	Morgan J.H.
09-Dec	Middx County Gr.	Civil Service	1-0		Alcock C.W.	Goldney J.T.	Kennedy G.G.
12-Dec	Brompton	London Athletic Club	2-3		Alcock C.W.	Kennedy G.G. 2	Goldney J.T.
19-Dec	Vincent Square	Crusaders	3-0		Alcock C.W. 1	Baker A. 1	Freeth E.
22-Dec	Westminster	Civil Service	0-0		Alcock C.W.	Nicholls A.	Shaw V.K.
14-Jan	Middx County Gr.	Old Bradfields	4-4		Alcock C.W.	Baker A.	Hooman T.C. 1
16-Jan	Middx County Gr	Old Etonians	1-1		Alcock C.W.	Kennedy G.G.	Baker A. 1
19-Jan	Middx County Gr.	Bedouins	4-0		Tebbut C.M.	Cutbill R. 2	Giffard J.H.
23-Jan	Woodford	Forest Club	3-0		Alcock C.W.	Reid C.F.	Yates J.M. 1
30-Jan	Hampstead	Hampstead Heathens	0-5		Wade	Hooman T.C.	Rhodes P.
06-Feb	Harrrow	Harrow School	0-2		Kennedy G.G.	Bowen E.E.	Cruikshank J.A.
13-Feb	Beaufort House	Royal Military Ac.	0-1				
17-Feb	Middx County Gr.	Charterhouse School	1-2		Tebbut C.M.	Yates J.M.	Baker A. 1
20-Feb	Middx County Gr.	West Kent	1-0		Dunn R. 1		
10-Mar	Vincent Square	Westminster School	3-1		Tebbut C.M.	Yates J.M.	Kinnaird A.F. 2
13-Mar	Upton Park	Upton Park	8-0		Yates J.M.	Kinnaird A.F. 3	Hammond T. 1
24-Mar	Charterhouse	Charterhouse School	3-2		Yates J.M.	Kinnaird A.F. 2	Tebbut C.M.
27-Mar	Woodford	Forest Club	0-0		Yates J.M.	Borwick A.	Cooper E.A.

Notes
24th Mar v Charterhouse - 12 Rees-Mogg W. *

* Emergancies
** report states as absent
$ lost by three goals to one touch down (Montgomery HH)
$$ looks like a clever way of saying a substitute was used
£ own
goal

Postponed

09-Jan	Islington	Crusaders	

4	5	6	7	8	9	10	11
Cockerill J.	Dixon W.J.	Kirkpatrick J.	Nash A.	Rhodes P.	Wylde E.W	Ogden L.	
Shillitoe F.	Baker A.	Kirkpatrick J.	*Lubbock E. 1*	Dunn	Brown	Barnes	
Borwick A.	Dixon W.J.	Fairfield E.	Kirkpatrick J.	Tebbut C.M.	Dunn R.	Tayloe J.E.	Shillitoe F.
Giffard J.P.	Ker R.N.	Luscombe F.	Rouguette P.G.	Gurton P.	Tayloe E.	Saxton P.	Thornton PM
Shaw V.R.	Dorling F.	Tuck A.J.	Pitt-Taylor F.H.	Walford O.S.	Emanuel H	Broughton H	E.Mergancy $$
Tuck A.J.	Gossett G.	Pelham Hon. T.H.	Rigden J.	Thompson A.C.	Thornton C	Walford O.S.	Hoare W.
Povah F.K.	Chamberlin AC	Sharland J.	Scott P.	Tebbut C.M.	Lubbock E. **	Head H. **	Lawrence H.W. **
Yates J.M.	Hewlett W.O.	Broughton H.E.	Bowen E.E.	Cruikshank J.A.	Young E.M	Torr G. *	Carry H. *
Dawson C.	Read H.	Reid C.F.	Thornton C.J.				
Smith W.	Reid C.F.	Povah F.K.	Tabor A.	Thompson A.	Ker R.	Bouch W.	Field J.
Lloyd H.	Borwick A.	Baker A.	Hudson M.	Tebbut C.M.	*Cutbill R. 1*	Kerr R.W.	Forester A *
Freeth E.	Kirkpatrick J.	Cutbill R.	Tayloe E.	Norman E.			
Pelham HF	Parry C.H.H.	*Gibson J.F. 1*	Lucas F.	Mackenzie K.A.M.	*Douglas SK 1*	Giles J.	Ainslie J.A.
Martin J 1	Norman E.	Reid C.F.	Borwick A.	Cutbill R.	Huggins C.L.	Baker A.	
Yates J.M.	Reid C.F.	Povah F.K.	Thompson A.	Dixon W.J.	Lubbock E. **		
Goldney JT	Hooman T.C.	Huggins C.L.	*Kennedy G.G. 1*	Kirkpatrick J.	Martin J.B.	Rhodes P.	Tebbut C.M.
Hooman T	Nepean C.E.B.	Higgins W.F.	Martin J.B.	Baker A.	Dixon W.J.	Rhodes P.	Tebbut C.M.
Higgins W	*Bowen E.E. 1*	*Fairfield E. 1*	*Kennedy G.G. 1*	Kirkpatrick J. **	Bradfield.A *	Hunt W.F.	
Bowen EE	Higgins W.F.	Vero Shaw	Wade R.E.L.	Yates J.M.	Hooman T.C.	Huggins C.L.	Fairfield E.
Wade REL	*Hooman TC 1*	Baker A.	*Luscombe F. 1*	Alcock C.W.	Higgins W.F **		
Stileman F.	*Wade R.E.L. 1*	*Hooman T.C. 1*	Shaw A.	Clementson C	James C.	Vero Shaw	Clementson F.
Cameron	Jutsum	Atkinson	Barnett	Brown	Gribble	Welch	
Crawford R	Fryer F.E.R.	Holland H.	Rhodes P.	Rodwell W.H.	Stileman F.	Tabor A.	Young E.W.
Dixon W.J.	Reid C.F.	Fairfield E.	Luscombe F.	Cutbill A.L.	Cutbill R.	Carter G.T. *	Huxley T.C. *
Lubbock E.	Baker A.	Kirkpatrick J.	Dixon W.J.	Wydle E.W.	Giffard J.H.	*Nepean C. 1*	Dunn R.
Sinclair A.	Kennedy GG	Ayers T.	*Nepean C.E.B. 2*	Dunn R.	Rhodes P.	Huggins C.L.	*Dixon W.J. 1*
Tayloe E.	*Lubbock E 1*	Huggins C.L.	Kirkpatrick J.	Way C.	Kennedy GG	Carter G.S. *	Harvey G.W. *
Sharpe H.	Tayloe J.E.	Tebbut C.M.	Borwick J. *	Roy *	Rouquette S. *	Twining *	

Stop Press

On Thursday 19th May 2005 the second F.A. Cup which was used between 1896 and 1910 and was later presented to Lord Kinnaird for his services to football was sold at Christies for £478,400.   It was later revealed to have been purchased by David Gold, Chairman of Birmingham City F.C. Mr Gold later said 'he was compelled to buy the trophy yesterday to stop it from going overseas. I have bought the cup not just for myself but on behalf of the nation's football fans.'

Date	Venue	Opponents	Res	Att	1	2	3
25-Sep	Clapham Common	Clapham Rovers	0-1		Alcock C.W.	Emanuel H.	Fairfield E.
02-Oct	Clapham Common	C.C.C.	0-0		Alcock C.W.	Borwick A.	Fairfield E.
09-Oct	Oval	West Kent	0-2		Alcock C.W.	Baker A.	Bowen E.E.
23-Oct	Oval	Old Etonians	0-2		Alcock C.W.	Borwick A.	Brown F.F.
27-Oct	Oval	Rochester Club	3-0		Alcock C.W.	Baker A.	Borwick A.
30-Oct	Woodford	Forest Club	5-0		*Alcock C.W. 1*	*Baker A. 1*	*Borwick A. 1*
03-Nov	Charterhouse	Charterhouse School	2-2		Alcock C.W.	*Baker A. 1*	Cotton R.B.
06-Nov	Oval	Upton Park	2-0		*Alcock C.W. 1*	Baker A.	Hogg Q.
08-Nov	Oxford	Oxford Amalgamation Cl.	0-0		Pelham H.F.	Parry C.H.	West S.H.
09-Nov	Walthamstow	Forest School	1-2		Alcock C.W.	*Baker A. 1*	Borwick A.
10-Nov	Oval	Royal Engineers	2-1		*Baker A 2*	Cotton R.B.	Cutbill R.
12-Nov	Parker's Piece, Camb	Christ's College	3-1 $ %		Foote J.H.	Stansfield R.	De Mattos W.
17-Nov	Vincent Square	Westminster School	1-0		Baker A.	Dixon W.J.	Fitzmaurice Lord E.
20-Nov	Oval	Gitanos	0-0		Baker A.	Bowen E.E.	Sherborne S.T.
23-Nov	Parker's Piece, Camb	Cambridge University	0-2 $$		Alcock C.W.	Fryer F.E.R.	Prior C.H.
27-Nov	Harrow	Harrow School	1-3		Alcock C.W.	Bowen E.E.	*Cruikshank J.A. 1*
01-Dec	Oval	Civil Service	4-2		Kinnaird A.F.	Baker A.	*Stephens H.P. 2*
04-Dec	Oval	Hampstead Heathens	2-0		*Alcock C.W. 1*	Borwick A.	Dixon W.J.
11-Dec	Oval	Crusaders	1-2		Alcock C.W.	Tebbut C.M.	Huggins C.L.
14-Dec	Oval	Desperadoes	1-2		*Alcock C.W. 1*	Hunt W.F.	Hogg Q.
05-Jan	Crystal Palace	Crystal Palace	1-0		Abbott R.W.	Baker A.	Crake W.P.
15-Jan	Oval	Gitanos	1-1		Alcock C.W.	Baker A.	Crake W.P.
19-Jan	Oval	Harrow Pilgrims	1-0 %		Kinnaird A.F.	Baker A.	Hogg Q.
22-Jan	Oval	Civil Service	3-0		*Alcock C.W. 1*	Vidal R.W.S.	Stephenson C.W.
05-Feb	Harrow	Harrow School	0-1		Alcock C.W.	Bowen E.E.	Cruikshank J.A.
07-Feb	Oxford	Oxford Amalgamation Cl.	0-0				
09-Feb	Oval	Crystal Palace	0-2		Alcock C.W.	Baker A.	Currie F.A.
23-Feb	Vincent Square	Westminster School	0-1		Alcock C.W.	Reid C.F.	Currie F.A.
26-Feb	Woodford	Forest Club	7-0		*Alcock C.W. 2*	*Baker A. 3*	*Kirkpatrick J. 1*
05-Mar	Clapham Common	Clapham Rovers	0-2		Vere Wright	Fleet A.	Noyes H.
12-Mar	Upton Park	Upton Park	3-0		*Alcock C.W. 1*	*Baker A. 1*	Currie F.A.
19-Mar	Charterhouse	Charterhouse School	1-1		Baker H.	Kinnaird A.F.	Emanuel H.
19-Mar	Oval	Hampstead Heathens	2-1		Alcock C.W.	*Fairfield E. 1*	Fleet A.

Notes

9th Nov v Forest School - Sportsman lists different team

12th March v Upton Park - 12 Vere Wright

19th March v Hampstead Heathens - 12 Kinnaird A.F.

* subsitue

** absent

$ 3 goals and 5 touch downs to one

$$ lost by 2 goals and one touch down to one touch down

% one scorer unknown

124

4	5	6	7	8	9	10	11
Kirkpatrick J.	Morten A.	Rhodes P.	Shillitoe F.	Wylde E.W.	Hartung F.N.	Gill R. *	
Kirkpatrick J.	Lubbock E.	Morten A.	Nash A.J.	Povah F.K.	Shillitoe F.	Tayloe J.E.	
Borwick A.	Dixon W.J.	Freeth E.	Huggins C.L.	Kirkpatrick J.	Morten A.	Povah F.K.	Wallace W.
Dixon W.J.	Huggins C.L.	King H.S.	Nepean C.E.B.	Nichols J.P.	Stephenson CW	Vidal R.W.S	Wallace W.
Borwick J.C.	*Emanuel H. 1*	Fairfield E.	*Martin J.B. 1*	*Nash A. 1*	Nash E.J.	Sinclair A.	Thompson A.
Borwick J.C.	*Fairfield E. 1*	Hogg Q.	Hunt W.F.	*Kinnaird A.F. 1*	Nash A.	Renshaw A.G.	Lubbock E.
Emanuel H.	Rivett-Carnac W	Hogg Q.	Martin J.B.	*Nash A. 1*	Norman E.	Thompson A.	Coombs T.
Hunt W.F.	Giffard J.H.	Morten A.	Smith J.C.	Wallace W.	*Harmar W. 1*	Rivett-Carnac W	Atkinson C.E.
Wilson F.H.	Brymer J.G.	Gibson E.C.S.	Hammick E.A.	Paulson F.G.	Povah F.K.	Paget Q.	Price B.
Borwick J.C.	Allport D.	Cotton R.B.	Nash A.J.	Nash J.C.	Thompson C.	Jutsum M.	Chingford W.
Hogg Q.	Kirkpatrick J.	Lubbock E.	Norman E.	Sherborne S.T.	Thompson A.	Tayloe J.E. **	Wallace W. **
Thornton C.J. 1	Barker G.F.	Strutt Hon C.H.	Pidcock C.A.	Giles C.T.	Tabor A.	*Gosset G. 1*	Fryer F.E.R.
Gosset G.	*Kinnaird A.F. 1*	Lubbock E.	Nash A.J.	Norman E.	Reid C.F.	Sherborne S.T.	Smith J.C.
Huggins C.L.	Lubbock E.	Morten A.	Nash A.J.	Nichols J.P.	Smith J.C.	Vidal R.W.S	Dixon H.B.
Gosset G.	Money W.B.	Radcliffe W.W.	Pidcock C.A.	Tabor A.	Bouverie E.		
Elliott F.A.	Fleet A.	Hunt W.F.	Rivett-Carnac W	Young Rev E.M.	Torr W.E. *	Welch R.C. *	Thomson J.C. *
Thompson A.	Nash A.J.	*Huggins C.L. 2*	Lubbock E.	Sherborne S.T.			
Lawrence H.W.	Nash A.J.	*Nicholls J.P. 1*	Stephenson CW	Vidal R.W.S.	Wallace W.	Whitmore F.J.	
Rhodes P.	Fleet A.	Nash A.J.	*Vere Wright 1*	Martin J.B.	Wallace W. **		
Kinnaird A.F.	Nash A.J.	Rhodes P.	Walford O.S.	Reid C.F.	Tabor A.	Tayloe J.E.	Thornton P.M.
Emanuel H.	Hogg Q.	Kinnaird A.F.	Nash A.J.	Rushworth H.	Sherborne S.T.	Stephenson C.W.	Tebbut C.M.
Fleet A.	*Kinnaird A.F. 1*	Morgan J.H.	Noyes H.	Stephenson CW	Barker G.F.	Smith J.C.	
Huggins C.L.	Rushworth H.	Barker G.F.	Emanuel H.	Nash A.	Walford O.S.		
Hall E.	Turner P.R.	*Kinnaird A.F. 2*	Hammond T.	Noyes H.	Lubbock E.	Barker G.F.	Walford O.S.
Elliott F.A.	Hammond T.	Howard A.W.	Kinnaird A.F.	Noyes H.	Thornton A.H.	Macan G. *	Grey A.H.G. *
Nash A.	Kinnaird A.F.	Rushworth H.	Tebbut C.M.	Martin J.B.	Stephens H.P.	Lubbock E. **	Hogg Q **
Fitzmaurice Lord E.	Baker A.	Freeth E.	Kirkpatrick J.	Fairfield E.	Hammond T.	Dixon W.J.	Nash A. **
Currie F.A. 1	Hamilton WAB	Hooman T.C.	Hammond T.	Nichols J.P.	Noyes H.	Wallace W.	
Wallace W.	Currie F.A.	Jutsum M.	Hooman T.C.	Bainbridge A.	Cooper E.A.		
Emanuel H.	Hamilton WAB	Hooman T.C.	*Huggins C.L. 1*	Kinnaird A.F.	Kirkpatrick J.	Nicholls J.P.	Wallace W.
Thornton A.H.	Bowen E.E.	Reid C.F.	Kirkpatrick J.	Stephenson CW	Currie F.D.	*Mackenzie HM 1*	Whitmore E.J.
Freeth E.	Giffard J.H.	Hooman T.C.	*Huggins C.L. 1*	Morten A.	Nichols J.P.	Rhodes P.	Stephens H.P.

Top scorers season by season

1861/62	J.Pardoe	3	**1862/63**	C.W. Alcock		4
1863/64	C,W. Alcock	5	**1864/65**	numerous		1
1865/66	J.B. Martin	7	**1866/67**	CW Alcock/PM Thornton		2
1867/68	C.W. Alcock	3	**1868/69**	A.F. Kinnaird		7
1869/70	A.Baker/ CW Alcock	9	**1870/71**	C.W. Alcock		17
1871/72	C.W. Alcock	10	**1872/73**	C.H.R. Wollaston		7
1873/74	C.H.R. Wollaston	6	**1874/75**	C.W. Alcock		11
	F.B. Maddison/					
1875/76	C.H.R. Wollaston	5	**1876/77**	H. Wace		7
1877/78	H. Wace/ W.J. Wylie	9	**1878/79**	J. Kenrick		2
1879/80	C.A Denton	3	**1880/81**	4 players		2

Date	Venue	Opponents	Res	Att	1	2	3	4
01-Oct	Oval	Clapham Rovers	0-1		Alcock C.W.	Baker A.J.	Fairfield E.	Goodbart E.C.
08-Oct	Oval	C.C.C	1-0		Alcock C.W.	Kinnaird A.F.	Hogg Q.	Vidal R.W.S.
12-Oct	Oval	Civil Service	1-0		*Alcock C.W. 1*	Thompson A.	Huggins C.L.	Reid C.F.
15-Oct	Oval	West Kent	0-0		Alcock C.W.	Hogg Q.	Hooman T.C.	Huggins C.L.
22-Oct	Oval	Harrow Pilgrims	2-0		Lubbock E.	Huggins C.L.	*Borwick A. 1*	Morten A.
25-Oct	Walthamstow	Forest School	4-1		*Alcock C.W. 2*	Allport D.	*Baker A. 1*	Betts M.P.
29-Oct	Upton Park	Upton Park	0-0		Alcock C.W.	Borwick A.	Nicholls J.P.	Hooman T.C.
02-Nov	Charterhouse	Charterhouse School	1-3		Alcock C.W.	Baker A.	*Borwick A. 1*	Field E.
05-Nov	Harrow	Harrow School	2-1		Alcock C.W.	Baker A.	Betts M.P.	*Bowen E.E. 1*
05-Nov	Woodford	Forest Club	2-0		Hooman T.C.	Wallace W.	Nicholls J.P.	Matthews H.L.
09-Nov	Oval	Brixton Club	5-1		*Alcock C.W. 2*	Baker A.	Field E.	*Hooman T.C. 3*
12-Nov	Oxford	Oxford Association Club	2-0		*Alcock C.W. 1*	Baker A.J.	Betts M.P.	Hogg Q.
16-Nov	Vincent Sq	Westminster School	0-0		Alcock C.W.	Baker A.J.	Chenery C.J.	Crake W.P.
23-Nov	Oval	Crystal Palace	2-0		*Alcock C.W. 1*	Betts M.P.	Borwick A.T.	Crake W.P.
26-Nov	Oval	Gitanos	5-0		*Alcock C.W. 1*	Bowen E.E.	*Hooman T.C. 2*	*Huggins C.L. 1*
29-Nov	Oval	Forest School	2-0		*Alcock C.W. 1*	Baker A.	Hooman T.C.	Chenery C.J.
01-Dec	Oval	Rochester Club	2-1		Alcock C.W.	Baker A.J.	Borwick A.	Lloyd A.
03-Dec	Oval	Royal Engineers	0-0		Alcock C.W.	Baker A.J.	Chenery C.J.	Hooman T.C.
10-Dec	Brighton	Brighton College	0-1		Alcock C.W.	Jacket P.	Stileman F.	Chenery C.J.
13-Dec	Oval	Harrow Rovers	4-0		Alcock C.W.	Morton M.T.	Kennedy G.G.	*Howard A.W.H. 1*
16-Dec	Oval	Eton College	0-0		Alcock C.W.	Kinnaird A.F.	Baker A.J.	Chenery C.J.
17-Dec	Hampstead	Hampstead Heathens	0-5		Reid C.F.	Nicholls J.P.	Stileman F.	Wallace W.
18-Jan	Oval	Crystal Palace	3-0		*Alcock C.W. 1*	Dixon H.B.	Hogg Q.	*Kinnaird A.F. 2*
21-Jan	Oval	West Kent	0-0		Alcock C.W.	Street F.E.	Dixon H.B.	Whitmore F.J.
25-Jan	Oval	Civil Service	6-1		*Alcock C.W. 4*	Whitmore F.J.	Stileman F.	Street F.E.
04-Feb	Harrow	Harrow School	0-0		Alcock C.W.	Baker A.J.	Betts M.P.	Bouverie H.P.
11-Feb	Oval	Gitanos	2-0		Alcock C.W.	Hogg Q.	Bouch A.	Baker A.J.
15-Feb	Oval	Brixton Club	1-0		Alcock C.W.	Hogg Q.	Reid C.F.	Stileman F.
18-Feb	Oval	Hampstead Heathens	2-0		*Alcock C.W. 1*	Hogg Q.	Kinnaird A.F.	Hooman T.C.
23-Feb	Vincent Sq	Westminster School	2-1		Alcock C.W.	Allport D.	Bonsor A.G.	Chenery C.J.
01-Mar	Charterhouse	Charterhouse School	2-2		*Alcock C.W. 1*	Allport D.	Reid C.F.	Stephens H.P.
04-Mar	Oval	Clapham Rovers	0-1		Alcock C.W.	Betts M.P.	Bowen E.E.	Currie F.A.
11-Mar	Chatham	Royal Engineers	0-1		Alcock C.W.	Betts M.P.	Chenery C.J.	Currie F.A.
18-Mar	Oval	Forest Club	2-0		*Alcock C.W. 1*	Bouch A.	*Crake W.P. 1*	Currie F.A.
18-Mar	Oval	Upton Park	1-0		Alcock C.W.	Baker A.J.	*Crake W.P. 1*	Currie F.A.
25-Mar	Oval	The World	1-1		Hogg Q.	Gladstone WH	Kinnaird A.F.	Alcock C.W.

Reserve Game								
05-Nov	Harrow	Harrow School	0-5		Kennedy G.G.	Howard A.W.	Lawrence H.W.	Reid C.F.

Notes

12th Oct v Civil Service - 12 Maclure H.D.
17th Dec v Hampstead Heathens - 12 Fairfield E. **
18th Mar v Forest Club - 12 Wace H.

* substitute

** listed as absent

5	6	7	8	9	10	11
Hall E.	Hogg Q.	Morten A.	Rhodes P.	Tebbut C.M.	Wallace W.	Whitmore F.J.
Hooman T.C.	*Hall E. 1*	Trower P.	Round F.R	Stileman F.	Whitmore F.J.	Wallace W. *
Hogg Q.	Stileman F.	Kennedy G.G.	Hartung F.H.	Tatham J.P.	Allport D.	Hall E.
Kennedy G.G.	Nicholls J.P.	Reid C.F.	Rhodes P.	Vidal R.W.S.	Walker R.S.F.	Stileman F. *
Trower P.	*Walker R.S.F. 1*	Hogg Q. **	Nichols J.P. **			
Borwick A. 1	Hooman T.C.	Lloyd A.	Stileman F.	Jones T.A. *	Huggins C *	Hutchinson A *
Stileman F.	Vidal R.W.S.	Rushworth H.	Kennedy G.G.	Pelham Hon. T. **	Hogg Q. **	Morten A. **
Hogg Q.	Kinnaird A.F.	Morten M.T.	Norman E.	Reid C.F.	Round F.R.	Thompson A.
Cruikshank J.A. 1	Crake W.P.	Hogg Q.	Smith C.J.	Thornton R.C.	Vidal R.W.S (A.W.?)	Kinnaird A.F. **
Rushworth H.	Morten A.	Jutsum M.	*Barnett F. 1*	*Jones A.M. 1*	Compton H.	Capper C.
Kinnaird A.F.	Morton M.T.	Reid C.F.	Thornton R.C.	Hogg Q.**	Howard A.W.H **	Stileman F. **
Hooman T.C.	Kinnaird A.F.	Law W.	Nepean C.E.B.	Pelham H.F.	*Vidal R.W.S 1*	Tait C. *
Huggins C.L.	Kennedy G.G.	Kinnaird A.F.	Norman E.	Morton M.T.	Reid C.F.	Trower P.
Howard A.W.H. 1	Pelham Hon. T.	Reid C.F.	Rushworh H.	Stephenson C.W.	Stileman F.	Thompson A.
Matthews H.L.	Morten A.	*Reid C.F. 1*	Wallace W.	Stileman F.	Nicholls J.P. **	Baker A.J. **
Douglas A.	Stileman F.	Matthews H.L.	Reid C.F.	Rushworth H.	Soden F.B.	*Spreckley T.F. 1*
Chenery C.J.	Stileman F.	Morten A.	*Huggins C.L. 1*	Thompson A.	Weaver F.	*Rushworth H. 1*
Miller F.	Hogg Q.	Round F.R.	Kennedy G.G.	Huggins C.L.	Morten A.	Lloyd A.
Huggins C.L.	Gladwyn P.	Cotterill J.M.	Battye M.	Stock J.O.	*	*
Stileman F.	Hogg Q.	Baker A.J.	*Kinnaird A.F. 2*	Street F.	Crake W.P.	*Chenery C.J. 1*
Hogg Q.	Morton H.J.	Pelham Hon. T.	Stileman F.	Trower P.	Hoare E. **	Norman E. **
Street F.	Dixon H.B.	Round F.R.	Bayley *	Leach *	Trower F. **	Matthews H. **
Morton M.T.	Street F.E.	Whitmore F.J.				
Pelham Hon. T.	Emanuel H.	Hogg Q.	Waring A.T.	Thornton A.H. **		
Hogg Q. 1	*Allport D. 1*					
Bowen E.E.	Chenery C.J.	Cruikshank J.A.	Hooman T.C.	Kinnaird A.F.	Bosworth-Smith H.R.	Walker C.W.
Hooman T.C 1	Rhodes P.	Whitmore F.J.	Walker R.S.F.	*Wallace W. 1*	Howard A.W.H.	
Stephenson C.W.	*Vidal R.W.S. 1*					
Baker A.J.	Wallace W.	*Pelham Hon. T. 1*	Currie F.A.	Crake W.P.	Bonsor A.G.	Betts M.P.
Cotton R.B.	Howard A.W.H.	Kinnaird A.F. (Harvey R.)	Kirkpatrick J.	*Pelham Hon. T. 2*	Roberts J.	Kitchen A.
Field E.	*Pelham Hon. T. 1*	Chenery C.J.	Crake W.P.	Cotton R.B.	Morgan J.H.	*
Stileman F.	Wallace W.	Jutsum M.	Wilton F.	Money W.B.	Stair A.	Soden F.B.
Dixon H.B.	Gosset A.	Kirkpatrick J.	Knight R.S.	Morten A.	Stephenson C.W.	Vidal R.W.S.
Hogg Q.	Hooman T.C.	Kinnaird A.F.	Matthews H.L.	Pelham Hon. T.	Smith R.	Vidal R.W.S.
Dixon H.B.	Hogg Q.	Hooman T.C.	Smith R.	Vidal H.S.	Vidal R.W.S.	Wallace W.
Baker A.J.	Crake W.P.	Hooman T.C.	*Howard A.W.H. 1*	Nepean C.E.B.	Pelham Hon. T.	Vidal R.W.S.
Rhodes P.	Smith R.B.	Stileman F.	Thornton R.	Peel F.	Young J.	AN Other *

Most F.A. Cup winners medals

A.F. Kinnaird	Wanderers & Old Etonians	5
C.H. Wollaston	Wanderers	5
J. Forrest	Blackburn Rovers	5
R. Keans	Manchester United	4
R. Giggs	Manchester United	4
M. Hughes	Manchester United	4

127

The Wanderers 1871/72

Date	Venue	Opponents	Res	Comp	Att	1	2	3
07-Oct	Oval	Clapham Rovers	0-0	F		Alcock C.W.	Kirkpatrick J.	Tatham S.R.
14-Oct	Oval	Harrow Chequers	0-0	F		Alcock C.W.	Dodd C.	Hooman T.C.
17-Oct	Oval	Civil Service	1-0	F		Alcock C.W.	Crawford R.E.W.	Crawford F.H.
21-Oct	Oval	Gitanos	4-0	F		Alcock C.W.	Crake W.P.	Crawford R.E.W.
24-Oct	Walthamstow	Forest School	3-0	F		*Alcock C.W. 1*	Kirkpatrick J.	Crawford R.E.W.
28-Oct	Oval	Upton Park	1-2	F		Hooman T.C.	Kirkpatrick J.	*Giffard J.H. 1*
04-Nov	Harrow	Harrow School	0-1	F		Alcock C.W.	Betts M.P.	Bowen E.E.
08-Nov	Charterhouse	Charterhouse	1-1	F		Betts M.P	Kennedy G.G.	Currie F.A.
11-Nov	Oval	Royal Engineers	1-1	F		Betts M.P	*Currie F.A. 1*	Paton W.P.
11-Nov	Camberwell	First Surrey Rifles	1-0 %	F		Welch R.C.	Rivett-Carnac P.T.	Ripple A.C.
13-Nov	Parker's Piece	Cambridge University	1-0	F		Alcock C.W.	Thompson A.C.	Welch R.C.
15-Nov	Vincent Square	Westminster School	4-0	F		Thompson A.C.	Fitzstephens C.W.	Welch R.C.
22-Nov	Oval	Windsor Home Park	1-0	F		Alcock C.W.	Morton P.	Childs C.
25-Nov	Oval	Crystal Palace Club	1-0	F		Alcock C.W.	Hooman T.C.	Stephenson C.W.
28-Nov	Oval	Forest School	5-0 %	F		*Alcock C.W. 1*	Chenery C.J.	Elliot E.H.M.
02-Dec	Oval	Hampstead Heathens	2-0	F		Hooman T.C.	Lubbock E.	*Kennedy G.G. 1*
12-Dec	Oval	Harrow Chequers	4-0	F		*Alcock C.W. 2*	Morton P.	Elliot E.H.M
16-Dec	Clapham Common	Clapham Rovers	1-0	FAC2		Lubbock E.	Welch R.C.	Stephenson C.W.
16-Dec		Chiswick	0-1	F				
19-Dec	Oval	Cambridge University	2-1	F		*Alcock C.W. 1*	Welch R.C.	Rivett-Carnac P.T.
13-Jan	Oval	Hampstead Heathens	3-0	F		*Alcock C.W. 2*	Betts M.P.	Elliot E.H.M.
20-Jan	Clapham Common	Crystal Palace	0-0	FAC3		Alcock C.W.	Betts M.P.	Bonsor A.G.
20-Jan	Oval	Gitanos	0-2	F		Welch R.C.	Hunt W.F.	Barker G.
03-Feb		Crystal Palace	1-0 %	F				
10-Feb	Oval	First Surrey Rifles	1-2	F		Bonsor A.G.	*Wollaston 1*	
14-Feb	Oval	Civil Service	6-1 %	F		Alcock C.W.	*Bonsor A.G. 2*	Childs C.
17-Feb	Harrow	Harrow School	0-2	F		Alcock C.W.	Bowen E.E.	Gibbon J.H.
21-Feb	Vincent Square	Westminster School	3-0	F		*Alcock C.W. 1*	Beaufort L.P.	*Bonsor A.G. 1*
04-Mar	Oval	Queens Park	0-0	FACsf		Alcock C.W.	Thompson A.C.	Bonsor A.G.
09-Mar	Clapham Common	Clapham Rovers	1-1	F		Alcock C.W.	Thompson A.C.	Elliot E.H.M.
16-Mar	Oval	Royal Engineers	1-0	FACf	2,000	Alcock C.W.	Bowen E.E.	Bonsor A.G
20-Mar	Charterhouse	Charterhouse	1-1	F		Alcock C.W.	Barker G.R.	Bonsor A.G
11-Nov		Harrow Chequers	w/o	FAC1				

Notes

13th Nov v Cambridge University - 12 Peel C.W., 13 Rivett-Carnac P.T.

22nd Nov v Windsor Home Park - 12 Heath A.J. **

25th Nov v Crystal Palace - 12 Dodd C. **

17th Feb v Harrow School - 12 McLaren J.S.

21st Feb v Westminster School - 12 Wollaston C.F.

* emergancy

** absent

% scorer unknown

128

4	5	6	7	8	9	10	11
Stephenson C.W.	Betts M.P.	Crawford R.E.W	Hooman T.C.	Lawrence P.	Pelham Hon TH	Giffard J.H.	Morten A.
Huggins C.L.	Kirkpatrick J.	Lawrence P.	Stephenson C.W.	Stileman J.	Thompson A.		
Emanuel H.	*Huggins C.L.*	Morten A.	Thornton A.H.	Welch R.C.	Williams A.	Wood S.	Soden F.B.
Hooman T.C. 1	*Huggins C.L. 1*	Thornton A.H.	*Vidal R.W.S. 2*	Welch R.C.	Miller F. **	Kirkpatrick J. **	Stephenson C **
Douglas A.	*Huggins C.L. 1*	*Morton P. 1*	Rivett-Carnac P.T.	Reid C.F.	Thornton A.H.	Welch R.C.	
Kennedy G.G.	Stephenson CW	Hibbert C.G.	Roughton J.W.	Wilson F.H.	Wade C.H.	Reid C.F.	Thompson A.
Crake W.P.	Cruikshank J.A.	Currie F.A.	Elkington G.B.*	Maltby E.C.	Rivett-Carnac PT	Vidal R.W.S	Welch R.C.
Heath A.J.	*Ernest F. 1*	Thompson A.C.	Miller F.	Welch R.C.	Fitzmaurice Ld E	Pelham Hon TH	Huggins C.L.
Vidal R.W.S.	Bowen E.E.	Lubbock E.	Stephenson C.W.	Thompson A.C.	Dodd C.	Miller F.	Childs C.
Crawford F.H.	Kennedy G.G.	Crompton A.					
Morton P.	Lucas W.T.	Gosset G.	*Matthews H.L. 1*	Thompson H.M.	Thompson A.C.	Sarl C.	Radcliffe A.C.
Alcock C.W. 2	Betts M.P.	Giffard J.H.	*Kennedy G.G. 1*	Barker G.R.	*Pelham Hon T.H. 1*	Rivett-Car. PT	Miller F.
Jay H.A.	Welch R.C.	Rivett-Car. PT	*Kennedy G.G. 1*	Kirkpatrick J.	Barker G.R.	Crawford RE.**	Crawford FH.**
Grace W.G.	Barker G.F.	*Roughton JW.1*	Huggins C.L.	Jones A.M.	Wilton F.	Thornton A.H.	Bouch A.
Giffard J.H. 1	Barker G.R.	*Bonsor A.G. 1*	Thompson A.C.	Reid C.F.	Thornton A.H.	*Rivett-Car P.T. 1*	Welch R.C.
Reid C.F.	Elliot E.H.M.	Wilson F.H.	Crompton A.	*Barker G.R. 1*	Vidal H.D.S.	Beaufort L.P.	
Reid C.F.	Fitzjames J.	Welch R.C.	Rivett-Carnac P.T.	*Bonsor A.G. 2*	Giffard J.H.	Bowen E.E.	
Alcock C.W.	Betts M.P.	Bowen E.E.	Bonsor A.G.	Crake W.P.	Rivett-Carnac PT	Hooman TC	*Pelham TH 1*
Elliot E.H.M.	Thornton A.H.	Kennedy G.G.	Morton P.	Barker G.R.	*Huggins C.L. 1*	Thompson A.	Smith J.
Beaufort.L.P.	Welch R.C.	Stephenson CW	Hooman T.C.	Howard A.W.H.	*Dixon H.B. 1*	Denton C.A.	
Crake W.P.	Elliot E.H.M.	Hooman T.C.	Kennedy G.G.	Lubbock E.	Stephenson CW	Thompson A.C.	Thornton A.H.
Beaufort.L.P.	Crawford J.C.	Crompton A.	Huggins C.L.	Roughton J.W.	Wylde E.W.		
Crawford REW	Elliot E.H.M.	Emanuel H.	Reid C.F.	Thompson A.C.	Thompson C.M.	Welch R.C.	*Wollaston CH 2*
Elliot E.H.M.	Crawford REW	Vidal R.W.S.	Welch A.W.	Welch R.C.	Rawson W.S.	Wollaston C.F.	Woodhouse AL
Chenery C.J.	Crawford REW	Morten A.	Pelham Hon T.H.	Stephenson CW	*Thompson CW 1*	Welch R.C.	Wilson F.H.
Crawford REW	Pelham Hon TH	Welch R.C.	Wollaston C.F.	Emanuel H.	Stewart H.H.	Elliot E.H.M	Parry W.
Wotherspoon D	Gardner R.H.	Crake W.P.	Wollaston C.H.	Thompson A	Bonsor A.G.	Hooman T.C.	*Grace W.G. 1*
Betts M.P. 1	Hooman T.C.	Crake W.P.	Lubbock E.	Thompson A.C.	Welch R.C.	Wollaston C.H.	Vidal R.W.S
Betts M.P (GK)	*Dixon H.B. 1*	Kirkpatrick J.	Morten A.	Parry W.	Thompson A.C.	Vidal R.W.S	Welch R.C.

Table of Wanderers F.C. players to scorer three or more in a game

31/10/1874	R.K. Kingsford	v	Farningham	5
25/1/1871	C.W. Alcock	v	Civil Service	4
31/10/1874	C.H.R. Wollaston	v	Farningham	4
10/11/1877	H. Heron	v	Panthers	4
18/12/1883	E.H. Parry	v	Harrow School	4
15/3/1862	J.Pardoe	v	Crystal Palace	3
13/3/1869	C.E.B. Nepean	v	Upton Park	3
13/3/1869	A.F. Kinnaird	v	Upton Park	3
26/2/1870	A. Baker	v	Forest Club	3
9/11/1870	T.C. Hooman	v	Brixton Club	3
5/10/1872	C.H.R. Wollaston	v	Clapham Rovers	3
2/12/1873	C.H.R. Wollaston	v	Civil Service	3
4/11/1874	C.W. Alcock	v	Civil Service	3
21/11/1874	C.W. Alcock	v	Barnes	3
9/1/1875	J. Kenrick	v	Harrow Chequers	3
27/11/1875	F.B. Maddison	v	Cricklewood	3
15/11/1876	H. Wace	v	Gitanos	3

Date	Venue	Opponents	Res	Comp	Att	1	2	3
05-Oct	Oval	Clapham Rovers	4-0	F		*Alcock C.W. 1*	Barker R.	Welch R.C.
12-Oct	Oval	Surrey Club	1-0	F		Kirkpatrick J.	*Crake W.P. 1*	Elliot E.H.M.
19-Oct	Oval	Upton Park	4-1 %	F		Alcock C.W.	Barker R.	Borwick A.
22-Oct	Snaresbrook	Forest School	0-0	F		Alcock C.W.	Absolom C.A.	Borwick A.
29-Oct	Oval	Forest School	4-1	F		*Alcock C.W. 1*	Borwick A.	Clarke A.F.
06-Nov	Vincent Sq.	Westminster School	2-0	F		*Alcock C.W. 1*	Clarke A.F.	Gosset G.
09-Nov	Oval	Gitanos	1-1 %	F		Alcock C.W.	Hooman T.C.	Bowen E.E.
12-Nov	Eton	Eton College	0-0	F		Kinnaird A.F.	Alcock C.W.	Thompson A.C.
25-Nov	Parker's Piece	Cambridge University	0-2	F		Welch	Philpot	Cursham
30-Nov	Oval	Royal Engineers	0-2	F		Kinnaird A.F.	Sturgis J.R.	Bonsor A.G.
07-Dec	Harrow	Harrow School	1-4	F		*Betts M.P. 1*	Welch R.C.	Bowen E.E.
11-Dec	Charterhouse	Charterhouse School	1-0	F		Kingsford R.K.	*Clarke A.F. 1*	Thompson A.
16-Dec	Oval	Cambridge University	2-1	F		Welch R.C.	Kingsford R.K.	*Vidal R.W.S. 1*
17-Dec	Oval	Harrow School Vacation C.	2-2	F		Welch R.C.	*Bowen E.E. 1*	*Kingsford R.K. 1*
18-Dec	Oval	Crystal Palace	5-2 &	F		*Betts M.P. 1*	*Vidal R.W.S. 2*	Pelham Hon. T.H.
21-Dec	Oval	Harrow Chequers	4-4 %	F		Bonsor A.G.	Chenery C.J.	Beaufoy M.
23-Dec	Oval	Old Reptonians	3-1	F		Betts M.P.	*Kinnaird A.F. 2*	*Powell R.W. 1*
29-Jan	Oval	Uxbridge	2-1	F		Kinnaird A.F.	*Wollaston C.H. 1*	*Erskine Hon. A.M.S. 1*
01-Mar	Chatham	Royal Engineers	0-4	F		Kinnaird A.F.	Giffard J.H.	Kirkpatrick J.
05-Mar	Vincent Sq.	Westminster School	2-4	F		Kinnaird A.F.	Wilson F.H.	Sturgis J.R.
12-Mar	Lille Bridge	Gitanos	2-2 %	F		Kinnaird A.F.	Elliot E.H.M.	Stewart Rev. H.H.
22-Mar	Upton Park	Upton Park	1-1	F		Williams A.	Vidal H.D.S.	*Wollaston C.H. 1*
29-Mar	Lille Bridge	Oxford University	2-0	FACf	3,000	*Kinnaird A.F. 1*	Welch R.C.	Howell L.S.

Reserve Games

Date	Venue	Opponents	Results	Comp	Att	1	2	3
26-Oct	Woodford	Woodford Wells	0-0	F		Alcock C.W.	Clarke A.F.	Clarke B.

Notes

16th Dec v Cambridge University - 12 Macnaughten H.A.
18th Dec v Crystal Palace - 12 Brockbank J.

* Emergancy
% scorers unknown
& goal listed as a scrimmage

130

4	5	6	7	8	9	10	11
Morten A.	Lockhart CWE	Elliot E.H.M.	*Wollaston C.H. 3*	Hooman T.C.	Bailey L.	Thompson A	Dixon H.B.
Bailey L.	Barker R.	Howell F.B.	Erskine Hon. A.	Giffard J.H.	Rawson WS	Thornton A.H.	Lockhart C.W.E.
Clarke A.F.	Crake W.P.	Erskine Hon. A	Powell R.W.	Stewart Rev. H	Thornton AH	Welch R.C.	Wollaston C.H.
Clarke A.F.	Elliot E.H.M.	Sheffield H.	Howell F.B.	Heath A.J.	Kennedy G.G.	Welch R.C.	Wollaston C.H.
Erskine Hon. A	Heath A.J.	*Howell F.B. 1*	Elliot E.H.M.	*Emanuel H. 1*	Kennedy G.G.	*Kinnaird A.F. 1*	Welch R.C.
Chenery C.J.	Stewart Rev. H	Powell R.W.	Stephenson C.W.	Broadmead J.B.	*Wollaston C.H. 1*	Welch R.C.	Thompson A.C.
Crake W.P.	Kinnaird A.F.	Inglis J.F.	Wollaston C.H.	Powell R.W.	Thompson A.C.	Tatham S.R.	Welch A.C. ? R?
Welch R.C.	Stewart H.H.	Pelham Hon.TH	Seymour H.S.	Powell R.W.	Greenwood C.G.	Wilson F.H.	Howard R.M. *
Giffard J.H.	Wilson F.H.	Thompson A.C.	Elliot E.H.M.	Wollaston C.H.	Kingsford R.K.	Kennedy G.G.	
Marshall F.C.	Colbeck C.	Kingsford R.J.	Kingsford J.	Kennedy G.G.	Howell F.B.	Elliot E.H.M.	Leyland F.D.
Grey W.H.	Inglis J.F.	Kingsford J.H.	Kingsford F.	Williams E.	Hanson J.C.	Foster H.	Corrie A.W.
Bonsor A.G. 1	Elliot E.H.M.	Kirkpatrick J.	Thomas H.C.	Stewart Rev H	Clarke A.F.	Beaufoy R.	Powell C.
Greg E.H.	Beaufoy M.	Pelham Hon TH	Beaufoy R.	Giffard J.H.	Thompson A.	Colbeck C.	Hamilton W.A.B.
Welch R.C.	Mews J.	Woodhouse AL	Bowen E.E.	Hamilton WAB	Bonsor A.G.	Denton C.A.	*Colbeck C. 1*
Stewart Rev. H	Sturgis J.R.	Brockbank J.	Denton C.A.	Howard A.W.H.	Miles E.		
Brockbank J.	Kingsford RK	Clarke A.F.	Denton C.A.	Mortimer L.E.	Mews J.	Heath A.J.	Thompson A
Kingsford R.K.	Morten A.	Childs C.	Elliot E.H.M.	Gallus A.C.	Thompson A.C.	Thompson C.M.	
Brockbank J.	Barker R.	Philpot R.	Rawson W.S.	Brune J.	Heath A.J.	Elliot E.H.M.	Hippisley G.C. *
Gosset G. 1	Stewart Rev. H	Elliot E.H.M.	*Kenyon-Sla. WS.1*	Giffard J.H.	Jackson H.S. *?	?	?
Borwick A.	Greg E.H.	Kingsford R.G.	Gibney E.S.	Kingsford J.P.	*Gosset G. 1*	Childs C.	Sturgis J.R.
Elliot E.H.M.	Bailey L.	M'Keand J.P.	Gibney E.S.	Dury J.B.	Wylde E.W.		
Bowen E.E.	*Wollaston C 1*	Kingsford R.K.	Bonsor A.G.	Kenyon-Sla. WS	Thompson C.M.	Sturgis J.R.	Stewart Rev H

4	5	6	7	8	9	10	11
Bowyer G.H.	Wallace W.	Inglis J.F.	Elliott E.H.M.	Kennedy G.G.	Welch R.C.	Bailey L.	

Table of highest appearances season by season

1861/62	numerous	2	1862/63	C.W. Alcock	3
1863/64	C.W. Alcock	8	1864/65	C.W. Alcock	3
1865/66	C.W. Alcock	16	1866/67	C.W. Alcock	14
1867/68	C.W. Alcock	20	1868/69	C.W. Alcock	15
1869/70	C.W. Alcock	22	1870/71	C.W. Alcock	33
1871/72	C.W. Alcock	23	1872/73	E.H.M. Elliot	12
1873/74	C.W. Alcock	12	1874/75	C.W. Alcock	11
1875/76	W.D.O. Greig/ A.H. Stratford	15	1876/77	H. Wace	15
1877/78	A.H. Stratford	16	1878/79	C.A. Denton/ T.N. Tyndale	6
1879/80	C.A. Denton	10	1880/81	3 players	5

The Wanderers 1873/74

Date	Venue	Opponents	Res	Comp	Att	1	2	3
04-Oct	Oval	Clapham Rovers	0-1	F		Alcock C.W.	Wollaston C.H.	Barker R.
21-Oct	Snaresbrook	Forest School	2-2	F		*Alcock C.W. 1*	Clarke A.F.	Birley F.H.
28-Oct	Oval	Forest School	4-3	F		Alcock C.W.	Morten A.	Kirkpatrick J.
30-Oct	Oval	Royal Engineers	0-1	F		Way C.	Kirkpatrick J.	Willis C.
05-Nov	Vincent Square	Westminster School	3-1	F		Deacon H.F.	Chappell C.	*Morris S. 1*
12-Nov	Oval	Swifts	0-5	F		Morris S.	Thompson C.M.	Way C.
15-Nov	Oval	Gitanos	1-0 %	F		Alcock C.W.	Barker R.	Birley F.H.
26-Nov	Charterhouse	Charterhouse	1-4	F		Alcock C.W.	Emmanuel H.	Stewart H.H.
02-Dec	Lille Bridge	Civil Service	4-0	F		Bowen E.E.	Gibney E.S.	Crawford J.C.
06-Dec	Oval	Oxford University	1-1	FAC3		*Alcock C.W. 1*	Thompson A.C.	Wollaston C.H.
15-Dec	Oval	Cambridge University	2-1	F		Alcock C.W.	Chenery C.J.	*Kingsford R.K. 2*
16-Dec	Oval	Harrow School	2-3	F		Alcock C.W.	*Courtenay C.J. 1*	Vidal R.W.S.
01-Jan	Oval	Harrow Chequers	2-1	F		Alcock C.W.	Kirkpatrick J.	Otter R.S.
07-Jan	Slough	Swifts	1-5	F		*Alcock C.W. 1*	Welch R.C.	Welch A.W.
14-Jan	Oval	Uxbridge	2-1	F		Alcock C.W.	Welch A.W.	Birley F.H.
17-Jan	Upton Park	Upton Park	1-2	F		*Alcock C.W. 1*	Welch R.C.	Welch A.W.
17-Jan	Oval	Gitanos	0-1	F		Lubbock E.	Giffard J.F.	Howard A.W.H.
31-Jan	The Parks, Ox.	Oxford University	0-1	FAC3r		Welch R. de C.	Stratford A.H.	Tatham S.R.
04-Mar	Vincent Square	Westminster School	4-0	F		*Wollaston C.H. 1*	Birley F.H.	Giffard J.H.
?	Harrow ?	Harrow School	1-2	F		*Burn C.M.P. 1*		
		Southall	w/o	FAC1				
		Trojans	w/o	FAC2				

* substitutes
% scorers unknown

The Wanderers 1874/75

Date	Venue	Opponents	Res	Comp	Att	1	2	3
03-Oct	Oval	Clapham Rovers	5-0	F		Alcock C.W.	Kingsford R.K.	Stratford A.H.
21-Oct	Oval	Uxbridge	1-1 &	F		Alcock C.W.	Cambrian R.C.	Stratford A.H.
24-Oct	Oval	Royal Engineers	0-2	F		Alcock C.W.	Birley F.H.	Lubbock E.
31-Oct	Oval	Farningham	16-0	FAC1		*Alcock C.W. 2*	Birley F.H.	Green F.T.
04-Nov	Oval	Civil Service	7-0	F		*Alcock C.W. 3*	Benson R.H.	Birley F.H.
21-Nov	Oval	Barnes	5-0	FAC2		*Alcock C.W. 3*	Birley F.H.	Green F.T.
15-Dec	Oval	Harrow School	5-0 &	F		*Alcock C.W. 1*	*Heron H. 2*	Heron F.
09-Jan	Oval	Harrow Chequers	9-1	F		*Alcock C.W. 1*	*Barker R. 1*	*Wollaston C.H. 1*
19-Jan	Oval	Gitanos	1-1	F		Alcock C.W.	Kirkpatrick J.	Kenrick J.
30-Jan	Oval	Oxford University	1-2 &	FAC3		Alcock C.W.	Maddison F.B.	Kingsford R.K.
03-Feb	Oval	England Trial Team	2-1	F		*Alcock C.W. 1*	Robson G.A.	Maddison F.B.
18-Mar	Chatham	Royal Engineers	1-1 $%	F				
		Harrow School	0-2	F				

Notes
15th Dec v Harrow School - 12 Stratford A.H.

$ no report listed in football annual
% scorer unknown

4	5	6	7	8	9	10	11
Welch R.C.	Huggins C.L.	Kirkpatrick J.	Giffard J.H.	Street J.E.	Dann E.R.	Capper A.	Wilkes F.
Wollaston C. 1	Kirkpatrick J.	Wylde E.W.	Chenery C.J.	*	*	*	*
Borwick A.	*Brockbank J. 1*	Street F.E.	*Allport R.L. 2*	Delrichs A.E.	Thompson CM	*Chenery C.J. 1*	
Wollaston C.H.	Stewart H.H.	Thompson C.M.	Street F.E.	Bouch W.	Chenery C.J.	Kingsford R.K.	
Giffard J.H.	Fitzstephen W.C.	Kirkpatrick J.	Thompson C.M.	Way C.	*Wollaston C.2*	Giles R. *	Bolton G. *
Bouch W.	Oelrichs A.E.	Kirkpatrick J.	Allport R.L.				
Borwick A.	Colbeck C.	Howell F.B.	Otter H.S.	Welch R.C.	Bailey W.R.	Wollaston C.H.	
Gibney E.C.	*Borwick A. 1*	Burrows L.H.	Reeve C.A.	Curzon R.	Page W.R.	Tod A.H.	Lucas C.
Crawford F.F 1	Kennedy G.G.	Colbeck C.	Way C.	*Wollaston C.H. 3*	Huggins C.L.		
Lubbock E.	Otter S.	Barker R.	Welch R.C.	Howell L.S.	Kingsford R.K	Chenery C.J.	Crake W.P.
Kingsford F.	Kirkpatrick J.	Giffard J.H.	Vidal R.W.S.	Stewart Rev. H	Borwick A.	Lubbock E.	
Bevington H.S.	*Brockbank J. 1*	Giffard J.H.	Geaves R.L.	Gibney E.S.	Colbeck C.	Wollaston C.H.	
Emanuel H.	Brockbank J.	*Beaufoy M. 1*	Field E.A.	*Field W. 1*	Mortimer T.	Ker H.C.	Deacon H.F.
Deacon H.F.	Otter H.S.	Chamberlain P. *	Aldworth F. *	Owthwaite *	Wright H. *		
Kenrick J.	Beaufoy M.	Howard A.W.H.	Kingsford R.K.	*Dixon S. (Z?) 1*	Otter R.S.	Kingsford F.	Deacon H.F.
Erskine Hon. A.	Stair A.	Mortimer L.G.	Heath A.J.	Greig W.D.O.	Bowen E.E.	Stratford E.H.	Kennedy G.G.
Norman P.	Dixon H.B.	Kenyon-Slaney W	Deacon H.F.	Kirkpatrick J.	Courthope C.J.	Smith J.	
Alcock C.W.	Barker R.	Chenery C.J.	Crake W.P.	Kingsford R.K.	Otter H.S.	Shaughnessy W	Kinnaird A.F.
Chenery C.J.	Erskine Hon. A.	*Edwards J.H. 1*	*Kingsford R.K. 2*	Sturgis J.G.	Kirkpatrick J.	Deacon H.F.	Heron H.

4	5	6	7	8	9	10	11
Welch R.C.	Barker R.	*Wollaston C.H. 2*	*Heron H. 1*	Daun G.R.	Heron F.	Geaves R.L.	*Otter H.S. 2*
Giffard J.H.	Crake W.P.	Jay K.	Smith C.E.	Greig W.D.O.	Bevington H.S	Kirkpatrick J.	
Stratford A.H.	Kingsford R.K.	Chenery C.J.	Heron H.	Wollaston C.H.	Welch R.C.	Barker R.C.	Morten A.
Stratford A.H.	*Kingsford R.K. 5*	*Chenery C.J. 2*	Barker R.C.	*Wollaston C.H. 4*	*Kenrick J. 1*	*Heron H. 2*	Welch R.C.
Chenery C.J.	Courtenay R.	Green F.T.	*Greig W.D.O. 2*	Heron H.	*Kenrick J. 1*	*Stratford A.. 1*	
Maddison F.B.	Heron H.	*Kenrick J. 1*	Kingsford R.K.	Beauchamp H.W.	Stratford A.H.	Welch R.C.	*Wollaston C.H. 1*
Wollaston C.H.	Beauchamp H.W.	Maddison F.B.	Roberts S.	Sparham H.H.	*Kenrick J. 1*	Birley F.H.	Green F.T.
Birley F.H.	*Maddison F.B. 1*	Kinnaird A.F.	Stratford A.H.	*Heron H. 2*	Toynbee W.N.	Otter H.S.	*Kenrick J. 3*
Cambrian R.	Welch A.W.	Green F.T.	Heron H.	*Heron F. 1*	Podger A.	Stratford A.H.	Wylie J.G.
Barker R.	Kenrick J.	Heron H.	Wollaston C.H.	Birley F.H.	Green F.T.	Toynbee W.N.	Welch R.C.
Chenery C.J.	*Heron H. 1*	Wollaston C.H.	Green F.T.	Birley F.H.	Welch R.C.		

Wanderers' F.C. Secretary's 1859-1883

1859-1864	A.W. Mackenzie (Forest F.C.)
1864-1875	C.W. Alcock
1875-1879	J. Kenrick
1879-1883	C.H. Wollaston

133

Date	Venue	Opponents	Res	Comp	Att	1	2	3
02-Oct	Balham	Clapham Rovers	0-0	F		Alcock C.W.	Kenrick J.	Kirkpatrick R.
09-Oct	Hampden Park	Queens Park	0-5	F	12,000	Alcock C.W.	Geaves R.L.	Otter H.S.
23-Oct	Oval	1st Surrey Rifles	5-0	FAC1		*Alcock C.W. 1*	Gibney E.S.	Heron H.
03-Nov	Vincent Square	Westminster School	3-2	F		Heron H.,	Heron F.	Greig W.D.O.
13-Nov	Harrow	Harrow School	0-1	F		Alcock C.W.	Bevington H.S.	Bowen E.E.
17-Nov	Oval	Gitanos	4-0 &	F		*Alcock C.W. 1*	Lloyd F.	*Geaves R.S. 1*
20-Nov	The Parks, Oxford	Oxford University	1-3	F		Birley F.H	Stratford A.H.	Green F.T.
23-Nov	Malvern	Malvern College		F				
24-Nov	Oval	Aldershot Division	0-0	F		Alcock C.W.	Daun E.R.	Smith C.E.
27-Nov	Cricklewood	Cricklewood	7-0	F		*Kenrick J. 1*	*Green F.T. 1*	*Maddison F.B. 3*
11-Dec	Oval	Crystal Palace	3-0	FAC2		Alcock C.W.	Heron H.	*Heron F. 1*
14-Dec	Oval	Harrow School	2-2	F		Alcock C.W.	Bevington H.S.	Brockbank J.
20-Dec	Oval	Royal Engineers	0-0	F		Birley F.H.	Rawson W.S.	Greig W.D.O.
22-Dec	Oval	Swifts	2-2	F		Alcock C.W.	Bevington H.S.	Barlow F.P.
29-Jan	Oval	Sheffield Club	2-0	FAC3		Birley F.H.	Green F.T.	Stratford A.H.
05-Feb	Oval	Queens Park	2-0	F		Birley F.H.	Maddison F.B.	Rawson W.S.
26-Feb	Oval	Swifts	2-1	FACsf		*Birley F.H 1*	Green F.T.	Stratford A.H.
29-Feb	Vincent Square	Westminster School	0-1	F		Kenrick J.	Kinnaird A.F.	Green F.T.
11-Mar	Oval	Old Etonians	1-1	FACf	2,000	Greig W.D.O	Stratford A.H.	Lindsay W.
18-Mar	Oval	Old Etonians	3-0	FACf r	4,000 $	Greig W.D.O	Stratford A.H.	Lindsay W.
01-Apr		Royal Engineers	0-3 $$	F				
?		Harrow School	1-1 $$	F		*Giles A.B. 1*		

Notes

14th Dec v Harrow School - 12 Giffard J.H.

$ Sportsman states 1,500

$$ no reports listed in the Football Annual

** absent

& own goal

134

4	5	6	7	8	9	10	11
Armitage C.C.	Wollaston C.H.	Brockbank J.	Smith C.E.	Otter H.S.	Lindsay W.	Bouch W.	Kirkpatrick J.
Heron H.	Turner J.	Chambers H.W.	Stratford A.H.	Kinnaird A.F.	Rawson W.S.	Kenrick J.	Grieg W.D.O
Heron F.	*Kenrick J. 2*	*Maddison F.B. 2*	Wollaston C.H.	Birley F.H.	Green F.T.	Stratford A.H.	Grieg W.D.O
Smith C.E.	Stratford A.H.	*Barlow F.P. 1*	*Kinnaird A.F. 1*	Sturgis J.R.	Green F.T.	Beaufoy M.	*Giffard J.H. 1*
Colbeck E.C.	Daun E.R.	Gibney E.S.	Howell F.S.	James H.S.	Macan G.	Maddison F.B.	Marshall F.E.
Heron H.	Bevington H.S.	Kenrick J.	*Heron F. 1*	Green F.T.	Stratford A.H.	Kirkpatrick J.	Grieg W.D.O
Greig W.D.O.	Wollaston C.H.	Kenrick J.	Heron H.	*Denton C.A. 1*	Fort R.	Gibney E.S.	Miles E.
Beaufoy M.	Kenrick J.	Lloyd F.	Birley F.H.	Green F.T.	Kirkpatrick J.	Greig W.D.O.	Heron F. **
Gibney E.S. 1	*Lloyd F. 1*	Alington E.H.	Marshall E.F.	Greig W.D.O.	Bowen E.E.	Welch R.C.	
Wollaston C.H. 2	Birley F.H.	Green F.T.	Stratford A.H.	Lindsay W.	Maddison J.M.	Kenrick J.	Grieg W.D.O.
Heron H.	Otter H.S.	*Simpson F.D. 1*	Robinson G.	*Colbeck C. 1*	Bowen E.E.	Green F.T.	Stratford A.H.
Otter H.S.	Heron H.	Heron F.	Howard A.W.H.	Beaufoy M.	Lindsay W.	Denton C.A.	Stratford A.H.
Geaves R.L.	*Smith C.E. 2*	Otter H.S.	Simpson F.D.	Foa E.C.	Stratford A.H.		
Lindsay W.	Maddison F.B.	*Heron F. 2*	Kenrick J.	Hughes T.B.	Heron H.	Wollaston C.H.	Grieg W.D.O.
Stratford A.H	Greig W.D.O	Metcalfe C.H.T	Otter H.S.	Heron F.	*Kenrick J. 1*	Heron H.	*Wollaston C.H. 1*
Lindsay W.	Heron H.	Hughes T.B.	Heron F.	*Wollaston C.H. 1*	Kenrick J.	Maddison F.B.	Grieg W.D.O.
Stratford A.H	Lindsay W.	Maddison F.B.	Greig W.D.O.	Bevington H.S.	Cloete W.B.	Wylde E.W.	Hughes T.B.
Maddison F.B.	Birley F.H.	Wollaston C.H.	Heron H.	Heron F.	*Edwards J.H. 1*	Kenrick J.	Hughes T.B.
Maddison F.B.	Birley F.H.	*Wollaston C.H. 1*	Heron H.	Heron F.	Edwards J.H.	Kenrick J.	*Hughes T.B. 2*

Wanderers F.C. highest scoring victories

1874/75	Wanderers	v	Farningham	16-0
1876/77	Wanderers	v	South Norwood	9-0
1877/78	Wanderers	v	High Wycombe	9-0
1874/75	Wanderers	v	Harrow Chequers	9-1
1877/78	Wanderers	v	Panthers	9-1
1877/78	Wanderers	v	1st Surrey Rifles	9-1
1868/69	Wanderers	v	Upton Park	8-0

Date	Venue	Opponents	Res	Comp	Att	1	2	3
18-Oct	Oval	Barnes	0-1	F		Kenrick J.	Morton P.	Kirkpatrick J.
21-Oct	Oval	Royal Engineers	3-0 £	F		Birley F.H.	Maddison F.B.	Lindsay W.
25-Oct	Vincent Square	Westminster School	2-0	F		Kirkpatrick J.	*Smith C.E. 1*	Kinnaird A.F.
01-Nov	Oval	Civil Service\	7-0	F		Birley F.H.	West F.	*Kenrick J. 1*
04-Nov	Oval	Queens Park	0-6	F		Birley F.H.	Maddison F.B.	Rawson W.S.
15-Nov	Oval	Gitanos	5-1	F		Betts M.P.	Green F.T.	Stratford A.H.
18-Nov	The Parks, Ox.	Oxford University	0-1	F				
21-Nov	Oval	Forest School	3-0	F		Morton P.	Green F.T.	*Fox C.J. 2*
25-Nov	Plaistow	Upton Park	0-0	F		Greig W.D.O.	Wollaston C.H.	Buchanan W.S.
25-Nov	Harrow	Harrow School	2-3	F		Betts M.P.	Bowen E.E.	Colbeck C.
09-Dec	Camberwell	1st Surrey Rifles	4-0 %	F		Birley F.H.	Haigh-Brown W.W.	Jackson H.S.
13-Dec	Oval	Oxford University	0-1	F		Birley F.H.	Green F.T.	Stratford A.H.
15-Dec	Oval	Cambridge University	2-0	F		Birley F.H.	Green F.T.	Fox C.J.
16-Dec	Southall	Southall	6-0 $%	FAC2		Birley F.H.	Green F.T.	Lindsay W.
18-Dec	Oval	Old Bradfieldians	0-1	F				
19-Dec	Oval	Harrow School	5-0 ?	F		*Betts M.P. 2*	Jarrett B.G.	*Alington E.H. 1*
23-Dec	Norwood	South Norwood	2-0 %	F		Maddison F.B.	Welch H.V.	Welch C.
06-Jan	Slough	Swifts	3-1 %	F				
13-Jan	Lille Bridge	Old Wykemists	3-2 %	F				
20-Jan	Oval	Pilgrims	3-0 £	FAC3		*Wollaston C.H. 1*	Heron H.	Wace H.
27-Jan	Oval	Old Harrovians	2-6 %	F				
03-Feb	Streatham	Clapham Rovers	3-1	F		Kirkpatrick J.	Lindsay W.	Jackson H.S.
03-Feb	Harrow	Harrow School	2-1 %	F				
08-Feb	Camberwell	Upton Park	0-1	F		Maddison F.B.	Stratford A.H.	Kinnaird A.F.
10-Feb	Chatham	Royal Engineers	0-1	F		Lindsay W.	Green F.T.	Stratford A.H.
17-Feb	Norwood	South Norwood	9-0 %	F				
21-Feb	Vincent Square	Westminster School	1-0 ??	F		*Kinnaird A.F. 1*	Kenrick C.	Sparkes C.
07-Mar	Barnes	Barnes	1-0 %	F				
10-Mar	Camberwell	1st Surrey Rifles	2-0 %	F				
17-Mar	Upton Park	S.R. Bastard's Team	4-1 %	F				
20-Mar	Oval	Cambridge University	1-0	FACsf		Birley F.H.	Green F.T.	Lindsay W.
24-Mar	Oval	Oxford University	2-1 aet	FACf	3,000	Birley F.H.	Green F.T.	Hughes T.B.
?	?	Saffron Walden	w/o	FAC1				
?	?	Bye		FAC4				

$ Three results printed in different books 6-1/5-0/6-0 - sportsman says 6-0 (one goal disputed)

£ goal described as a rush/scrimmage

% scorers unknown

? The Sportsman states Maddison scored yet he is not included in the team line up

?? Team differs in various publications

136

4	5	6	7	8	9	10	11
Barlow F.T.	Courtney R.	Richmond W.F.	Denton C.A.	Smith C.E.	Greig W.D.O.	Heron H.	Wace H.
Haygarth E.B.	*Wollaston C.H. 1*	Heron H.	Smith C.E.	*Wace H. 1*	Green F.T.	Barker R.	Greig W.D.O.
Greig W.D.O.	Maddison F.B.	Richmond W.F.	Stanley A.J.	*Betts M.P. 1*	Courtney R.	Green F.T.	Haygarth E.B.
Wace H. 2	*Smith C.E. 2*	Stanley A.J.	*Heron H. 1*	*Buchanan W.S. 1*	Chenery C.J.	Lawford H.F.	Hudson H.A.
Haygarth E.B.	Greig W.D.O.	Kenrick J.	Otter H.S.	Heron H.	Wollaston C.H.	Smith C.E.	Wace H.
Kenrick J. 1	Smith C.E.	*Wace H. 3*	Spilman J.	Beaufoy M.	*Kirkpatrick J. 1*		
Stratford A.H.	Rawson F.L.	Jackson H.S.	Lloyd F.	Beaufoy M.	Stanley A.J.	*Chenery C.J. 1*	
Wace H.	Kenrick J.	Morice C.J.	Jackson H.S.	Birley F.H.	Haygarth E.B.		
Kinnaird A.F.	Longman C.J.	Maddison F.B.	Marshall F.E.	*Paton W.B. 2*	Rivett-Carnac L.W.	Welch R.C.	Hodgson C.H.
Stratford A.H.	Kinnaird A.F.	Wollaston C.H.	Heron H.	Maddison F.B.	Kenrick J.	Wace H.	Smith C.E.
Lindsay W.	Kinnaird A.F.	West H.B.	Kenrick J.	Smith C.E.	Rawson F.L.	Alington E.H.	Wace H.
Stratford A.H.	Betts M.P.	Vidal R.W.S.	*Parry E.H. 1*	*Otter H.S. 1*	Hills A.F.	Wace H.	Alington E.H.
Stratford A.H.	Kinnaird A.F.	Wollaston C.H.	Heron H.	Wace H.	Smith C.E.	Kenrick J.	Maddison F.B.
Webbe A.J.	Hargreaves W.Y.	Hills A.F.	Bowen E.E.	Kinnaird A.F.	Chenery C.J.	*Heron H. 1*	Webb P.G.
Jarrett B.G.	Jackson H.S.	Barker R.	*Smith C.E. 1*	Colbeck C.	Other A.N.		
Smith C.E.	Hughes T.B.	Heron F.	Green F.T.	*Maddison F.B. 1*	Stratford A.H.	Kinnaird A.F.	
Kinnaird A.F.	Maddison J.B.	*Wollaston C.H. 2*	Kenrick J.	*Wace H. 1*	Heygate L.	Denton C.A.	Govett F.L.
Green F.T.	Wylie J.G.	Daly J.	Foa E.C.	Maynard W.J.	Allport R.L.	Macan G.	Fox C.J.
Weldon J.	Betts M.P.	Kinnaird A.F.	Wace H.	Wollaston C.H.	Heron H.	Barker R.	Kenrick J.
Heron H.	Field E.	Maddison F.B.	Betts M.P.	Jackson H.S.	Stafford C.	Chenery C.J.	Other A.N.
Stratford A.H.	Kinnaird A.F.	Wollaston C.H.	*Heron H. 1*	Wace H.	Hughes T.B.	Denton C.A.	Kenrick J.
Kenrick J. 1	Wollaston C.H.R.	Stratford A.H.	*Lindsay W. 1*	Denton C.A.	Heron H.	Wace H.	Kinnaird A.F.

Wanderers F.C. highest scoring defeats

1879/80	Wanderers	v	Clapham Rovers	2-8
1876/77	Wanderers	v	Queens Park	0-6
1878/79	Wanderers	v	Old Etonians	2-7
1875/76	Wanderers	v	Queens Park	0-5
1873/74	Wanderers	v	Swifts	0-5
1870/71	Wanderers	v	Hampstead Heathens	0-5
1868/69	Wanderers	v	Hampstead Heathens	0-5
1876/77	Wanderers	v	Old Harrovians	2-6
1878/79	Wanderers	v	Clapham Rovers	1-5
1873/74	Wanderers	v	Swifts	1-5

The Wanderers 1877/78

Date	Venue	Opponents	Res	Comp	Att	1	2	3
06-Oct	Oval	Old Harrovians	1-2	F		Kenrick J.	Heron F.	*Wace H. 1*
13-Oct	Oval	Clapham Rovers	1-3	F		*Wollaston C.H. 1*	Wylie J.G.	Denton C.A.
20-Oct	Oval	Runnymede	7-0	F		*Wollaston C.H. 2*	*Denton C.A. 2*	Brockbank J.
03-Nov	Oval	Royal Engineers	4-0	F		Kirkpatrick J.	Haygarth E.B.	Stratford A.H.
10-Nov	Sandhurst	Panthers	9-1	FAC1		*Heron H. 4*	Wollaston C.H.	Kirkpatrick J.
21-Nov	Vincent Sq.	Westminster School	1-0	F		Kinnaird A.F.	Stratford A.H.	Dun O.L.
08-Dec	Oval	Old Wykehamists		F				
15-Dec	Wycombe	High Wycombe	9-0 &	FAC2		*Kinnaird A.F. 1*	Green F.T.	Stratford A.H.
18-Dec	Oval	Harrow School	3-1	F		Kinnaird A.F.	Page W.R.	Short E.M.
05-Jan	Snaresbrook	Old Foresters	0-0	F		Kinnaird A.F.	Heron F.	Stratford A.H.
12-Jan	Oval	Barnes	1-1	FAC3		Wollaston C.H.	Heron H.	Wace H.
26-Jan	Oval	Barnes	4-1	FAC3r		*Wollaston C.H. 1*	Heron H.	Kenrick J.
02-Feb	Streatham	Clapham Rovers		F				
09-Feb	Oval	Runnymede		F				
13-Feb	Vincent Sq.	Westminster School	5-2	F		Kinnaird A.F.	Green F.T.	Jackson H.S.
16-Feb	Oval	Sheffield	3-0	FAC4		Wollaston C.H.	*Wylie J.G. 1*	*Wace H. 1*
02-Mar		Clapham Rovers	5-1 %	F				
09-Mar	Camberwell	First Surrey Rifles	9-1 %	F		Kinnaird A.F.	Green F.T.	Stratford A.H.
23-Mar	Oval	Royal Engineers	3-1	FACf	5,000 $	Kirkpatrick J.	Stratford A.H.	Lindsay W.
13-Apr	Oval	Vale of Leven	1-3	F	2,000	Kinnaird A.F.	Bailey N.C.	Lindsay W.
?	Harrow ?	Harrow School	2-2	F		*Colbeck C. 1*	*Prior H.T. 1*	
?	?	Bye		FACsf				

$ Sportsman gives it as 3,000
% scorers unknown
& own goal

5 games were played and the results are unknown - 4 were won and 1 drawn

The Wanderers 1878/79

Date	Venue	Opponents	Res	Comp	Att	1	2	3
05-Oct	Oval	Old Harrovians	2-3	F		*Wollaston C.H. 1*	Wylie M.	*Kinnaird A.F. 1*
12-Oct	Oval	Clapham Rovers	1-5	F		Wollaston C.H.	*Cuppage W.A. 1*	Wylie M.
19-Oct	Snaresbrook	Old Foresters	1-1 %	F				
04-Nov	Oval	Clapham Rovers	2-2 %	F	4,000	Wollaston C.H.	Maynard W.J.	Tyndale T.N.
09-Nov	Oval	Old Etonians	2-7 £	FAC1		Wollaston C.H.	Maynard W.J.	Wace H.
16-Nov	Barnes	Barnes	5-0 %	F		Wollaston C.H.	Kenrick J.	Heygate
pre 21 nov	Harrow	Harrow School	2-4 %	F		Welch R.C.	Bowen E.E.	Colbeck C.
20-Nov	Vincent Sq.	Westminster School	1-1	F		*Kenrick J. 1*	Denton C.A.	Tyndale T.N.
30-Nov	Oxford	Oxford University	1-1 %	F				
14-Dec	Oval	Hertfordshire Rang.		F				

Notes
12th Oct v Clapham Rovers - 12 Stratford A.H.
4th Nov v Clapham Rovers - 12 Reffey D.J.

*
Emergency
% scorers unknown
£ goal given as a scrimmage

138

4	5	6	7	8	9	10	11
Brockbank J.	Baker E.E.	Howell L.J.	Jackson H.S.	Wylie W.J.	Haygarth E.B.	Stratford A.H.	Baker C.E.
Wace H.	Armstrong E.	Govett F.A.	Heron F.	Foa E.C.	Haygarth E.B.	Stratford A.H.	Jackson H.S.
Wylie J.G. 2	*Cuppage W.A. 1*	Wace H.	Abernethy H.W.	Mead R.	Haygarth E.B.	Stratford A.H.	Jackson H.S.
Kinnaird A.F.	Green F.T.	*Wace H. 2*	*Wylie J.G. 1*	Wollaston C.H.	Rawson F.L.	*Denton C.A. 1*	Kenrick J.
Stratford A.H.	Tatham S.R.	Green F.T.	Kinnaird A.F.	*Wylie J.G. 2*	*Wace H. 2*	*Kenrick J. 1*	Denton C.A.
Jackson H.S.	Heron F.	Sparks F.J	Kenrick J.	Rawson F.L.	Denton C.A.	Pitchford E.	*Stanley A.J. 1*
Haygarth E.B.	Kirkpatrick J.	*Wollaston C.H. 2*	Heron H.	*Wylie J.G. 2*	*Wace H. 2*	Kenrick J.	*Denton C.A. 1*
Benson R.H.	*Wylie J.G. 1*	*Denton C.A. 1*	Colbeck C.	Green F.T.	*Stratford A.H. 1*	Smith G.M.	
Haygarth E.B.	Wollaston C.H.	Heron H.	Baker E.E	Kenrick J.	Inglis F.J.	Widnell A.	
Benson R.H.	Kenrick J.	*Denton C.A. 1*	Kirkpatrick J.	Stratford A.H.	Haygarth E.B.	Lindsay W.	Green F.T.
Denton C.A.	*Wylie J.G. 1*	Wace H.	*Kinnaird A.F. 1*	*Green F.T. 1*	Lindsay W.	Stratford A.H.	Kirkpatrick J.
Kirkpatrick J.	*Tyndale T. 1*	Stratford A.H.	*Wace H. 1*	Short E.M.	*Kenrick J. 2*	*Denton C.A. 1*	Heron F.
Heron H.	Kenrick J.	*Denton C.A. 1*	Kinnaird A.F.	Green F.T.	Lindsay W.	Stratford A.H.	Kirkpatrick J.
Kenrick J.	Wace H.	Wylie J.G.	Barker R.	Denton C.A.	Baker E.E.	Wollaston C.H.	
Kinnaird A.F. 1	Green F.T.	Wollaston C.H.	Heron H.	Wylie J.G.	Wace H.	Denton C.A.	*Kenrick J. 2*
Stratford A.H.	*Wollaston C.H. 1*	Otter H.S.	Denton C.A.	Kenrick J.	Wace H.	Wylie J.G.	Jackson H.S.

4	5	6	7	8	9	10	11
Foa E.C.	Stratford A.H.	Denton C.A.	Tyndale T.N.	Wylie J.G.	Shearman M.	Vardon P.J.	
Tyndale T.N.	Denton C.A.	Wylie J.G.	Wace H.	Smith K.	Maynard W.F.	Maddison F.F.	Foa E.C.
Wace H.	Wylie J.G.	Denton C.A.	Kenrick J.	Maddison F.B.	Green F.T.	Lindsay W.	Stratford A.H.
Wylie J.G.	*Kenrick J. 1*	Tyndale T.N.	Green F.T.	Haygarth E.B.	Lindsay W.	Stratford A.H.	Denton C.A.
Tyndale T.N.	Oldfield	Denton C.A.	Maynard W.F.	Fox	Maddison F.F.	Mason	
Welch A.W.	Hodgson C.H.	Hotham F.W.	Branson J.C.E.	Law Rev W.	Marshall F.E.	Easton E.G. *	Ewing C.L.O. *
Maynard W.F.	Heygate	Newman E.H.A.	Kinnaird A.F.	Stanley A.J.	Stratford A.H.	Hotham F.W.	Hill G.R.

Most Appearances in the F.A. Cup final

A.F. Kinnaird	Wanderers & Old Etonians	9
R. Keane	Manchester United	7

The Wanderers 1879/80

Date	Venue	Opponents	Res	Comp	Att	1	2	3
11-Oct	Oval	Clapham Rovers	2-8 %	F		Stratford A.H.	Kennedy A.	Stratford F.W.
18-Oct	Oval	Old Foresters	2-2 %	F	100	*Wollaston C.H. 1*	Denton C.A.	Hughes T.B.
25-Oct	Cambridge	Cambridge Univ		F				
01-Nov	Oval	Barnes	4-0 %	F		Wollaston C.H.	Stratford A.H.	Kennedy A.G.
08-Nov	Chatham	Royal Engineers	1-2 %	F		Wollaston C.H.	Wylie J.G.	Tyndale T.N.
15-Nov	Bat & Ball Grd.	Rochester	6-0 %	FAC1		Hammond C.E.	Kennedy A.G.	Stratford A.H.
19-Nov	Vincent Square	Westminster School	1-0	F		Denton C.A.	Stanley A.J.	Rawson L.F.
22-Nov	Oval	Old Carthusians		F				
29-Nov	The Parks, Ox.	Oxford University	1-2	F		Wollaston C.H.	Kennedy A.G.	Vincent J.E.
16-Dec	Oval	Harrow School		F				
27-Dec	Upton Park	Upton Park	4-5 %	F				
03-Jan	Oval	Old Harrovians	4-3	F		*Denton C.A. 2*	Hughes T.B.	*Lyttleton Hon. A. 1*
10-Jan	Oval	Old Carthusians	1-0	FAC2		Rawson W.S.	Stratford F.W.	Stratford A.H.
17-Jan	Barnes	Barnes		F				
24-Jan	Oval	Old Etonians	1-3	FAC3		Hammond C.E.	Stratford A.H.	Kennedy A.G.
31-Jan	Wandsworth	Clapham Rovers		F				
12-Feb	Vincent Square	Westminster School	1-0	F		*Denton C.A. 1*	Bastard S.R.	Sparks F.J.
21-Feb	Oval	Royal Engineers	0-0	F				
28-Feb	Upton Park	Upton Park	0-3	F				
13-Mar	Snaresbrook	Forest School	0-0	F				

Notes
1st Nov v Barnes - 12 Denton C.A.
% scorer unknown

The Wanderers 1880/81

Date	Venue	Opponents	Res	Comp	Att	1	2	3
02-Oct	Oval	Old Harrovians	6-2	F		Kennedy A.G.	Hotham F.W.	Stratford F.W.
09-Oct	Oval	Clapham Rovers	0-4	F		Wollaston C.H.	Stratford F.W.	Tepper C.W.R.
16-Oct	Oval	Old Foresters	3-1	F	200	Wollaston C.H.	Stratford F.W.	*King R.B. 1*
23-Oct	Oval	Upton Park	0-2	F		Wollaston C.H.	Hughes C.	Tyndale T.N.
06-Nov	Chatham	Royal Engineers		F				
13-Nov		Rangers F.C., Lond.	w/d	FAC1				
17-Nov	Vincent Square	Westminster School	0-1	F		Crowdy C.W. *	Foley C.W.	Whitehead C.W.
20-Nov	Harrow ?	Harrow School	0-4	F		Bowen E.E.	Brougham H.	Colbeck C.
13-Dec	Oval	Oxford University	3-2	F		Warner C.	Kennedy A.G.	Hotham F.W.
14-Dec	Oval	Harrow School	2-1 &	F		Bowen E.E.	Sandwith W.F.	Hotham F.W.
12-Feb	Vincent Square ?	Westminster School	0-1	F				

Notes
9th Oct v Clapham Rovers - 12 Brown H.F.
* Emergancy Sub
& own goal

The Wanderers 1881/82

Date	Venue	Opponents	Res	Comp	Att	1	2	3
?	?	Harrow School	2-1 %	F				
		St Bartholomews H	w/d	FAC1				

% scorers unknown

The Wanderers 1882/83

Date	Venue	Opponents	Res	Comp	Att	1	2	3
19-Dec	Oval	Harrow School	1-1	F		Betts M.P.	Eyre D.	Humphrey E.J.

The Wanderers 1883/84

Date	Venue	Opponents	Res	Comp	Att	1	2	3
18-Dec	Oval	Harrow School	6-1	F		Rawlinson J.F.P.	Bowen E.E.	Nickisson J.L.

4	5	6	7	8	9	10	11
King	*Wollaston C.H. 1*	Denton C.A.	Barker R.	Roffey D.B.	Wylie M.	Foa E.C.	Denny G.W.
Maynard W	Tyndale T.N.	Benbow H.C.	Brooks R.	King	Stratford F.W.	Stratford A.H.	Kennedy A.A.
Stratford F	King R.B.	Wylie J.G.	Maynard W.J.	Tyndale T.N.	Barker R.	Roffey S.R.	Hughes T.B.
Roffey D.B.	Maynard W.J.	Hemsley A.M.	Denton C.A.	Stratford F.W.	King B.B.	Lindsay W.	Kennedy A.S.
Maddison F	Hughes T.B.	Wollaston C.H	Wace H.	Wylie J.G.	Tyndale T.N.	Stratford F.W.	Denton C.A.
Hughes F.J.	Tyndale T.N.	Maynard W.J.	Wylie D.J.	*Hemsley A.N. 1*	Brockbank J.	Stratford A.H.	Denton E.B.
Stratford F	Savory J.H.	Gillett H.	Wace H.	Wylie J.G.	Denton C.A.	Stanley A.J.	*Bartholomew A. 1*
Tyndale T 1	Garnet-Clarke H.	Maddison T.B.	Stratford F.W.	Stratford A.H.	Kennedy A.G.	Jackson H.S.	
Kennedy AS	Hammond C.E.	Wollaston C.H.	Denton C.A.	Hughes T.B.	Tyndale T.N.	*Wace H. 1*	Wylie M.
Lindsay W.	Stratford F.W.	Wollaston C.H.	Tyndale T.N.	Hughes T.B.	*Wace H. 1*	Denton C.A.	Roffey D.B.
Janson F.W.	Bayliss C.G.	King R.B.	Mortlock C.	Stratford F.W.	Abernethy H.W.	Stratford A.H.	Barnett F.

4	5	6	7	8	9	10	11
Tepher CW	*Benbow H.C. 2*	*Barker R. 1*	*Hughes T.B. 2*	Wollaston C.H.	Wild E.J.	*Hughes C. 1*	Janson F.W.
Stratford A	Kennedy A.G.	Hughes T.B.	Hughes C.	Benbow H.C.	Morice W.S.	Jansen F.	Tyndale T.N.
Stratford A	Hotham F.W.	Wace H.	*Sparks F.W. 2*	Janson F.W.	Tyndale T.N.	Wild W.	Mortlock C.
Morcie W.S.	Hughes T.B.	Wace H.	King R.B.	Whitehead H.C.	Kennedy A.G.	Stratford A.H.	Stratford F.W.
Janson F.W.	Sandwith W.F.	Webb P.G.L.	Mortlock C.	Maynard W.J.	Barry F.	Stratford A.H.	
Hughes T.B.	Hargreaves F	Janson F.W.	Morice W.S.	Field Rev. T.	Spiro D.G.	Prentice G.F.	
Fletcher C	Stratford F.W.	Hughes T.B.	Bastard S.R.	Brougham H.	*Stanley A.J. 1*	*Lloyd-Jones C 2*	Anderson W.J.
Vidal A.	Maynard W.J.	Des-Graz C.	Colbeck C.	Davidson A.H.	*Morton P.H. 1*	Phillips J.H.	Lawson W.E.

4	5	6	7	8	9	10	11

4	5	6	7	8	9	10	11
Anderson W	*Parry E.H. 1*	Hughes T.B.	Holden-White C.	Kinnaird A.F.	Foley C.W.	Bowen E.E.	Hotham F.W.

4	5	6	7	8	9	10	11
Whitfield H.	*Parry E.H. 4*	Bain F.W.	Colbeck C.	*Holden-White C. 1*	*Sandwith W.F.G. 1*	Kinnaird A.F.	Fletcher C.

141

England Full Internationals

This list only contains players who listed Wanderers as their primary club.

30th November 1872 – Scotland 0 England 0

England – R.C. Welch

8th March 1873 – England 4 Scotland 2

England – L.S. Howell, A.G. Bonsor (1 goal), W.S. Kenyon-Slaney (2 goals)

Scotland – A.F. Kinnaird

7th March 1874 – Scotland 2 England 1

England – A.H. Stratford, C.H. Wollaston, R.K. Kingsford (1 goal)

6th March 1875 – England 2 Scotland 2

England – F.H. Birley, C.H. Wollaston (1 goal), C.W. Alcock (1 goal), A.G. Bonsor, H. Heron

4th March 1876 – Scotland 3 England 0

England – F.T. Green, H. Heron, F. Heron

3rd March 1877 – England 1 Scotland 3

England – W. Lindsay, C.H. Wollaston

2nd March 1878 – Scotland 7 England 2

England – H. Wace, J.G. Wylie (1 goal), H. Heron

18th January 1879 – England 2 Wales 1

England – H. Wace

5th April 1879 – England 5 Scotland 4

England – H. Wace

13th March 1880 – Scotland 5 England 4

England – C.H. Wollaston

Pseudo-Internationals

Note the players listed appeared for the Wanderers Football Club during the season in question. Wanderers F.C., was not always their primary club.

5th Mar 1870 – England 0 Scotland 0

England – C.W.Alcock, E.E. Bowen, A.Baker, W.P. Crake, E. Freeth, E. Lubbock, A.Nash, J.C. Smith, A.H. Thornton, R.W.S. Vidal

Scotland – J. Kirkpatrick, A.F. Kinnaird, A. Morten

19th Nov 1870 - England 1 Scotland 0

England – C.W. Alcock, A.J. Baker, W.P. Crake, T.C. Hooman, E. Lubbock, R.W.S. Vidal, R.S.F. Walker

Scotland – J. Kirkpatrick, A.F. Kinnaird, C.E.B. Nepean, Q. Hogg, G.G. Kennedy

25th Feb 1871 - England 1 Scotland 1

England – C.W. Alcock, A.J. Baker, M.P. Betts, W.P. Crake, T.C. Hooman, E. Lubbock, C.W. Stephenson, R.W.S. Vidal, R.S.F. Walker

Scotland – A.F. Kinnaird, W.H. Gladstone, Q. Hogg, J. Kirkpatrick, C.E.B. Nepean

18th Nov 1871 - England 2 Scotland 1

England – C.W. Alcock, M.P. Betts, E. Lubbock, C.W. Stephenson, A.C. Thompson, R.W.S. Vidal, W.P. Crake

Scotland – R.E.W. Crawford, F.H. Crawford, J. Kirkpatrick, E. Elliot

24th Feb 1872 - England 1 Scotland 0

England – C.W. Alcock, A.G. Bonsor, C.J. Chenery, E. Lubbock, T.C. Hooman, C.W. Stephenson, A.C. Thompson, R.W.S. Vidal, C.H. Wollaston

Scotland – R.E.W. Crawford, E. Elliot, F.H. Crawford, Rev. H.H. Stewart, C. Thompson

Wanderers all time season by season record

Season	P	W	D	L	F	A
1861/62	2	2	0	0	4	0
1862/63 1	3	3	0	0	4	1
1863/64	11	8	3	0	27	2
1864/65 2	4	4	0	0	5	0
1865/66	16	11	4	1	31	10
1866/67 3	15	6	4	5	12	8
1867/68 4	28	9	8	11	26	27
1868/69 5	30	12	8	10	45	35
1869/70 6	33	14	7	12	47	31
1870/71	36	21	9	6	57	21
1871/72	32	18	8	6	50	16
1872/73	23	11	7	5	43	33
1873/74	20	8	2	10	31	35
1874/75	13	7	3	3	54	13
1875/76	21	9	7	5	38	22
1876/77	32	22	1	9	77	29
1877/78 7	23	16	4	3	82	26
1878/79	9	1	4	4	17	24
1879/80	15	6	3	6	28	28
1880/81	9	4	0	5	14	18
1881/82	1	1	0	0	2	1
1882/83	1	0	1	0	1	1
1883/84	1	1	0	0	6	1
Total	378	194	83	101	701	382

Notes
1 One game v Crystal Palace is unaccounted for
2 No games reported on after November
3 One game v CCC is unaccounted for
4 also scored two touchdowns and conceded seven
5 also scored one touchdown
6 also scored six touchdowns and conceded two
7 Five games included which no reports have been found

Grey highlighted seasons, indicate Wanderers won the F.A. Cup

Bibliography

Books

Alcock, C.W.	The Association Game	George Bell & Sons	1890
Alcock, C.W.	Football Annual 1868	John Lillywhite	1868
Alcock, C.W.	Football Annual 1869	Sportsman	1869
Alcock, C.W.	Football Annual 1870	Sportsman	1870
Alcock, C.W.	Football Annual 1871	Virtue & Co.	1871
Alcock, C.W.	Football Annual 1872	Virtue & Co.	1872
Alcock, C.W.	Football Annual 1873	Virtue & Co.	1873
Alcock, C.W.	Football Annual 1874	Virtue & Co.	1874
Alcock, C.W.	Football Annual 1875	Virtue & Co.	1875
Alcock, C.W.	Football Annual 1876	Ward, Lock & Tyler	1876
Alcock, C.W.	Football Annual 1877	Ward, Lock & Co.	1877
Alcock, C.W.	Football Annual 1878	The Cricket Press	1878
Alcock, C.W.	Football Annual 1879	The Cricket Press	1879
Alcock, C.W.	Football Annual 1880	The Cricket Press	1880
Alcock, C.W.	Football Annual 1881	The Cricket Press	1881
Alcock, C.W.	Football Annual 1882	The Cricket Press	1882
Alcock, C.W.	Football Annual 1883	The Cricket Press	1883
Alcock, C.W.	Football Annual 1884	Wright & Co.	1884
Alcock, C.W.	Football Annual 1885	Wright & Co.	1885
Alcock, C.W.	The Book of Football		1906
Alcock, C.W. & Marriott C.J.B.	Football	George Routledge & Sons	1890
Alverstone, Lord & Alcock, C.W.	Surrey Cricket – It's History & Associations	Longmans, Green & Co.	1902
Arrowsmith, J.L.	Charterhouse Register 1769-1872	Phillimore	1974
Bailey, Thorn & Wynne-Thomas	Who's who of Cricketers	Newines	1984
Bettesworth, W.	Chats on the Cricket Field	Merritt & Hatcher Ltd	1900
Blythe Smart, J.	The Wow Factor	Blythe Smart Publications	2003
Booth, Keith	The Father of Modern Sport, the Life & Times of Charles W Alcock	The Parrs Wood Press	2002
Brailsford, D.	British Sport, A Social History	The Lutterworth Press	1997
Butler, Byron	The Official Illustrated History Of the F.A.Cup	Headline Book Publishing	1996
Catton, J.A.	The Real Football	Sands & Co.	1900
Collett, Mike	The Complete Record of the F.A. Cup	Sportsbooks	2003
Crouzet, F.	The Victorian Economy	Methuen & Co Ltd	1982
Dauglish, M.G. & Stephenson,	The Harrow School Register 1800-1911	Longmans, Green & Co.	1911
Fabian, A.H. & Green, Geoffrey	Association Football	Caxton Publishing Co.	1960
Formack-Peck, J	New Perspectives on the late Victorian Economy	Cambridge University Press	1991
Gibbs, Nick	England – The Football Facts	Facer Books	1988

Grace, W.G.	Cricketing Reminiscences & Personal Recollections	James Bowden	1899
Green, Geoffrey	A History of the Football Association	The Naldrett Press	1953
Green, Geoffrey	The Official History of the F.A. Cup	William Heinemann Ltd	1960
Green, Geoffrey	Soccer: The World Game, A Popular History	Pan Books	1958
Jackson, N.L.	Association Football	George Newnes Ltd	1900
Jeffrey, Robert	Pictorial History of English Football	Dempsey Pan	1998
Lowndes, W.	The Story of Football	Thorsons Publishing	1952
MacDonald, R.	Soccer A Pictorial History	Collins	1977
McCord, N.	British History 1815-1906	Oxford University Press	1991
Moore, Isabel & Soar, Phil	The Story of Football	Marshall Cavendish Ltd	1976
Pawson, Tony	100 Years of the F.A.Cup	William Heinemann Ltd	1972
Russell Barker,& Stemming,	The Record of Old Westminsters vol 1 & 2	Chiswick Press	1928
Sportsman, The	British Sports & Sportsmen	J.G. Hammond & Co Ltd	1917
Titley, U.A. & McWhirter, Ross	Centenary History of the R.F.U.	Redwood Press	1970
Ward, Andrew	Scotland The Team	Breedon	1987
Williams, G.	The Code War	Yore Publications	1994
	Eton School Register Part 3 1862-1868	Spottiswoode & Co. Ltd	1906
	Burke's Peerage, Baronetange & Knightage	Burke's Peerage Ltd	1949

Articles

Reynolds, Adrienne Forest School and the F.A.Cup

Newspapers, Handbooks & Journals

Alpine Journal
Bell's Life & Sporting Chronicle
Carthusian – March 1981
The Sportsman
Field
London Football Association Directory 1999/2000
The Eton College Chronicle
The Tyro (Harrow)
The Triumvirate (Harrow)
The Harrovian
Harrow Notes
The Elizabethan

Websites

www.cricinfo.com
www.kenaston.org
http://en.wikipedia.org
www.arthurianleague.com
www.lords.org
www.englandfc.com

Acknowledgements

David Barber, Football Association
Norman Epps
British Newspaper Library, Colindale
Roger Banks, Forest School
Trevor Jones, Surrey County Cricket Club
Sue Cole, Charterhouse School
John Mills
The Phillips Brothers, Corinthian-Casuals F.C.
Oliver Pollard
Gerald Wright, Forest School
Peter Holmes, National Football Museum
Jed Smith, Rugby Football Union
Suzanne Foster, Winchester College
Penny Hatfield, Eton College
Rita Boswell-Gibbs, Harrow School
Eddie Smith & Selma Thomas, Westminster School
Keith Booth
Dr Janet Pennington, Lancing College Archives
Tony Walters, Shrewsbury School
Jenny Dixon-Gough, Bradfield College
Geoff Hewitson, Corinthian-Casuals F.C.
Tom Blackbourn
Rachel Cripps
Colin Walton
Dave Tywdell